William Morris

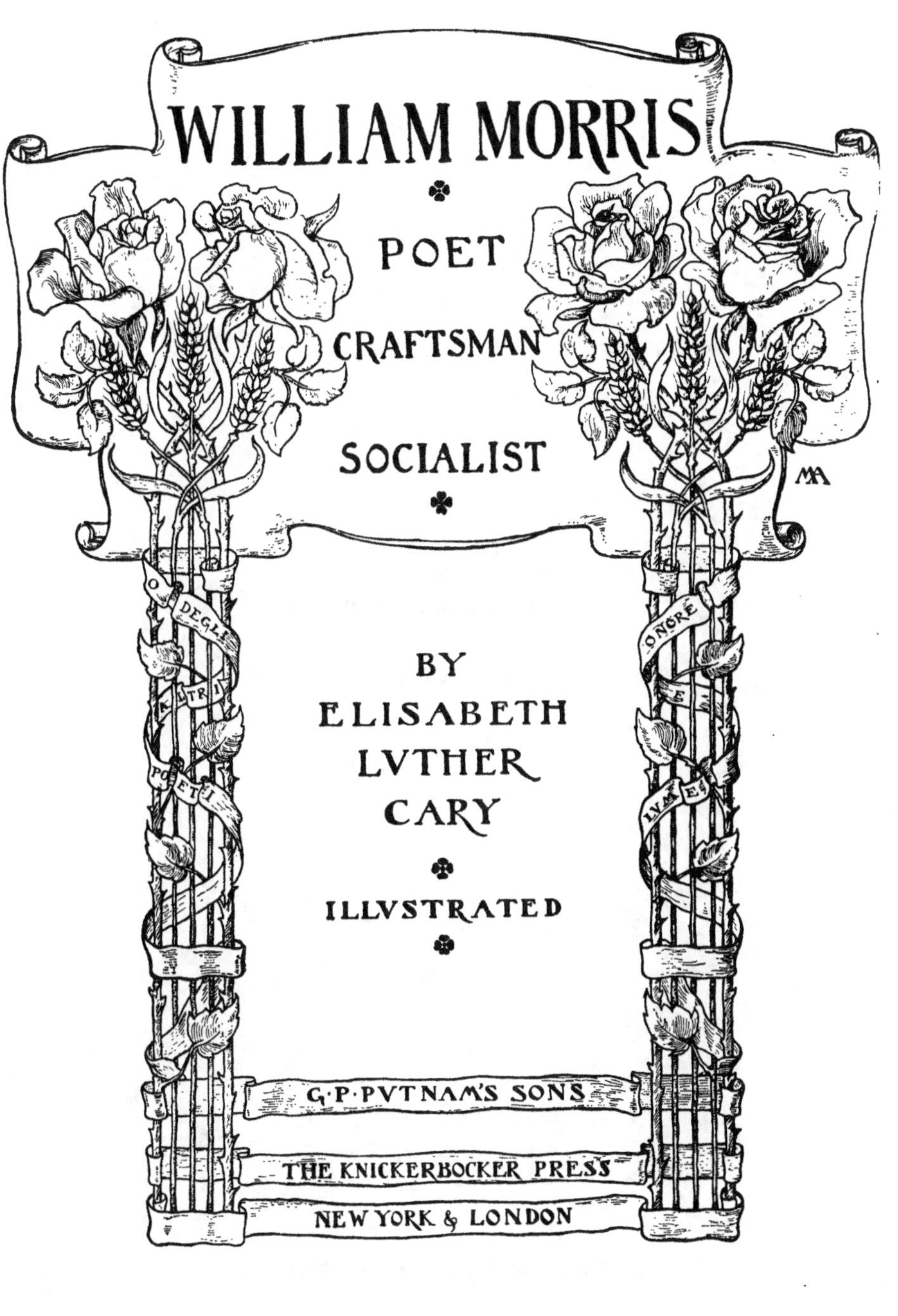
WILLIAM MORRIS
POET
CRAFTSMAN
SOCIALIST
BY
ELISABETH
LVTHER
CARY
ILLVSTRATED
G·P·PVTNAM'S SONS
THE KNICKERBOCKER PRESS
NEW YORK & LONDON

Published, October, 1902

The Knickerbocker Press, New York

PREFACE.

THE personal life of William Morris is already known to us through Mr. Mackail's admirable biography as fully, probably, as we shall ever know it. My own endeavour has been to present a picture of Morris's busy career perhaps not less vivid for the absence of much detail, and showing only the man and his work as they appeared to the outer public.

I have used as a basis for my narrative, the volumes by Mr. Mackail; *William Morris, his Art, his Writings, and his Public Life,* by Aymer Vallance; *The Books of William Morris,* by H. Buxton Forman; numerous articles in periodicals, and Morris's own varied works.

I wish to express my indebtedness to Mr. Bulkley of 42 East 14th Street, New York City, for permission to reproduce a number of Morris patterns in his possession, notably a fragment of the St. James's wallpaper.

Much material for the letter-press and for the illustrations I have obtained through the Boston Public

Library. The *Froissart* pages were found there and most of the Kelmscott publications from which I have quoted.

The bibliography is that prepared by Mr. S. C. Cockerell for the last volume of Mr. Morris issued by the Kelmscott Press, under the title of *A Note by William Morris on His Aims in Founding the Kelmscott Press.* To the Cockerell bibliography have been added a few notes of my own.

E. L. C.

Brooklyn, Sept. 10, 1902.

CONTENTS.

ILLUSTRATIONS.

"These designs must not be taken as exact as to colour afterwards used, Mr. Morris using the colours to his hand and afterwards superintending the actual colouring in the course of manufacture; in most cases many experimental trials being made before the desired colouring was actually decided upon."

Reproduced from examples obtained by courtesy of Mr. A. E. Bulkley.

The Morris designs in this book were reproduced by permission of Messrs. Morris & Company.

CHAPTER I.

BOYHOOD.

THERE is, perhaps, no single work by William Morris that stands out as a masterpiece in evidence of his individual genius. He was not impelled to give peculiar expression to his own personality. His writing was seldom emotionally autobiographic as Rossetti's always was, his painting and designing were not the expression of a personal mood as was the case with Burne-Jones. But no one of his special time and group gave himself more fully or more freely for others. No one contributed more generously to the public pleasure and enlightenment. No one tried with more persistent effort first to create and then to satisfy a taste for the possible best in the lives and homes of the people. He worked toward this end in so many directions that a lesser energy than his must have been dissipated and a weaker purpose rendered impotent. His tremendous vitality saved him from the most humiliating of failures, the failure to make good extravagant promise. He never lost sight of the result in the endeavour, and his discontent with existing mediocrity was neither formless nor empty. It was the motive power of all his labour; he was always trying to make everything "something different from what it was," and this instinct was, alike for strength and weakness, says his chief biographer, "of the very essence of his nature." To tell the story of his life is to write down the record of dreams made real, of nebulous theories brought swiftly to the test of experiment, of the spirit of the distant past reincarnated in the present. But, as with most natures of similar mould, the man was greater than any part of his work, and even greater than the sum of it all. He remains one of the not-to-be-forgotten figures of the nineteenth century, so interesting was he, so impressive, so simple-hearted, so nearly adequate to the great tasks he set himself, so well beloved by his companions, so useful, despite his blunders, to society at large.

The unity that held together his manifold forms of expression was maintained through the different periods of his life, making him a "whole man" to a more than usual degree. From the earliest recorded incidents of his childhood we gain an impression not unlike that made by his latest years, and by all the interval between. The very opposite of Rossetti, with whose "school" he has been so long and so mistakenly identified, his nature was as single as his accomplishment was complex, and the only means by which it is possible to get a just idea of both the former and the latter is to regard him as a man of one preoccupation amounting to an obsession, the reconstruction of social and industrial life according to an ideal based upon the more poetic aspects of the Middle Ages. From first to last the early English world, the English world of the thirteenth and fourteenth centuries, was the world to which he belonged. "Born out of his due time," in truth, he began almost from his birth to accumulate associations with the time to which he should have been native and whose far off splendour lured him constantly back toward it.

The third of nine children, he was born at Walthamstow, in Essex, England, on the 24th of March, 1834. On the Morris side he came of Welsh ancestry, a fact accounting perhaps for the mingled gloom and romance of his temperament. His father was a discount broker in opulent circumstances, and his mother was descended from a family of prosperous merchants and landed proprietors. On the maternal side a strong talent for music existed, but in the Morris family no more artistic quality can be traced than a devotion to general excellence, to which William Morris certainly fell heir. For a time he was a sickly child, and used the opportunity to advance his reading, being "already deep in the Waverley novels" when four years old, and having gone through these and many others before he was seven.

In 1840 the family removed to Woodford Hall, a house belonging to the Georgian period, standing in about fifty acres of park, on the road from London to Epping, and here Morris led an outdoor life with the result of rapidly establishing his health, steeping mind and sense in the sights and sounds of nature dear to him forever after, and gaining intimate acquaintance with the romantic and mediæval surroundings by which his whole career was to be influenced. The county of Essex was well adapted to feed his prodigious appetite for antiquities. Its churches, in numbers of which Norman masonry is to be found, its ancient brasses (that of the schoolboy Thomas Heron being among many others within easy reach of Woodford), and its tapestry-hung houses, all stimulated his inborn love of the Middle Ages and started him fairly on that path through the thirteenth century which he followed deviously as long as he lived. Even in his own home, we are told, certain of the habits of mediæval England persisted, such as the brewing of beer, the meal of cakes and ale at "high prime," the keeping of Twelfth Night, and other such festivals. The places he lived in counted for much with him always, and the impressions of this childish period remained, like all his later impressions, keen and permanent. Toward the end of his life he printed at the Kelmscott Press the carol *Good King Wenceslas,* which begins with a lusty freshness:

> Good King Wenceslas look'd out,
> On the feast of Stephen,
> When the snow lay round about,

Deep and crisp and even.
Brightly shone the moon that night,
Though the frost was cruel,
When a poor man came in sight
Gath'ring winter fuel.

"The legend itself," he comments, "is a pleasing and genuine one, and the Christmas-like quality of it, recalling the times of my boyhood, appeals to me at least as a memory of past days."

Beside angling, shooting, and riding, he very early occupied much of his time with visits to the old churches, a pursuit of which he was never to weary, studying their monuments and accumulating an amount of genuine erudition concerning them quite out of proportion to his rather moderate accomplishment along the ordinary lines of study. At an age when Scott was scouring his native heath in search of Border ballads and antiquities, this almost equally precocious boy was collecting rubbings from ancient inscriptions, and picturing to himself, as he wandered about the region of his home on foot or on horseback, the lovely face of England as it looked in the thirteenth or fourteenth century. In one of the earliest of the boyish romances that appeared in the *Oxford and Cambridge Magazine,* he imagines himself the master-mason of a church built more than six centuries before, and which has vanished from the face of the earth with nothing to indicate its existence save earth-covered ruins "heaving the yellow corn into glorious waves." His description of the carving on the bas-reliefs of the west front and on the tombs shows with what loving intensity he has studied the most minute details of the work of the ancient builders in whose footsteps he would have rejoiced much to tread. How far his family sympathised with his tastes it is impossible to say, but probably not deeply. We have few hints of the personal side of his home-life; we know that a visit to Canterbury Cathedral with his father was among the indelible experiences of his first decade, and that he possessed among his toys a little suit of armour in which he rode about the park after the manner of a Froissart knight, and that is about all we do know until we hear of the strong disapproval of his mother and one of his sisters for the career that finally diverted his interest from the Church for which they had designed him.

His formal education began when he was sent at the age of nine to a preparatory school kept by a couple of maiden ladies. There he remained until the death of his father in 1847. In February, 1848, he went to Marlborough College, a nomination to which his father had purchased for him. The best that can be said for this school seems to be that it was situated in a part of England ideally suited to a boy of archæological tastes, and was provided with an excellent archæological and architectural library. Here his eager mind browsed on the literature of English Gothic, and his restless feet carried him far afield among pre-Celtic barrows, stone circles, and

Roman villas. Savernake Forest was close at hand and he spent many of his holidays within it. It was doubtless the familiarity with all aspects of the woods, due to his pilgrimages through Savernake and Epping Forests and the long roving days idled away among their shadows, that gave rise to the allusions in his books—early and late—to woodland life. The passage through the thick wood and the coming at last to the place where the trees thin out and the light begins to shimmer through them is a constantly recurring figure of his verse and of his prose. Frequently the important scene of a romance or of a long poem is laid in a wildwood, as in the story entitled *The Wood beyond the World,* or in *Goldilocks and Goldilocks,* the concluding poem of the volume of *Poems by the Way,* in which the great grey boles of the trees, the bramble bush, the "woodlawn clear," and the cherished oaks are as vivid as the human actors in the drama. His heroes seldom fail of being deft woodsmen, able to thread the tangle of underbrush by blind paths, and observant of all the common sights and sounds of the woodland, rabbits scuttling out of the grass, adders sunning themselves on stones in the cleared spaces, wild swine running grunting toward close covert, hart and hind bounding across the way. They know the musty savour of water dipped from a forest brook, they know how to go straight to the yew sticks that quarter best for bow-staves, they know the feeling of the boggy moss under their feet, and the sound of the "iron wind" through the branches in the depth of winter; there is no detail of wild wood life of which they are ignorant. This intimacy with Nature in her most secluded moments, in her shyest and most mysterious aspect, forms an element of inexpressible charm in the lovely backgrounds against which Morris delighted to place his visionary figures. He never tired of combining the impressions stored away in his mind on his boyish rambles into pictures the delicate beauty of which can hardly be overestimated.

While he was at school, his already highly developed imagination found an outlet in constant fable-making, his tales of knights and fairies and miraculous adventures having a considerable popularity among his comrades, with whom, however, he himself was not especially popular, making friends with them only in a superficial fashion. Judging from the autobiographic fragments occasionally found in his work, he was a boy of many moods, most of them tinged with the self-conscious melancholy of his early poetry. Sentiment was strong with him, and a peculiar reticence or detachment of temperament kept him independent of others during his school years, and apparently uninfluenced by the tastes or opinions of those about him, if we except the case of his Anglo-Catholic proclivities, which obviously were fed by the tendencies of the school, but which, so far from diverting him from the general scheme of his individual interests, fitted into them and served him as another link between the present and the much preferred past.

Outwardly he can hardly have seemed the typical dreamer he has described himself as being. Beautiful of feature, of sturdy build, with a shouting voice, extraordinary muscular strength, and a gusty temper, he impressed himself upon his comrades chiefly by his impetuosity in the energetic game of singlestick, by the surplus vigour that led him at times to punch his own head with all his might to "take it out of himself," and by the vehemence and enthusiasm of his argumentative talk.

He was little of a student along the orthodox lines, and Marlborough College was not calculated to increase his respect—never undue—for pedagogic methods. A letter written when he was sixteen to his eldest and favourite sister reflects quite fully his pre-occupations. It has none of the genuine wit and literary tone of the juvenile letter written by Stevenson to his father, presenting his claims for reimbursements. It shows no such zest for bookish pursuits as Rossetti's letters, written at the same age, reveal. But it is entirely free from the shallow flippancy that frequently characterises the correspondence of a young man's second decade—that characterised Lowell's, for example, to an almost painful degree; nor has it a shade of the self-magnification to which any amount of flippancy is preferable. It is straightforward and boyish, and remarkable only as showing the thorough and intelligent method with which its writer followed up whatever commanded his interest. Commencing with the description of an anthem sung at Easter by the trained choir of Blore's Chapel connected with his school, he passes on to an account of his archæological investigations, giving after his characteristic fashion all the small details necessary to enable his correspondent to form a definite picture of the places he had visited. After he had made one pilgrimage to the Druidical circle and Roman entrenchment at Avebury, he had learned of the peculiar method of placing the stones which, from the dislocated condition of the ruins, had not been obvious to him. Therefore he had returned on the following day to study it out and fix the original arrangement firmly in his imagination, and, at the time of writing the letter, was able to explain it quite clearly, a result, derived from the expenditure of two holidays, that was completely satisfactory to him. He winds up with a purely boyish plea for a "good large cake" and some biscuit in addition to a cheese that had been promised him, and for paper and postage stamps and his silkworm eggs and a pen box to be sent him from home.

At school he was "always thinking about home," and when the family moved again to Walthamstow, within a short distance of his first home, and to a house boasting a moat and a wooded island, he was eagerly responsive to the poetic suggestions conveyed by these romantic accessories. When at the end of 1851 he left school to prepare under a private tutor for Oxford, he renewed his early familiarity with Epping Forest and spent most of his holidays among the trees that had not apparently changed since the time of Edward the Confessor. The great age of the wood and its peculiarly English character made a profound impression upon him, and it is easy to imagine the fury with which he must have received the suggestion, made forty years later by Mr. Alfred Wallace, that in place of "a hideous assemblage of stunted mop-like pollards rising from a thicket of scrubby bushes," North American trees should be planted and a part of the forest made into an "almost exact copy" of North American woodland. Indeed, a suppressed but unmistakable fury breathes from the letters written to the *Daily Chronicle,* as late as 1895, regarding the tree-felling that was going on ruthlessly in the forest, destroying its native character and individual charm. These letters, curiously recalling those written half a century before concerning boyish excursions through the same region, are well worth quoting here, where properly they belong, as they are inspired by the earliest of the associations and ideals cherished by Morris to the end of his life. They are fine examples of his own native character in argument, his humbly didactic tone early caught from Ruskin and never relinquished, his militant irony, his willingness to fortify his position by painstaking investigation, his moral attitude toward matters artistic, his superb rightness of taste in the special problem under discussion. They show also how closely his memory had held through his manifold interests the details that had appealed to him in his boyhood. The first letter is dated April 23rd, and addressed to the editor of the *Daily Chronicle.*

"SIR: I venture to ask you to allow me a few words on the subject of the present treatment of Epping Forest. I was born and bred in its neighbourhood (Walthamstow and Woodford), and when I was a boy and young man I knew it yard by yard from Wanstead to the Theydons, and from Hale End to the Fairlop Oak. In those days it had no worse foes than the gravel stealer and the rolling-fence maker, and was always interesting and often very beautiful. From what I can hear it is years since the greater part of it has been destroyed, and I fear, Sir, that in spite of your late optimistic note on the subject, what is left of it now runs the danger of further ruin.

"The special character of it was derived from the fact that by far the greater part was a wood of hornbeams, a tree not common save in Essex and Herts. It was certainly the biggest hornbeam wood in these islands, and I suppose in the world. The said hornbeams were all pollards, being shrouded every four or six years, and were interspersed in many places with holly thickets, and the result was a very curious and characteristic wood, such as can be seen nowhere else. And I submit that no treatment of it can be tolerable which does not maintain this hornbeam wood intact.

"But the hornbeam, though an interesting tree to an artist and reasonable person, is no favourite with the landscape gardener, and I very much fear that the intention of the authorities is to clear the forest of native trees, and to plant vile weeds like deodars and outlandish conifers instead. We are told that a committee of 'experts' has been formed to sit in judgment on Epping Forest; but, Sir, I decline to be gagged by the word 'expert,' and I call on the public generally to take the same position. An 'expert' may be a very dangerous person, because he is likely to narrow his views to the particular business (usually a commercial one) which he represents. In this case, for instance, we do not want to be under the thumb of either a wood bailiff whose business is to grow timber for the market, or of a botanist whose business is to collect specimens for a botanical garden; or of a landscape gardener whose business is to vulgarise a garden or landscape to the utmost extent that his patron's purse will allow of. What we want is reasonable men of real artistic taste to take into consideration what the essential needs of the case are, and to advise accordingly. Now it seems to me that the authorities who have Epping Forest in hand may have two intentions as to it. First, they may intend to landscape-garden it, or turn it into golf grounds (and I very much fear that even the latter nuisance may be in their minds); or second, they may really think it necessary (as you suggest) to thin the hornbeams, so as to give them a better chance of growing. The first alternative we Londoners should protest against to the utmost, for if it be carried out then Epping Forest is turned into a mere place of vulgarity, is destroyed in fact.

"As to the second, to put our minds at rest, we ought to be assured that the cleared spaces would be planted again, and that almost wholly with hornbeam. And, further, the greatest possible care should be taken that not a single tree should be felled unless it is necessary for the growth of its fellows. Because, mind you, with comparatively small trees, the really beautiful effect of them can only be got by their standing as close together as the emergencies of growth will allow. We want a thicket, not a park, from Epping Forest.

"In short, a great and practically irreparable mistake will be made if, under the shelter of the opinion of 'experts,' from mere carelessness and thoughtlessness, we let the matter slip out of the hands of the thoughtful part of the public; the essential character of one of the greatest ornaments of London will disappear, and no one will have even a sample left to show what the great north-eastern forest was like. I am, Sir, yours obediently,

"William Morris

"Kelmscott House, Hammersmith."

The second letter is written two or three weeks later, and shows Morris as characteristically prompt and thorough in action as he is positive in speech.

"Yesterday," he says, "I carried out my intention of visiting Epping Forest. I went to Loughton first, and saw the work that had been done about Clay Road, thence to Monk Wood, thence to Theydon Woods, and thence to the part about the Chingford Hotel, passing by Fair Mead Bottom and lastly to Bury Wood and the wood on the other side of the road thereby.

"I can verify closely your representative's account of the doings on the Clay Road, which is an ugly scar originally made by the lord of the manor when he contemplated handing over to the builder a part of what he thought was his property. The fellings here seem to me all pure damage to the forest, and in fact were quite unaccountable to me, and would surely be so to any unprejudiced person. I cannot see what could be pleaded for them either on the side of utility or taste.

"About Monk Wood there had been much, and I should say excessive, felling of trees apparently quite sound. This is a very beautiful spot, and I was informed that the trees there had not been polled for a period long before the acquisition of the forest for the public; and nothing could be more interesting and romantic than the effect of the long poles of the hornbeams rising from the trunks and seen against the mass of the wood behind. This wood should be guarded most jealously as a treasure of beauty so near to 'the Wen.' In the Theydon Woods, which are mainly of beech, a great deal of felling has gone on, to my mind quite unnecessary, and therefore harmful. On the road between the Wake Arms and the King's Oak Hotel there has been again much felling, obviously destructive.

"In Bury Wood (by Sewardstone Green) we saw the trunks of a great number of oak trees (not pollards), all of them sound, and a great number were yet standing in the wood marked for felling, which, however, we heard had been saved by a majority of the committee of experts. I can only say that it would have been a very great misfortune if they had been lost; in almost every case where the stumps of the felled trees showed there seemed to have been no reason for their destruction. The wood on the other side of the road to Bury Wood, called in the map Woodman's Glade, has not suffered from felling, and stands as an object lesson to show how unnecessary such felling is. It is one of the thickest parts of the forest, and looks in all respects like such woods were forty years ago, the growth of the heads of the hornbeams being but slow; but there is no difficulty in getting through it in all directions, and it has a peculiar charm of its own not to be found in any other forest; in short, it is thoroughly *characteristic.* I should mention that the whole of these woods are composed of pollard hornbeams and 'spear'—*i. e.,* unpolled—oaks.

"I am compelled to say from what I saw in a long day's inspection, that, though no doubt acting with the best intentions, the management of the forest is going on the wrong tack; it is making war on the natural aspect of the forest, which the Act of Parliament that conferred it on the nation expressly stipulated was to be retained. The tendency of all these fellings is on the one hand to turn over London forest into a park, which would be more or less like other parks, and on the other hand to grow sizable trees, as if for the timber market. I must beg to be allowed a short quotation here from an excellent little guidebook to the forest by Mr. Edward North Buxton, verderer of the forest (Sanford, 1885). He says, p. 38: 'In the drier parts of the forest beeches to a great extent take the place of oaks. These "spear" trees will make fine timber for future generations, provided they receive timely attention by being *relieved of the competing growth of the unpicturesque hornbeam pollards.* Throughout the wood between Chingford and High Beech, *this has been recently done,* to the great advantage of the finer trees.'

"The italics are mine, and I ask, Sir, if we want any further evidence than this of one of the verderers as to the tendency of the fellings. Mr. Buxton declares in so many words that he wants to change the special character of the forest; to take away this strange, unexampled, and most romantic wood, and leave us nothing but a commonplace instead. I entirely deny his right to do so in the teeth of the Act of Parliament. I assert, as I did in my former letter, that the hornbeams are the most important trees in the forest, since they give it its special character. At the same time I would not encourage the hornbeams at the expense of the beeches, any more than I would the beeches at the expense of the hornbeams. I would leave them all to nature, which is not so niggard after all, even on Epping Forest gravel, as *e. g.*, one can see in places where forest fires have denuded spaces, and where in a short time birches spring up self-sown.

"The committee of the Common Council has now had Epping Forest in hand for seventeen years, and has, I am told, in that time felled 100,000 trees. I think the public may now fairly ask for a rest on behalf of the woods, which, if the present system of felling goes on, will be ruined as a natural forest; and it is good and useful to make the claim at once, when, in spite of all disfigurements, the northern part of the forest, from Sewardstone Green to beyond Epping, is still left to us, not to be surpassed in interest by any other wood near a great capital. I am, Sir, yours obediently,

"WILLIAM MORRIS."

These letters emphasise in a single instance what the close student of Morris will find emphasised at every turn in his career, — the persistent and strong influence over him of the tastes and occupations of his boyhood. Unless this is kept constantly in mind, it is easy to fall into the common error of regarding the various activities into which he threw himself as separate and dissociated instead of seeing them as they were, component parts of a perfectly simple purpose and unalterable ideal. With most men who are on the whole true to the analogy of the chambered nautilus and cast off the outworn shell of their successive phases of individuality as the seasons roll, the effect of early environment and tendency may easily be exaggerated, but Morris grew in the fashion of his beloved oaks, keeping the rings by which his advance in experience was marked; at the end all were visible. His education began and continued largely outside the domain of books and away from masters. His wanderings in the depths of the quaint and beautiful forest, his intimate acquaintance with the nature of Gothic architecture, his familiarity with Scott, his prompt adoption of Ruskin, all these formed the foundation on which he was to build his own theory of life, and all were his before he went up to Oxford. They prepared him for the many-sided profession, if profession it can be called, which was to absorb and at last to exhaust his mighty energy. It was the tangible surface of the world that most inspired him in boyhood and in maturity. Loving so much even as a child its aspects, its lights and shadows, the forms of trees and birds and beasts, the changes of season, the lives of men living close to "the kind soil" and in touch with it through hearty manual labour, it was but a step to the occupations that finally engrossed him. He never got so far away from the visions of his youth as to forget them. In one form or another he was constantly trying to embody them that others might see them with his eyes and worship them with his devotion. "The spirit of the new days, of our days," says the old man in *News from Nowhere,* "was to be delight in the life of the world, intense and almost overweening love of the very skin and surface of the earth on which man dwells."

CHAPTER II.

OXFORD LIFE.

LIKE the majority of the students who went up to Oxford in the fifties, Morris matriculated with the definite intention of taking holy orders. Unlike the majority, he was impelled not only by the sensuous beauty of ritualistic worship, to which, however, no one could have been more keenly alive than he, but by a genuine enthusiasm for a life devoted to high purposes. A fine buoyant desire to better existing conditions and sweep as much evil as possible off the face of the earth early inspired him. His mind turned toward the conventual life as that which combined the mediæval suggestions always alluring to him with the moral beauty of holiness. He planned a "Crusade and Holy Warfare against the Age," sang plain song at daily morning service, read masses of mediæval chronicles and ecclesiastical Latin poetry, and hovered just this side of the Roman Communion. Had the ecclesiology of the University been supported at that time by an inward and spiritual grace sufficient to hold the heart of youth to a sustained allegiance, there is little doubt that Morris would have thrown himself ardently into the religious path. But Oxford had become an indolent and indifferent mother to her children. The storm of feeling aroused by the Tractarian movement had died down and the reaction from it was evident. At Balliol Jowett's energy had made its mark, but at Exeter, where Morris was, the educational system deserved (and received) the contempt of an ambitious boy with an unusually large supply of stored-up intellectual force seeking outlet and guidance. Nor was the social life more stimulating to moral activity. The abuses recorded in 1852 by the University Commission were in essence so shameful that in the light of that famous report "the sweet city with her dreaming spires" seems to have only the beauty of the daughter of Helios, under whose enchantments men were turned to swine for loving her. The clean mind and honest nature of Morris revolted from the excesses that went on about him. He wrote to his mother two years after his matriculation, defending the proposition that his Oxford education had not been thrown away: "If by living here and seeing evil and sin in its foulest and coarsest forms, as one does day by day, I have learned to hate any form of sin and to wish to fight against it, is not this well too?" It is proof of his purity of taste and strength of will that, despite his ample means, the wanton extravagance of the typical undergraduate had for him no allurement. It is certain that he was never seen at those dinners which were pronounced by an official censor "a curse and a disgrace to a place of Christian education," and as certainly he played no part in the mad carnivals at which novices were initiated into a curriculum of vice. Yet he could not indeed say with any truth what Gibbon had said a hundred years before, that the time he spent at Oxford was the most idle and unprofitable of his whole life. If he felt, as Gibbon did, that his formal studies were "equally devoid of profit and pleasure," and if he found nothing ridiculous in Ruskin's bitter complaint that Oxford taught him all the Latin and Greek that he would learn, but did not teach him that fritillaries grew in Iffley meadow, he did find a little band of helpful associates. With these he realised the priceless advantages which Mr. Bagehot says cannot be got outside a college and which he sums up as found "in the books that all read because all like; in what all talk of because all are interested; in the argumentative walk or disputatious lounge; in the impact of fresh thought on fresh thought, of hot thought on hot thought; in mirth and refutation, in ridicule and laughter." The first of the few strong personal attachments in the life of Morris dates from his first day at Oxford. At the end of January, 1853, he went up for his matriculation, and beside him at the examination in the Hall sat Burne-Jones, who within a week of their formal entrance to the college became his intimate. The friendship thus spontaneously formed on the verge of manhood lasted until Morris died. In their studies, in their truant reading, in their later aims and work, the two, diametrically as they differed in aspect and in temperament and in quality of mind, were sympathetic and dear companions. Together they joined a group of other happily gifted men—Fulford, Faulkner, Dixon, Cormell Price, and Macdonald—who met in one another's rooms for the disputatious lounge over the exuberant ideals by which they were in common inspired. Tennyson, Keats, and Shelley, Shakespeare, Ruskin, Carlyle, Kingsley, Thackeray, Dickens, and Miss Yonge were the gods and half gods of their young and passionate enthusiasm. The last, curiously enough, was an influence as potent as any. The hero of her novel of 1853, *The Heir of Redclyffe,* was the pattern chosen by Morris, according to Mr. Mackail's account, to build himself upon. Singular as it seems to-day that any marked impression should have been made upon an even fairly well-trained mind by a writer of such slight literary quality, it is true that the author of *The Daisy Chain* counted among her devoted readers men of brilliant and dominant intellectual power. She had the lucky touch to kindle in young minds that fire of sympathy with which they greet whatever shows them their own world, their age, themselves as they best like to see them. To Morris in particular the young heir of Redclyffe made the appeal of a congenial temperament in a position similar to his own. Like Morris, he was headstrong and passionate, given to excessive bursts of rage and to repentances not less excessive; like Morris, he united to his natural pride an unnatural and slightly obtrusive humility; like Morris, he was rich and beautiful, generous and lovable. It was no great wonder that Morris, poring with his characteristic absorption over the pleasant pages on which Guy Morville's chivalrous life is portrayed, said as Dromio to Dromio, "Methinks you are my glass and not my brother; I see by you I am a sweet-faced youth."

Mr. Mackail notes with an accent of surprise that Kingsley was much more widely read than Newman, thinking the choice a curious one in the case of passionate Anglo-Catholics. So far as Morris was concerned, however, there was little enough to relish in Newman's subtle theology and relentless logic. The man to whom religion as a mere sentiment was "a dream and a mockery" could hardly appeal to one to whom all life was a sentiment. Kingsley, on the other hand, although he was anti-Catholic in temper, and disposed to overthrow the illusions by which such romanticists as Scott, such dreamers as Fouqué, had surrounded the Middle Ages, picturing their coarse and barbarous side with harsh realism, was happy in rendering the charms of outdoor life and bold adventure, and the songs of the Crusaders in his *Saint's Tragedy* must have gone farther toward winning Morris than pages of Newman's reasoning devotion.

Gradually the monastic ideal faded before the brightness of art and literature and the life of the world as these became more and more impressed upon Morris's consciousness. To live in the spirit and in the region of purely intellectual interests could not have been his choice after the passing of the first fanatic impulse of youth to dedicate itself to what is difficult, ignorant of the joy of choosing. Many influences united to determine the precise form into which he should shape the future that for all practical purposes was under his control. His interest in pictorial art was stimulated by Burne-Jones, who was already making fantastic little drawings, and studies of flowers and foliage. Of great art he knew nothing until he spent the Long Vacation of 1854 in travelling through Belgium and Northern France, where he saw Van Eyck and Memling, who at once became to him, as they were to Rossetti, masters of incontestable supremacy. On this trip he saw also the beautiful churches of Amiens, Beauvais, and Chartres, which in his unbridled expansiveness of phrase he called "the grandest, the most beautiful, the kindest, and most loving of all the buildings that the earth has ever borne." The following year he repeated the experience, with Burne-Jones and Fulford for companions. This time the journey was to have been made on foot from motives of economy, as Burne-Jones was poor and Morris embraced the habits of poverty when in his company with unaffected delicacy of feeling. At Amiens, however, Morris went lame, and, "after filling the streets with imprecations on all boot-makers," bought a pair of gay carpet slippers in which to continue the trip. These proved not to serve the purpose, and the travellers were obliged to reach Chartres by the usual methods of conveyance, Morris arguing with fury and futility in favour of skirting Paris, "even by two days' journey, so as not to see the streets of it." They had with them one book, *Keats,* and their minds were filled with the poetic ideas of art as the expression of man's pleasure in his toil, and of beauty as the natural and necessary accompaniment of productive labour, which Ruskin had been preaching in *The Stones of Venice* and in the Edinburgh lectures. By this time they had become acquainted with the work of the Pre-Raphaelites, and Burne-Jones had announced that of all men who lived on earth the one he wanted to see was Rossetti. Morris had used his spare time, of which we may imagine he had a considerable amount, in the study of mediæval design as the splendid manuscripts in the Bodleian Library illustrate it. An architectural newspaper also formed part of his regular reading outside of his studies. Thus primed for definite action, on this holiday filled with stimulating interests and the delicious freedom of roaming quite at will with the best of companions through the sweet fertile country of Northern France, Morris put quite aside all aims that had not directly to do with art. He and Burne-Jones, walking late one night on the quays of Havre, discussed their plans. Both gave up once and for all the idea of taking orders; both decided to leave Oxford as quickly as they could; both were to be artists, Burne-Jones a painter and Morris an architect.

Although Morris was never to become a practising architect, this choice of a profession at the beginning of his career is both characteristic and significant. Buildings, as we have seen, had interested him from his childhood. His favourite excursions, long and short, had been to the region of churches. In the art of building he saw the means of elevating all the tastes of man. Architecture meant to him "the art of creating a building with all the appliances fit for carrying on a dignified and happy life." It seemed to him even at the outset, before the word "socialism" had come into his vocabulary, incredible that people living in pleasant homes and engaged in making and using these appliances of which he speaks, should lead lives other than dignified and happy. It was much more in accordance with his ideal of a vocation, a ministry to man, that he should contribute to the daily material comfort and pleasure of the world, that he should make places good for the body to live in and fair for the eye to rest upon, and therefore soothing to the soul, than that he should construct abstract spiritual mansions of which he could at best form but a vague conception. It was, then, with a certain sense of dedication, an exchange of method without a change of spirit, that he gave up the thought of holy orders and turned to the thought of furthering the good of mankind by working toward the beauty and order of the visible world.

From the point of view of his later interests as a decorator of houses, he was showing the utmost wisdom in beginning with the framework, which must exist before any decoration can be applied. "I have spoken of the popular arts," he says himself, in one of his lectures, "but they might all be summed up in that one word Architecture; they are all parts of that great whole, and the art of house-building begins it all. If we did not know how to dye or to weave; if we had neither gold nor silver nor silk, and no pigments to paint with but half a dozen ochres and umbers, we might yet frame a worthy art that would lead to everything, if we had but timber, stone and lime, and a few cutting tools to make these common things not only shelter us from wind and weather but also express the thoughts and aspirations that stir in us. Architecture would lead us to all the arts, as it did with the earlier men; but if we despise it and take no note of how we are housed, the other arts will have a hard time of it indeed."

And again: "A true architectural work," he says, "is a building duly provided with all the necessary furniture, decorated with all due ornament, according to the use, quality, and dignity of the building, from mere mouldings or abstract lines to the great epical works of sculpture and painting, which except as decorations of the nobler form of such buildings cannot be produced at all. So looked upon, a work of architecture is a harmonious, co-operative work of art, inclusive of all the serious arts—those which are not engaged in the production of mere toys or ephemeral prettinesses."

Morris communicated his momentous decision to his family as soon as it was made, and they received it with amazement and distress. While their origin was not especially aristocratic, their tastes ran toward the symbols of aristocracy. When Morris was nine years old, his father obtained a grant of arms from the Heralds' College, and the son had no small liking for the bearings assigned—bearings which included a horse's head erased argent between three horse-shoes. The horse's head he introduced on the tiles and glass of the house he built for himself in later years, and he was in the habit of making a yearly pilgrimage to the famous White Horse of the Berkshire Downs, connecting it in some obscure way with his ancestry. In England, during the fifties, nothing was less calculated to appeal to an aristocratic tendency than any form of art considered as a profession. In *The Newcomes* Mr. Honeyman remarks with bland dignity to his aspiring young relative; "My dear Clive, there are degrees in society which we must respect. You surely cannot think of being a professional artist." In much this spirit, apparently, Mrs. Morris received her son's announcement, conveyed in a long and affectionate letter stating in detail the motives that had led him to his resolution. After defending his chosen profession at some length, calling it with characteristic avoidance of pompous phraseology, "a useful trade," he dwells upon the moderation of his hopes and expectations. He does not hope "to be great at all in anything," but thinks he may look forward to reasonable happiness in his work. It will be grievous to his pride and self-will, he says, to have to do just as he is told for three long years, but "good for it, too," and he looks forward with little delight to the drudgery of learning a new trade, but is pretty confident of success, and is happy in being able to pay "the premium and all that" without laying any fresh burden of expense upon his mother. Finally he proposes taking as his master George Edmund Street, who was living in Oxford as architect of the diocese, and whose enthusiasm for the thirteenth century could hardly have failed to claim the sympathy of Morris. Certainly it seemed precisely the fitting opportunity that offered. There could have been no better moment for him to follow the advice he so frequently gave to others—to turn his back upon an ugly age, choose the epoch that suited him best, and identify himself with that. Gothic to the core, he had come to Oxford, not, as Mr. Day has suggested, to catch the infection of mediævalism abroad there, but to assimilate and thrive upon all the influences to which his independently mediæval spirit was acutely susceptible. Scott, Pugin, Shaw, Viollet-le-Duc, had broken the way through popular prejudice, and Street was engaged at the time Morris went to him in the work of restoring ancient churches and designing Gothic buildings. "Restoration" had not then so evil a sound to Morris as it later came to have. Some thirty years after, he was to say: "No man or no body of men, however learned they may be in ancient art, whatever skill in design or love of beauty they may have, can persuade, or bribe, or force our workmen of to-day to do their work in the same way as the workmen of King Edward I. did theirs. Wake up Theodoric the Goth from his sleep of centuries and place him on the throne of Italy, turn our modern House of Commons into the Witenagemote (or Meeting of the Wise Men) of King Alfred the Great!—no less a feat is the restoration of an ancient building." In 1855, however, he had not fully arrived at this conviction. It was then the period of "fresh hope and partial insight" which, regarding it retrospectively, he says, "produced many interesting buildings and other works of art, and afforded a pleasant time indeed to the hopeful but very small minority engaged in it, in spite of all vexations and disappointments." There seemed no reason to suppose that, helped as he was by his predilections and by his environment, he could not become the master-builder of the house beautiful that constantly haunted his imagination.

He was not to begin at once, however. In deference to his mother's wish he went through his final term, passed in the Final Schools without difficulty,

No. I. JANUARY, 1856. PRICE 1*s*.

THE

Oxford & Cambridge Magazine,

CONDUCTED BY MEMBERS OF THE

TWO UNIVERSITIES.

CONTENTS.

LONDON:
BELL AND DALDY, FLEET STREET.

[PRI]NTED BY C. WHITTINGHAM, TOOKS COURT, CHA[NCERY] LANE.

TITLE-PAGE OF "THE OXFORD AND CAMBRIDGE MAGAZINE"

and, together with his companions—The Brotherhood as they now called themselves,—gave distinction to his last year at the University, where despite all drawbacks he had been aboundingly happy, by founding the since famous little *Oxford and Cambridge Magazine.*

Like the Pre-Raphaelite *Germ,* this periodical aimed at an unusually high standard. It was printed at the Chiswick Press with some pretensions to typographical beauty. Each number had upon its title-page an ornamental heading designed by one of Charles Whittingham's daughters and engraved by Mary Byfield. On the green wrappers the name of the magazine was printed in the old-fashioned type which the Chiswick Press was the first to revive, and although, unlike *The Germ,* it was not illustrated, photographs of Woolner's medallions of Carlyle and Tennyson were mounted to bind with it and sold at a shilling apiece to subscribers. The price of each number was also a shilling, and twelve monthly numbers appeared, making it thrice as long lived as its prototype, *The Germ.* The financial responsibility, says Mr. Mackail, was undertaken wholly by Morris, and he at first attempted the general control. This he was soon glad to relinquish, paying a salary of a hundred pounds a year to his editor. The title, which in full read *The Oxford and Cambridge Magazine, Conducted by Members of the Two Universities,* indicates rather more co-operation than existed, the magazine being conducted entirely by Oxford men and fully two-thirds written by them. The tone of the contributions was to be impeccable. "It is unanimously agreed," wrote Price, "that there is to be no shewing off, no quips, no sneers, no lampooning in our Magazine." Politics were to be almost eschewed, "Tales, Poetry, friendly Critiques, and social articles" making up the body of the text.

First among the contributors in quantity and regularity of supply was Morris. During his second year at the University he had discovered that he could write poetry, and had communicated the fact to his companions without loss of time. Canon Dixon, recalling the very thrilling occasion of his reading his first poem to the group gathered in the old Exeter rooms occupied by Burne-Jones, affirms that he reached his perfection at once, that nothing could have been altered for the better, and also quotes him as saying, "Well, if this is poetry, it is very easy to write." He was not one to let a capability fust in him unused. Poetry and prose, equally easy to him, poured after this from his pen, giving expression with some confusion and incoherence to his boyish raptures over the things he best loved and most thought about. During the twelve months of the magazine's life he contributed to it five poems, eight prose tales, a review of Browning's *Men and Women*, and two special articles, one on a couple of engravings by Alfred Bethel and one on the Cathedral at Amiens. In all this early work, filled with superabundant imagery, self-conscious, sensuous, unsubstantial, pictorial, we have Morris the writer as he was at the beginning and much as he was again at the end. His first strange little romances pass before the eyes as his late ones do, like strips of beautiful fabric, deeply dyed with colours both dim and rich, and printed with faintly outlined figures in postures illustrating the dreamy events of dreamy lives. Many of the pages echo with the sound of trumpets and the clash of arms, but the echo is from so far away that the heart of the reader declines to leap. Passionate emotions are portrayed in passionate language. Men and women love and die with wild adventure. Splendid sacrifices are made, and dark revenges taken. But the effect is of marionettes, admirably costumed and ingeniously managed yet inevitably suggesting artifice and failing to suggest life. Nevertheless Morris wrote in the fashion commonly supposed to impart vitality if nothing else to composition. He sat up late of nights, after the manner of young writers, and let his words stand as they fell hot and unpremeditated on the page. The labour of learning the art, as his favourite, Keats, learned it, by indefatigable practice in finding the perfect word, the one exquisite phrase, was quite outside his method. As long as he lived, he preferred rewriting to revising a manuscript. The austerity of mind that leads to impatience of superfluous colour or tone, and that dreads as the plague superfluous sentiment, was foreign to him, nor did he ever acquire it as even the Epicurean temperament may do by ardent self-restraint. In most of the romances and poems the scene is laid somewhat vaguely but unmistakably in the Middle Ages. We rarely surprise the young writer in a date, but the atmosphere is that of the thirteenth century though with many thirteenth-century characteristics left out. The incidents appeal to what Bagehot calls "that kind of boyish fancy which idolises mediæval society as the 'fighting time.'" The distinction lies in the fertility and beauty of the descriptions. On nearly every page is some passage that has the quality of a picture. In *The Hollow Land,* in *Gertha's Lovers,* in *Svend and his Brethren,* and especially in the article on the Amiens Cathedral, are exquisite landscapes and backgrounds against which the personages group themselves with perfect fittingness. "I must paint Gertha before I die," said Burne-Jones, after Morris himself was dead, recalling the charm of this story which was written in his company, under the willows by the riverside. "The opening and the closing sentences always invited me in an indescribable way, but the motive *par excellence* was that of Gertha after death, in the chapter entitled 'What Edith the Handmaiden Saw from the War Saddle,' where the beautiful queen lies on the battlefield with the blue speedwell about her pale face, while a soft wind rustles the sunset-lit aspens overhead."

To his genius for evoking a scene from memory or imagination with a grace and delicacy missing in the designs he was later to make with tools more rebellious than words, Morris added a

Portrait of Rossetti

By Watts

D G Rossetti

singular ability to convey to his readers the most significant quality of what he admired, to impress them with the feature that had most impressed him. The fancy for gold, inspired perhaps by study of mediæval illumination, runs like a glittering thread through the story of *Svend and his Brethren.* Cissela's gold hair, her crown of gold, the golden ring she breaks with her lover, the gold cloth over which she walks across the trampled battle-field, the samite of purple wrought with gold stars, the golden letters on the sword-blade,—all these recur like so many bright accents from which the attention cannot escape. Again, in the description of Amiens Cathedral, we get from simple verbal repetition the effect of massive modelling, the sense of weight in the design as Morris felt it in one of the sculptured figures of the niches: "A stately figure with a king's crown on his head, and hair falling in three waves over his shoulders; a very kingly face looking straight onward; a great jewelled collar falling heavily to his elbows: his right hand holding a heavy sceptre formed of many budding flowers, and his left just touching in front the folds of his raiment that falls heavily, very heavily to the ground over his feet. Saul, King of Israel." In another passage describing with minute detail the figures of the Virgin and Child, a similar emphasis is laid on the quality of restfulness. "The two figures are very full of rest; everything about them expresses it from the broad forehead of the Virgin, to the resting of the feet of the Child (who is almost self-balanced) in the fold of the robe that she holds gently, to the falling of the quiet lines of her robe over her feet, to the resting of its folds between them." And if the effect to be rendered is one of colour, a touch of finer eloquence is added to this somewhat crude method. The final passage of the account of the great Cathedral is a genuine triumph of poetic observation, carrying the fancy of the reader lightly over the silvery loveliness of the picture as it lay before the boy enraptured by it: "And now, farewell to the church that I love, to the carved temple-mountain that rises so high above the water-meadows of the Somme, above the grey roofs of the good town. Farewell to the sweep of the arches, up from the bronze bishops lying at the west end, up to the belt of solemn windows, where, through the painted glass, the light comes solemnly. Farewell to the cavernous porches of the west front, so grey under the fading August sun, grey with the wind-storms, grey with the rain-storms, grey with the beat of many days' sun, from sunrise to sunset; showing white sometimes, too, when the sun strikes it strongly; snowy-white, sometimes, when the moon is on it, and the shadows growing blacker; but grey now, fretted into deeper grey, fretted into black by the mitres of the bishops, by the solemn covered heads of the prophets, by the company of the risen, and the long robes of the judgment-angels by hell-mouth and its flames gaping there, and the devils that feed it; by the saved souls and the crowning angels; by the presence of the Judge, and by the roses growing above them all forever."

The review of Browning's *Men and Women,* then recently published, is more valuable as testifying to the impression produced by Browning upon his young contemporary, than for any especial illumination it throws upon the poems themselves. Browning was popular with the students of Oxford long before he gained his wider audience, and although Morris did not follow him far in his investigation of the human soul and came heartily to dislike "his constant dwelling on sin and probing of the secrets of the heart," he placed him at the time of writing his criticism "high among the poets of all time" and he "hardly knew whether first or second in our own," and his defence of him, bristling with ejaculations, and couched in boyish phrases, shows in part a more than boyish divination. "It does not help poems much to *solve* them," he says, after what, in truth, is a somewhat disastrous attempt to interpret the meaning of *Women and Roses,* "because there are in poems so many exquisitely small and delicate turns of thought running through their music, and along with it, that cannot be done into prose, any more than the infinite variety of form, and shadow, and colour in a great picture can be rendered by a coloured woodcut." It was "a bitter thing" to him to see the way in which the poet had been received by "almost everybody," and he assured his little world that what the critics called obscurity in

Browning's poems resulted from depth of thought and greatness of subject on the poet's part, and on his readers' part, "from their shallower brains and more bounded knowledge," if not indeed from "mere wanton ignorance and idleness," and to this kind of obscurity one had little right to object. It was the first tilt in the lists, the beginning of the long combat against the Philistines upon which Morris entered with high resolve and firm conviction, which he lustily enjoyed, and in which despite many a broken lance he bore himself as a bold and skilful knight.

In the little tale called *The Hollow Land*, written for the magazine just before it "went to smash," to use Burne-Jones's expressive phrase, an amusingly significant sentence occurs: "Then I tried to learn painting," says the hero, "till I thought I should die, but at last learned through very much pain and grief." Here it is not difficult to recognise an autobiographic touch. Painting was already beginning to beckon Morris away from the profession he had so recently chosen. At the end of 1855, during the Christmas vacation, and just before Morris entered Street's office, Burne-Jones had made a visit to London, where at a monthly meeting at the Working Men's College he for the first time saw Rossetti, and later heard him rend in pieces the opinions of those who differed with him, and stoutly support his infrangible theory that all men should be painters. How ready Burne-Jones was to yield himself to this potent influence, how promptly Rossetti's vivid and original temperament acted upon his admirer, is clear from the latter's description, written many years after, of the first encounter—the young undergraduate sitting half-frightened, embarrassed and worshipping, among strangers, eating thick bread and butter, and listening to speeches about the progress of the college, until the entrance of his idol, whose sensitive, gentle, indolent face, with its flickering of humour and the fire of genius, entirely satisfied his poetic imagination. The great qualities of Rossetti in those days revealed themselves in his face, and his imperious will and keen intellect were no less obvious in his talk. Burne-Jones returned to Oxford with the idea of dedicating himself to art more than ever firmly fixed in his mind. Rossetti had approved the drawings which he had brought to him for consideration, and had pronounced the seven months still to elapse before he could take his degree time too valuable to waste outside of art, counselling him to fling the University and all its works behind him and begin painting at once. With mingled delight and terror Burne-Jones, in spite of small means and weak health, followed his leader, who, however rash to advise, was not one to neglect his charge, and who worked loyally to bring him through with triumph, criticising, teaching, approving, encouraging without stint, and presently, after his own inimitable fashion, bringing patrons to him, bidding them buy, which obediently they did.

It was inevitable that Morris should be stirred to emulation by this step on the part of his friend. After Burne-Jones went to London to begin painting under Rossetti's direction, Morris spent nearly all his Sundays with him at his lodgings in Chelsea. These holidays were full of excitement. It was a glorious little world that opened out under Rossetti's enthusiastic, dogmatic, and continuous talk and argument. Morris was deeply impressed by his notion that everyone should be a painter, and after Street moved his office to London and Morris and Burne-Jones took lodgings together, the former tried the characteristic experiment of combining painting with architecture, attempting to get six hours a day at his drawing in addition to his office work. It is interesting to find him writing at this juncture that he cannot enter into politico-social subjects with any interest, that things are in a muddle and that he has no power to set them right in the smallest degree, that *his* work is the embodiment of dreams in one form or another. What Rossetti thought of his two disciples is seen in a letter written by him to William Allingham in December, 1856, when Morris had been nearly a year with Street. He found both "wonders after their kind." "Jones is doing designs which quite put one to shame," he wrote, "so full are they of everything—Aurora Leighs of art. He will take the lead in no time." Morris he deemed "one of the finest little fellows alive—with a touch of the incoherent, but a real man," and "in

ILLUSTRATION BY ROSSETTI TO "THE LADY OF SHALOTT" IN THE MOXON "TENNYSON." THE HEAD OF LAUNCELOT IS A PORTRAIT OF MORRIS

all illumination and work of that kind" he considered him quite unrivalled by anything modern that he knew. With a guide thus confident and inspiring, it is not strange that Morris presently yielded to the spell, and renounced architecture to pursue painting as an end and aim in itself, although, like the hero of his romance, he learned with much pain and grief.

Rossetti's service to Morris is difficult to estimate. For a brief period his influence over him was supreme. Perhaps in the work and temper of this Italian, Morris saw more deeply into the heart of the mediæval world than all his churches and illuminated manuscripts could help him to see. At all events, he was for the time close to genius and dominated by it. His devotion to his master partook of the violence inseparable from his temperament. He was soon ready to say, when Burne-Jones complained that he worked better in Rossetti's manner than in his own: "I have got beyond that; I want to imitate Gabriel as much as I can." But he was never to be for very long under any personal influence. Nor could he be persuaded by the most brilliant eloquence in the world that good could be got out of doing what he did not enjoy; and he never enjoyed any labour that required long patience and persistent concentration of effort. Without being fickle, his mind was so restless as to produce the effect of fickleness and to preclude the possibility of his doing really great work. While he was trying, under Rossetti's stimulating but peremptory rule, to master a painter's methods he became gloomy and despondent. "How long Rossetti's daily influence might have kept him labouring at what he could not do," writes Mr. Mackail with a tinge of bitterness, "when there was work all round that he could do, on the whole, better than any man living, it is needless to inquire." But that Rossetti did manage to keep him for a couple of years at the study of painting cannot be counted a misfortune. Probably that experience, together with his brief term under Street, did as much as anything to save his design from mediocrity and imitativeness. He did not make himself an architect, and he never learned to draw anything that remotely resembled the actual structure of the human form, but he must have gained through his study some knowledge of the inviolable laws of art that he could not have gained by passive observation however keen, or by sympathy however ardent. Rossetti can hardly have been the best master for him. His own nature was too undisciplined, and he had as few of the academic virtues as any man on record of the same technical ability. But his was the supreme faculty of rousing enthusiasm. It may be doubted whether any other painter in England could have kept Morris at the appointed and impossible task for so long a time. It is easy to imagine how the impatient spirit of the latter rebelled against the slow process of learning to draw the human figure in its complicated and subtle beauty of construction and surface. The fact that he stopped so far short of satisfactory accomplishment seems to account for many of the defects to be found in his later designs, which at their best were never to be entirely beautiful, though full of zest and freedom. His tendency to drop any branch of his work as soon as it became tedious to him, to turn to something else, kept his creative impulse continually fresh and effective; but kept him also from achieving the penetrating distinction of artistic self-possession. Whatever helped him in any degree toward this self-possession, whatever he got in the way of discipline of mind and hand, should be acknowledged by his admirers with gratitude, and it is but just to recognise in Rossetti the one man who seems to have kept the prodigious impetuosity of Morris down without promptly losing hold upon his interest. Add to this the clear vision of a romantic ideal which all who worked with Rossetti were privileged to share, and the constant inspiration of the drama of sentiment and emotion rendered in his colour and line and in his exotic treatment of form, and we must own that nowhere else could Morris have found such food for an imagination already quickened by influences reaching it from a remote time and an alien world. Nowhere else could he have come so close to the concealed mysteries of the human soul, despite the disillusionment he was bound to feel in daily contact with a character as contradictory as it was compelling.

CHAPTER III.

FROM ROSSETTI TO THE RED HOUSE.

ALTHOUGH a blight of discouragement seems to have fallen upon Morris under Rossetti's tuition, there were some blithe compensations. Not the least of these was the fitting up of the rooms at 17 Red Lion Square where he and Burne-Jones took quarters. "Topsy and I live together," wrote Burne-Jones, "in the quaintest room in all London, hung with brasses of old knights and drawings of Albert Dürer." For the furniture, Morris, who, Rossetti said, was "bent on doing the magnificent," made designs to be carried out in deal by a carpenter of the neighbourhood. Everything was very large and heavy, intensely mediæval, and doubtless rather ugly in an honest fashion, but in the end it was furniture to be coveted, for it offered great spaces for decoration, and Rossetti as well as Morris and Burne-Jones painted on it subjects from Chaucer and Dante and the Arthurian stories. The panels of a cupboard glowed with Rossetti's beautiful pictures representing Dante and Beatrice meeting in

Florence and meeting in Paradise, and on the wide backs of the chairs he painted scenes from some of the poems Morris had written. The wardrobe was decorated by Burne-Jones with paintings from *The Prioress's Tale.* On the walls of the room were hung, no doubt, the several water-colours bought from Rossetti, to the lovely names of which Morris promptly wrote ballads. An owl was co-tenant with the young artists, and they were served and also criticised by a housemaid of literary ambitions. In this highly individual apartment, where, curiously enough, Rossetti and his friend Deverell had had their studio together five or six years before, life was not all labour and striving. There were, moreover, holidays spent at the Zoölogical Gardens, evenings at the theatre, night-long sessions in Rossetti's rooms, and excursions on the Thames. One of the latter is vividly described in Dr. Birkbeck Hill's *Letters of Gabriel Rossetti to William Allingham,* giving a joyous picture of Morris at the mercy of his ungovernable temper. The party, consisting of Hill, Morris, and Faulkner, had started out to row down the Thames from Oxford to a London suburb. By the time they had reached Henley they had spent all their money except enough for Faulkner's return ticket to Oxford, where he was to attend a college meeting. For this he departed, promising to bring back a supply of money in the evening. "The weather was unusually hot," writes Dr. Hill, "Morris and I sauntered along the river-side. I have not forgotten the longing glances he cast on a large basket of strawberries. He had always been so plentifully supplied with money that he bore with far greater impatience than I did this privation. At last the shadows had grown long and the heat was more bearable. We went with light hearts to the railway station to meet our comrade. 'Well, Faulkner,' cried out Morris, cheerfully, 'how much money have you brought?' Our friend gave a start. 'Good heavens,' he replied, 'I forgot all about it.' Morris thrust both his hands into his long dark curly hair, tugged at it wildly, ground his teeth, swore like a trooper, and stamped up and down the platform — in fact, behaved just like Sinbad's captain when he found that his ship was driving upon the rocks. His outbursts of rage, I hasten to say, were always harmless. They left no sullenness behind, and as each rapidly passed away he was ready to join in a hearty laugh at it. Faulkner, who was not the most patient of men, noticed that passengers, station-master, porters, engine-driver, and stoker were all gazing in astonishment. He, too, lost his temper, and, though in a far lower key, stormed back. Morris soon quieted down, and a council of war was held. He fortunately had a gold watch-chain on which he raised enough to pay all needful expenses. I remember well how the rest of our journey we rowed by many a tavern on the bank as effectually constrained as ever was Ulysses not to listen to its siren call. It was through no earthly paradise that the young poet and artist passed on the afternoon of our last day." When they landed they had just a penny among them, and were still some six or seven miles from their destination, so they were obliged to hire a cab and trust to good fortune for not coming to a turnpike gate before arriving at Red Lion Square.

About this time also Rossetti and Morris made an excursion to Oxford for the purpose of visiting Benjamin Woodward, the architect and Rossetti's friend. Mr. Woodward had recently erected a building for the Oxford Union, a society composed of past and present members of the University. In exhibiting the building to Rossetti it was suggested that the blank stretch of wall which ran around the top of the Debating Room afforded an admirable opportunity for decoration, and Rossetti with prompt enthusiasm evolved a plan for a coöperative enterprise. He and Morris, with several other willing spirits, — Burne-Jones, of course, Arthur Hughes, Valentine Prinsep, Spencer Stanhope, and J. Hungerford Pollen, — were to go up to Oxford in a body. Each was to choose a subject from the *Morte d'Arthur,* and execute it to the best of his ability on the walls of the Debating Room. The whole affair was to be a matter of a few weeks. The artists offered their services for nothing; their expenses (which turned out to be as free as their offer) were to be paid by the Union. It is easy to imagine the ensuing bustle and ardour. Rossetti eagerly managing, Morris delighted with the charmingly mediæval situation,— a few humble painters working together piously, without hope of glory or thought of gain, — the others following their leader with lamb-like docility. Had their knowledge of methods been equal to their zeal, the walls of the Debating Room must have become the loveliest of realised visions and the delight of many generations. The young workmen sat for each other, Morris, Burne-Jones, and Rossetti all possessing fine paintable heads. They clambered up and down endless ladders to gain a satisfactory view of their performance, and attacked the most stupendous difficulties with patience and ingenuity. The faces in the subject undertaken by Burne-Jones were painted, for example, in three planes at right angles to one another, owing to the projection of a string-course of bricks straight across the space to be filled by the heads of the figures. Some studies by Rossetti have been preserved, and show that his part at least of the decoration was conceived in a fresh poetic spirit, with fulness and quaintness of expression and suggestion. But the congenial band had entered upon their labours with a carelessness that can only be described as wanton. Not one of them knew how to paint in tempera, and the new damp walls were smeared over with a thin coat of white lime wash laid upon the bare bricks as sole preparation for a sort of water-colour painting that blossomed like a flower under the gifted hands of the artists, and faded almost as soon away. The effect at the time was so brilliant as to make the walls, according to Mr.

Coventry Patmore's contemporaneous testimony, "look like the margin of an illuminated manuscript," but in the course of a few months the colours had sunk into the sponge-like surface to such an extent that the designs were already dim and indistinguishable.

Morris, with characteristic promptness, was the first on the field, and his picture was finished in advance of any of the others. He was, however, no better instructed than his companions in the special requirements of his material, and presently all that was left of his painting was the head of his brave knight peering over the tops of multitudinous sunflowers. The decoration of the ceiling was also assigned to him, and he made his design for it in a single day. Later, in 1875, he repainted it, but most of the art of this merry period has receded into complete oblivion. The stay in Oxford lengthened into months as complications increased, and finally the enterprise was abandoned with the work unfinished. It had led, however, to an event of paramount importance to Morris, and of considerable importance to Rossetti — the meeting with Miss Burden, who was to figure in so many of Rossetti's symbolic pictures, and who became the wife of Morris. Her remarkable beauty had attracted the attention of the young men one night at the little Oxford theatre. "My brother was the first to observe her," writes William Rossetti; "her face was at once tragic, mystic, passionate, calm, beautiful, and gracious — a face for a sculptor and a face for a painter — a face solitary in England,

and not at all like that of an English woman, but rather of an Ionian Greek." In Rossetti's portrait of her at eighteen, painted shortly after this meeting, we see the grave, unusual features almost precisely as they are drawn with words in a poem by Morris, entitled *Praise of My Lady,* which Mr. Mackail says was written during a visit to the Manchester Exhibition of 1857, but which assuredly is no earlier than the date of his acquaintance with Jane Burden. The description, Pre-Raphaelite in its detail, runs through the first half of the poem :

My Lady seems of ivory
Forehead, straight nose, and cheeks that be
Hollow'd a little mournfully.
Beata mea Domina!

Her forehead, overshadow'd much
By bows of hair, has a wave such
As God was good to make for me.
Beata mea Domina!

Not greatly long my lady's hair,
Nor yet with yellow color fair,
But thick and crisped wonderfully;
Beata mea Domina!

Heavy to make the pale face sad,
And dark, but dead as though it had
Been forged by God most wonderfully;
Beata mea Domina!

Of some strange metal, thread by thread,
To stand out from my lady's head,
Not moving much to tangle me.
Beata mea Domina!

Beneath her brows the lids fall slow,
The lashes a clear shadow throw
Where I would wish my lips to be.
Beata mea Domina!

Her great eyes, standing far apart,
Draw up some memory from her heart,
And gaze out very mournfully;
Beata mea Domina!

So beautiful and kind they are,
But most times looking out afar,
Waiting for something, not for me.
Beata mea Domina!

I wonder if the lashes long
Are those that do her bright eyes wrong,
For always half tears seem to be.
Beata mea Domina!

Lurking below the underlid,
Darkening the place where they lie hid—
If they should rise and flow for me!
Beata mea Domina!

Her full lips being made to kiss,
Curl'd up and pensive each one is;
This makes me faint to stand and see.
Beata mea Domina!

It was the force of this attraction that kept Morris long at Oxford after Rossetti and Burne-Jones had returned to London, leaving the walls of the Oxford Union to their sad fate. But it was no love in idleness for him, rather a time of many beginnings. He was carving in stone, modelling in clay, making designs for stained glass windows, even "doing worsted work," in Rossetti's contemptuous phrase for his efforts at reviving the lost art of embroidery, with a frame made from an old model and wools dyed especially for him. Most of all he was writing poetry, the proper occupation of a lover so æsthetically endowed. Early in 1858 he had *The Defence of Guenevere,* a collection of thirty poems, ready to bring out. Save for a slim little pamphlet entitled *Sir Galahad: A Christmas Mystery,* the contents of which were included in it, it was his first volume and, like Swinburne's *Rosamond* published two years later, it was dedicated to Rossetti.

In this youthful, fantastic, emotional poetry we get the very essence of the writer's early spirit without the strange shadow of foreboding, the constant sense of swiftly passing time, that comes into the poetry of his maturity. Technically, the poems could hardly be more picturesquely defective than they are. The one giving the volume its name is nearly unintelligible in parts, even when the reader is aware of the incidents of Guenevere's story, and prepared to interpret the hysterical ravings of a woman overcome by sorrow, shame, and love.

But no poems, except Rossetti's own, have so suggested romantic art in strange shapes and unbridled colour. They, too, like the wall-paintings of that early and unrivalled time, resemble the margins of an illuminated manuscript, reminding one of nothing in nature, but flashing the richness of mediæval symbolism upon the imagination in more or less awkward forms. If Morris could not "imitate Gabriel" in his pictures, he could at least imitate Gabriel's pictures in his poems. From the *Beata Beatrix,* from the *Ghirlandata,* from the *Proserpine,* from almost any of Rossetti's paintings of women, these curious and affected lines, for example, might have been gleaned:

See through my long throat how the words go up
  In ripples to my mouth; how in my hand
The shadow lies like wine within a cup
  Of marvellously colour'd gold.

In *The Eve of Crecy* we have the glitter of gold and the splendour of material things, rendered with a childish abandon, as in the prose romances:

Gold on her head and gold on her feet,
And gold where the hems of her kirtle meet,
And a golden girdle round my sweet;—
        Ah! qu'elle est belle, La Marguerite.

Yet even now it is good to think

. . . .

Of Margaret sitting glorious there,
In glory of gold and glory of hair,
And glory of glorious face most fair;
        Ah! qu'elle est belle, La Marguerite.

The full hues that had for the decorators of mediæval missals a religious significance recur again and again in lines that have much more to do with earth than with heaven, and show less concern with the human soul than with the human heart. Damozels hold scarlet lilies such as Maiden Margaret bears "on the great church walls;" ladies walk in their gardens clad in white and scarlet; the vision of Christ appears to Galahad "with raiment half blood-red, half white as snow"; angels appear clad in white with scarlet wings; scarlet is the predominating colour throughout, if we except gold, which serves as background and ornament to everything. Next to scarlet comes green, which Morris was later to call "the workaday colour," and we find occasional patches of blue and of grey in painted boats and in hangings. The following stanza shows a favourite method of emphasising the prevailing colour of a poem:

> The water slips,
> The red-bill'd heron dips,
> Sweet kisses on red lips,
> Alas! the red rust grips,
> And the blood-red dagger rips,
> Yet, O knight, come to me!

For pure incoherence, the quality that Rossetti discerned in Morris at their first meeting, the song from which this stanza is taken is unsurpassed. Yet an emotional effect is gained in it. What we chiefly miss in the little craft sailing under such vivid colours, is that "deep-grasping keel of reason" which, Lowell says, "alone can steady and give direction" to verse. Excitable and impatient, in pursuit of a vague ideal, gifted with the power to bring out the pictorial quality of detached scenes, but without a fine metrical sense, and averse to lucid statement, the young poet introduced himself to the world as a symbolist in the modern acceptation of the word. One of his poems, *Rapunzel,* has been said to forecast Maeterlinck's manner and spirit, and the general characteristics of the poem — a fairy tale somewhat too "grown-up" in treatment — certainly suggest the comparison. In all this work physical characteristics play an important part. Long hands with "tenderly shadowed fingers," "long lips" that "cleave" to the fingers they kiss, lips "damp with tears," that "shudder with a kiss," lips "like a curved sword," warm arms, long, fair arms, lithe arms, twining arms, broad fair eyelids, long necks, and unlimited hair, form an equipment somewhat dangerous for a poet with anything short of genius to sustain him. For themes Morris had gone chiefly to the Arthurian stories and to the chronicles of Froissart. His style, he himself thought, was more like Browning's than anyone else's, though the difference that lay between him and Browning even at the beginning forbade any essential likeness. Browning's effort was always to render an idea which was perfectly clear in his own mind. His volubility and obscurity and roughness frequently arose from his over-eagerness to express his idea in a variety of ways, leading him to break off with half statements and begin afresh, to throw out imperfect suggestions and follow them with others equally imperfect. But all his stutterings and broken sentences failed to disguise the fact that an intellectual conception underlay the turbulent method, giving substance and life to the poem however much it might lack grace and form. With Morris the intellectual conception was as weak as with Browning it was strong, and apparently existed chiefly to give an excuse for the pictures following one another in rapid succession through every poem, short or long, dramatic or lyric, of both his youth and maturity. In this early volume there was, to be sure, an obvious effort toward rendering psychological effects. Most of the longer poems are miniature dramas with a march toward some great event in the lives of the actors. The author observes the dramatic requirement of sinking himself in the identity of his characters. Knights are slain and ladies die of love and witch-bound maidens are rescued by their princes without the sounding of a personal note on the part of their creator. And in two instances, *Sir Peter Harpdon's End* and *The Haystack in the Floods,* there is ruddy human blood in the tortured beings whose extremity moves the reader with a genuine emotion. In these two poems the voice might indeed be the voice of Browning, though the hand is still unmistakably the hand of Morris. In the main, however, the appeal that is made is to the imagination concerned with the visible aspect of brilliantly coloured objects and with the delirious expression of overwrought feelings.

One defect, calculated to interfere with a warm reception of the volume on the part of the general public, Morris shared with Browning, possessing even

Portrait of Jane Burden (Mrs. Morris)

By Rossetti

Oxford

more than Browning the merit attending it. Familiarity with the art and literature of the Middle Ages made it natural for him to preserve the thin new wine of his youthful poetry in the old bottles of the defunct past, using motives and scenes and accessories alien to our modern life, and only dimly understood by the modern reader. The true spirit of that past it is hardly necessary to say he did not revive,—no writer has ever revived the true spirit of any age antecedent to his own,—and Morris, with his remarkable faculty for eliminating from his mental conceptions whatever did not please his taste, was wholly unfitted by temperament, however well fitted by his acquirements, to carry through successfully a task so tremendous.

The Defence of Guenevere was received by the public without enthusiasm. About half an edition of five hundred copies was sold and given away, and the remainder lingered for a dozen years or more until the publication of *The Earthly Paradise* stimulated the interest of readers in the previous work of its author.

Whatever disappointment Morris may have felt must soon have given way to the excitement of the plunge he now made into a new life and the most intense personal interests. On the twenty-sixth of April, 1859, he was married to Jane Burden, and after a brief interval of travel he began to build the beautiful house which he then supposed would be his home for the rest of his days.

His personal attractiveness at this time was keenly felt by his companions. He had been "making himself," as the phrase is, since his childhood, and if Stevenson's dictum—to know what you like is the beginning of wisdom and of old age—be applied to him he can never have been wholly ignorant or a child. Knowledge of what he liked, and even more definitely of what he did not like, was his earliest as well as his most notable acquirement. But he was a boy, too, in his excessive restless vitality, and hitherto with all his enthusiasms he had been a somewhat cold boy. Just now he was beginning to "take a fancy for the human," as one of his friends put it. He was connecting his vague schemes and ambitions with a personal and practical enterprise. His ideals dropped from a region always too rare for them to an atmosphere of activities and interests in which the vast general public could breathe as easily as he. In building his new home to his fancy he was unconsciously laying the corner-stones of the many homes throughout England into which his influence was afterward to enter. He was just twenty-five, filled with energy, generous impulse, honesty, and kindness. The bourgeois touch which his biographer declares was inherent in his nature was far from obvious as yet. Society for its own sake he liked little, and was not above getting out of unwelcome invitations by subterfuge, if fair means would not avail. He affected a Bohemian carelessness in dress, and his hair was uniformly wild. His language was

"ACANTHUS" WALL-PAPER

"PIMPERNEL" WALL-PAPER

"AFRICAN MARIGOLD" COTTON-PRINT

WALL-PAPER AND COTTON-PRINT DESIGNS

(Reproduced from examples obtained by courtesy of Mr. A. E. Bulkley)

generally forcible, often violent, always expressive. He lived in the company of his intimates and cared for nothing beyond the range of his fixed interests. The remark made long after—"Do you suppose that I should see anything in Rome that I can't see in Whitechapel?"—was perfectly indicative of his mood toward everything that failed to arouse his intellectual curiosity. But the places and things that did arouse it were never tawdry or valueless, and his reasons for caring for them, of which he was always remarkably prolific, were such as appeal strongly to the mind in which homely associations hold a constant place. It must be an out and out classicist who fails to detect in himself a pulsation of sympathy in response to the wail which Morris once sent home from Verona: "Yes, and even in these magnificent and wonderful towns I long rather for the heap of grey stones with a grey roof that we call a house north-away."

His first house, in which he took unlimited delight, was not, however, a heap of grey stones, but a structure of brick, its name, the Red House, indicating its striking and then unusual colour. Its architect was Philip Webb, who had been an associate of Morris during the brief period passed in Mr. Street's office. Situated not far from London, on the outskirts of the village of Upton and in the midst of a pleasant orchard, whose trees dropped their fruit into its windows, the Red House wore an emphatically Gothic aspect. It was L-shaped, with numerous irregularities of plan, and entirely without frippery of applied ornament. Its great sloping roof, the pointed arches of its doorways, the deep simple porches, the large hall, with its long table in place of an entrance alley the open-timbered roof over the staircase, the panelled screen dividing the great hall from a lesser one, —all these were characteristic of the old English house before the day of Italian invasion, while the mobile Gothic style, adapting itself readily to individual needs, prevailed. It stood among the old and gnarled trees, only two stories in height, but with an effect of rambling spaciousness and hospitality, and the garden that lay close to it was as individual and old-fashioned as itself. Morris prided himself, Mr. Mackail tells us, on his knowledge of gardening, and his advice to the Birmingham Society of Artists in one of the lectures of his later years shows how thoughtfully he considered the subject. As he always acted so far as he could upon his theories, we may be fairly sure that the Red House garden was planned in conformity with the ideal place sketched in this lecture, and may assume in it a profusion of single flowers mixed to avoid great masses of colour, among them the old columbine, where the clustering doves are unmistakable and distinct, the old china aster, the single snowdrop, and the sunflower, these planted in little squares, divided from each other by grassy walks, and hedged in by wild rose or sweetbriar trellises. We may be sure the place contained no curiosities from the jungle or tropical waste, that everything was excluded which was not native to the English soil, and that ferns and brakes from the woodland were not enticed from the place of their origin to take away the characteristic domestic look of a spot that ought to seem "like a part of the house." "It will be a key to right thinking about gardens," says Morris, "if you consider in what kind of places a garden is most desired. In a very beautiful country, especially if it be mountainous, we can do without it well enough, whereas in a flat and dull country we crave after it, and there it is often the very making of the homestead; while in great towns, gardens both private and public are positive necessities if the citizens are to live reasonable and healthy lives in body and mind."

Passing from this first necessity of reasonable and healthy living through the rose-masked doorway into the Red House itself, we find it equally suggestive of its master's personal tastes and beliefs. For everything Morris had his persuasive reason. His windows had small leaded panes of glass, because the large windows found "in most decent houses or what are so called," let in a flood of light "in a haphazard and ill-considered way," which the indwellers are "forced to obscure again by shutters, blinds, curtains, screens, heavy upholsteries, and such other nuisances." By all means, therefore, fill the window with moderate-sized panes of glass set in solid sash bars — "we shall then at all events feel as if we were indoors on a cold day" — as if we had a roof over our heads. The fact that small windows were used in mediæval times and must therefore of necessity be superior is not brought forward in this argument, and the charm of the reasoning is not marred by any reminder of the actual conditions of which small heavily leaded windows are a survival — such as the fortress style of building belonging to a warlike time, and the great costliness of glass, and the inability to support large panes by leads.

Morris could always be trusted to support his fundamental liking for a thing by a host of assurances as to its sensible merits and practical advantages, but the mere fact that he liked it was quite sufficient for his own satisfaction of mind. When one of his comrades once suggested to him that personal feeling ought not to count for too much, and that not liking a thing did not make it bad, he replied: "Oh, don't it though! What we don't like *is* bad." And he had a fashion which must have produced an irritating effect upon some of his hearers, of declaring that the people who did not hold his ideas must be unhealthy either in body or mind or both. Certainly the aspect of the Red House suggested health within its walls. With a slight stretch of imagination one could argue from its furnishings that its master was a northerner, a middle-class man, the admirer of a rough age, a sturdy art, a plain habit of life; that he was a worker whose dreams tormented him to speedy and vigorous action, a creature whose vitality was too great even for his strong frame and physical power. He liked a massive chair, and well he might, for one of his amusements was to twist his legs about it in such a way that a lightly built affair must instantly succumb. He liked a floor that he could stamp on with impunity; he liked a table on which he could pound with his fists without danger to its equilibrium. In the Red House these requirements were fully met. In the lecture called *The Beauty of Life* is an account of the fittings "necessary to the sitting-room of a healthy person." Beside the table that will "keep steady when you work upon it," and the chairs "that you can move about," the good floor, and the small carpet "which can be bundled out of the room in two minutes," there must be "a bookcase with a great many books in it," a bench "that you can sit or lie upon," a cupboard with drawers, and, "unless either the bookcase or the cupboard be very beautiful with painting or carving," pictures or engravings on the wall, "or else the wall itself must be ornamented with some beautiful and restful pattern," then a vase or two, and fireplaces as unlike as possible to "the modern mean, miserable, and showy affairs, plastered about with wretched sham ornament, trumpery of cast iron, and brass and polished steel, and what not — offensive to look at and a nuisance to clean." To these necessaries, "unless we are musical and need a piano, in which case as far as beauty is concerned we are in a bad way," we can add very little without "troubling ourselves, and hindering our work, our thought, and our rest."

In accordance with these opinions, but with a fulness and richness of ornament not suggested by the simplicity of their expression, the pleasant building at Upton gradually took on great beauty and individuality. The walls were hung with embroidered fabrics worked by Mrs. Morris and her friends, or painted by Burne-Jones, who, undeterred by the Oxford episode, started an elaborate series of mural decorations in illustration of the wonderful adventures of Sire Degravant, the hero of an ancient romance. Another series of scenes from the War of Troy was started for the walls of the staircase, and although both schemes were abandoned, enough was done to give an effect of splendour to the rooms. Up to the large drawing-room came the ponderous and mighty settle which had cost so many expletives in the course of its adjustment to the old room in Red Lion Square, and which was now embellished by a balcony at the top to which a stairway led up. All minor accessories were thoughtfully considered and for the most part designed by Morris or by friends pressed into service at his eager demand. He found little to content him in the articles of commerce on sale at the orthodox shops in the early sixties. "In looking at an old house," he says in one of his books, "we please ourselves by thinking of all the generations of men that have passed through it, remembering how it has received their joy and borne their sorrow and not even their folly has left sourness on it; and in looking at a new

"THE STRAWBERRY THIEF" DESIGN FOR COTTON PRINT

house if built as it should be, we feel a pleasure in thinking how he who built it has left a piece of his soul behind him to greet the newcomers one after another, long after he is gone." Such an impress he left upon the Red House, so that no one passing it or even hearing of it can fail to think of it as belonging to William Morris, whoever may have the fortune to live in it hereafter, and fall heir to the associations with which he invested it.

During the time of building and furnishing he was exuberantly happy and wholly in his element. Turning constantly from one thing to another, yet keeping along the line of his united interests, giving his magnificent energy free scope in doing and accomplishing, seeing grow into visible form the theories and tastes so dear to his heart, letting out his enthusiasms and carrying others along on their current, setting a practical example in what he believed to be of the deepest importance by requiring for himself artistic handicraft, acting out a vigorous protest against the mechanical arts and the shams of the commercial world,—all this was meat and drink to him, and out of it grew an enterprise representing what to the public has been probably the most valuable side of his many-sided career, the establishment of a firm engaged in various forms of decorative art. At about this time he adopted, after the fashion of the master-workman of the Middle Ages, a device or legend expressive in one way or another of his aim. He chose the one used by Van Eyck, "Als ich kanne,"—if I can,—and distributed it in French translation and in English over his house, on windows and tiles and in tapestry hangings. The modesty of the words was no doubt as sincere in his case as in the case of the old Flemish painter who excelled all his contemporaries, but the extent to which he could and did in the new business on which he was about to enter has been the wonder of his followers.

CHAPTER IV.

MORRIS AND COMPANY.

THE formation of the firm of "Morris, Marshall, Faulkner, & Company," as it was first called, appears to have been highly incidental in character, despite the assertion of Morris himself in a letter to his old tutor, that he had long meant to be a decorator, and to that end mainly had built his fine house. "One evening a lot of us were together," says Rossetti, in the account given by Mr. Watts-Dunton, "and we got to talking about the way in which artists did all kinds of things in olden times, designed every kind of decoration and most kinds of furniture, and someone suggested — as a joke more than anything else — that we should each put down five pounds and form a company. Fivers were blossoms of a rare growth among us in those days, and I won't swear that the table bristled with fivers. Anyhow the firm was formed, but of course there was no deed or anything of that kind. In fact it was a mere playing at business, and Morris was elected manager, not because we ever dreamed he would turn out a man of business, but because he was the only one among us who had both time and money to spare. We had no idea whatever of commercial success, but it succeeded almost in our own despite."

In the mind of Morris it doubtless promised to be the sort of association about which he was constantly dreaming; a group of intelligent craftsmen interested in making the details of daily life as full as possible of beauty, each man fitted to his task and loving it, each in his way a master-workman of the guild, counting his craft honourable and spending his best thought and labour on it. There was ground enough for faith in the artistic if not in the commercial outcome of the enterprise. The associates, beside Morris, Rossetti, and Burne-Jones, were Madox-Brown, then an artist of established reputation, Webb, the architect of the Red House, who was also a designer of furniture and ornament; Peter Paul Marshall, to whom Mr. William Rossetti ascribes the first suggestion of the formation of the firm, a "capable artist" although an amateur; and Charles Faulkner of the Oxford group, who had followed his mates to London unable to endure the loneliness of Oxford without them. They proposed to open what Rossetti called "an actual shop," and sell whatever their united talent produced. "We are not intending to compete with ——'s costly rubbish or anything of that sort," Rossetti wrote to his friend Allingham, "but to give real good taste at the price as far as possible of ordinary furniture."

TULIP DESIGN FOR AXMINSTER CARPET

In the Spring of 1861, premises were taken over a jeweller's shop at 8 Red Lion Square. Two floors and a part of the basement were used by the firm, and about a dozen men and boys were presently employed. There were regular weekly meetings carried on with the boisterousness of youth and high spirits, but with thorough efficiency, nevertheless, where plans that were to modify and influence the household decoration of all England were gaily formed and put into practice.

The prospectus, in which Mr. Mackail discerns Rossetti's "slashing hand and imperious accent," was not entirely calculated to mollify rival decorators, calling attention to the fact that attempts at decorative art up to that time had been crude and fragmentary, and emphasising the want of some one place where work of "a genuine and beautiful character could be obtained." The new firm pledged itself to execute in a business-like manner:

"I. Mural Decoration, either in Pictures or in Pattern Work, or merely in the arrangement of Colours, as applied to dwelling-houses, churches, or public buildings.

"II. Carving generally, as applied to Architecture.

"III. Stained Glass, especially with reference to its harmony with Mural Decoration.

"IV. Metal Work in all its branches, including Jewellery.

"V. Furniture, either depending for its beauty on its own design, on the application of materials hitherto overlooked, or on its conjunction with Figure and Pattern Painting. Under this head is included Embroidery of all kinds, Stamped Leather, and ornamental work in other such materials, besides every article necessary for domestic use."

Clearly this was not the usual thing, nor was the business conducted in the usual way. According to Mr. William Rossetti, the young reformers adopted a tone of "something very like dictatorial irony" toward their customers, permitting no compromise, and laying down the law without concession to individual taste or want of taste. You could have things such as the firm chose them to be or you could go without them.

The finance of the company began, Mr. Mackail says, with a call of one pound per share and a loan of a hundred pounds from Mrs. Morris of Leyton. In 1862 a further call of nineteen pounds a share was made on the partners, raising the paid-up capital to one hundred and forty pounds, which "was never increased until the dissolution of the firm in 1874." A few hundred pounds additional were loaned by Morris and his mother. Each piece of work contributed by any member of the firm was paid for at the time, and Morris as general manager received a salary of a hundred and fifty pounds a year.

It is obvious that with this slender financial basis the business required the utmost energy, industry, skill, and talent to keep it from being promptly wrecked on the very uncertain coast of public opin-

PEACOCK DESIGN FOR COARSE WOOL HANGINGS

ion. During the first year all the members of the firm were active, although even at the first Morris led the rest. A stimulus was provided by the International Exhibition of 1862, whither they sent examples of their work, at the cost, wrote Faulkner, of "more tribulation and swearing to Topsy than three exhibitions will be worth." The exhibits attracted attention, and were awarded medals, in the case of the stained glass, "for artistic qualities of colour and design," and in the case of the furniture, hangings, and so forth, for the "closeness with which the style of the Middle Ages was rendered." It happened that the chief work in stained glass in the exhibit of the firm consisted of a set of windows designed by Rossetti, and giving, according to a Belgian critic, "an impression of colour, dazzling and magnificent, velvety and harmonious, resembling the Flemish stained glass windows decorating the Gothic cathedrals." Thus, fortunately, the first appearance of the firm was distinguished by the splendour which Rossetti alone among the group of workers could achieve, but his interest and activity shortly flagged and were absorbed in his individual work outside the company.

At first, despite the lordly prospectus, there were occasional blunders. Dr. Birkbeck Hill tells of a study table and an arm-chair, neither one of which was so thorough a piece of workmanship as the firm would have turned out later on, and Mr. Hughes remembers a sofa with a long bar beneath projecting six inches at each end so that it tripped up anyone who hastily went round it. These, however, were blunders of a kind soon remedied by experience. So long as the associates kept up their enthusiasm there were among them ample skill to grapple with technicalities, and ample artistic faculty to defy all ordinary competition. Whoever dropped behind from time to time in this most essential quality of enthusiasm it was never Morris, and all accounts agree in attributing to his energy and industry and unutterable zest the success of the novel and interesting experiment. "He is the only man I have known," said Rossetti once, "who beats every other man at his own game." The men he had to beat at this game of decoration were for the most part unworthy foes. Decorative art was at a low ebb in the early Victorian age, the age of antimacassars, stucco, and veneer. From this cheap vulgarity and pretentiousness Morris turned back — as he was wont to do on every occasion that offered excuse — to the thirteenth century as the purest fount of English tradition, where, if anywhere, could be found models showing logical principles of construction and genuine workmanship. His companions either caught from him the infection of the mediæval attitude or were already in sympathy with it, and the work of the firm took on an emphatically Gothic aspect from the beginning. How great or how important a part each member played in the sum of the production is very difficult to estimate owing to the coöperative plan by which several artists frequently united in executing one and the same piece of work. Sometimes Burne-Jones would draw the figures, Webb the birds, and Morris the foliage for a piece of drapery or wall-paper. Again portions of separate designs would be used over and over in different combinations for different places. This free coöperation, this moving about within the limits of a general plan, suited the restless spirit of Morris, and chimed also with his profound admiration for the way in which the mediæval works of art were brought about, no one man standing high above the others or trying to preserve his name and the fame of his performance. Working for the pleasure of the work was of the very essence of his philosophy, and nothing could be more unjust than the sneers from time to time launched at him because his venture proved a commercial triumph. Perhaps it would be going too far to say that money-getting was never in his mind, but there is no question that it was never first in his mind, and never in the slightest degree crowded his desire to put forth sincere, fine work, worth its price to the last detail, and worthy of praise and liking without regard to its price. There was not the slightest suggestion of pose or sham of any kind in his thought when he wrote, as he often did, against the greed of gain and in praise of the kind of labour that may be delighted in without regard to pounds and pence. He could say quite faithfully that he shared the humility of the early craftsmen, of whom he speaks with reverence.

"In most sober earnest," he says in one of his

lectures, "when we hear it said, as it often is said, that extra money payment is necessary under all circumstances to produce great works of art, and that men of special talent will not use those talents without being bribed by mere gross material advantages, we, I say, shall know what to reply. We can appeal to the witness of those lovely works still left to us, whose unknown, unnamed creators were content to give them to the world, with little more extra wages than what their pleasure in their work and their sense of usefulness in it might bestow on them." There is no room for doubt that he approached his work in precisely the spirit here described by him. He was willing to exercise his faculties on the humblest undertakings, with no other aim than to make a common thing pleasant to look upon and agreeable to use. Half a century ago "craft" was not the fashionable word for the kind of work with which the firm chiefly concerned itself, and in doing the greater part of what he did Morris was merely writing himself down, in the language of the general public, an artisan. Conforming to the truest of principles he raised his work by getting under it. Nothing was too laborious or too lowly for him. Pride of position was unknown to him in any sense that would prevent him from indulging in manual labour. His real pride lay in making something which he considered beautiful take the place of something ugly in the world. If it were a fabric to be made lovely with long disused or unfamiliar dyes, his hands were

PAINTED WALL DECORATION DESIGNED BY MORRIS

in the vat. If tapestry were to be woven, he was at the loom by dawn. In his workman's blouse, steeped in indigo, and with his hair outstanding wildly, he was in the habit of presenting himself cheerfully at the houses of his friends, relying upon his native dignity to save appearances, or, to speak more truly, not thinking of appearances at all, but entirely happy in his rôle of workman, though frankly desirous that the business should prosper beyond all danger of the "smash" that would, he owned, "be a terrible nuisance." "I have not time on my hands," he said, "to be ruined and get really poor." It was to the peculiar union of the ideal and the practical in his nature that his success in the fields on which he ventured is due.

It must be admitted, however, that while his soul and vigour found vent in his designing and in the journeyman work—"delightful work, hard for the body and easy for the mind"—at which he was so ready to lend a hand, his artistic product lacked somewhat in the qualities that come from the exercise of the higher intellectual gifts. It was more than an attempt to revive old Gothic forms; it was an adoption of old forms with an infusion of modern spirit; but it missed the native and personal character of work growing out of contemporaneous conditions and tastes. Imaginative craftsman as he was, Morris was never quite an artist in the strict sense of the word. He had a fine sense of colour and, within certain limits, a right feeling for pattern; but his invention was too exuberant for repose, and he displayed in the greater part of his work an ornamental luxuriance that destroyed dignity and simplicity of effect. He did not like the restraints of art, and he seems to have been incapable of entering the sphere of abstract thought in which the principles governing great art are found. "No schools of art," he says with his superbly inaccurate generalisation, "have ever been contented to use abstract lines and forms and colours — that is, lines and so forth without any meaning." Such ornament he deemed "outlandish." He wanted his patterns, especially his wall-paper patterns, to remind people of pleasant scenes: "of the close vine trellis that keeps out the sun by the Nile side; or of the wild woods and their streams with the dogs panting beside them; or of the swallows sweeping above the garden boughs toward the house eaves where their nestlings are, while the sun breaks the clouds on them; or of the many-flowered summer meadows of Picardy," — all very charming things to think about, but as really pertinent to wall-paper designing as the pleasant memory of a hard road with a fast horse speeding over it would be to the designing of a carpet. He preached the closest observation of nature and the most delicate understanding of it before attempting conventionalisation, but he did not hesitate to break all the laws of nature in his designs when he happened to want to do so. He did not hesitate, as Mr. Day has said, to make an acorn grow from two stalks or to give a lily five petals. Fitness in ornament was one of his fundamental principles, and he made his designs for the place in which they were to be seen and with direct reference to the limitations of opportunities of that place. It was never his way to turn a wall-paper loose on the market for any chance purchaser. He must know, if possible, something of the walls to which the design was to be applied and of the room in which it was to live, and he then adapted his design to his idea of what was required. This idea, however, was commonly much influenced by certain pre-conceived theories. He believed, for example, that there should be a sense of mystery in every pattern designed. This mystery he tried to get, not by masking the geometrical structure upon which a recurring pattern must be based, but by covering the ground equably and richly, so that the observer may not "be able to read the whole thing at once." Thus many of his designs are so over-elaborated as to give the effect of restlessness, whereas "rest" was the word oftenest on his lips in connection with domestic art. In common with most designers who derive their ideals from mediæval sources, he was less impressed by the tranquillity gained from calm clean spaces, the measure, order, and stateliness brought about by the simple relation of abstract lines, the repose of the rhythmical play of mass in perfect proportion, undisturbed by decorative detail, than by the charm of highly vitalised imagery. But though he erred on the side of luxuriance—while preaching simplicity—he never allowed his design to sink into vulgarity or petty picturesqueness. He might be intricate but he was not vague. "Run any risk of failure rather than involve yourself in a tangle of poor weak lines that people can't make out," he says. "Definite form bounded by firm outline is a necessity for all ornament. You ought always to go for positive patterns wnen they may be had." They might always be had from him. And it is due to his positive quality, his uncompromising certainty of the rightness of the thing that he is doing, that even when he is most imitative he gives an impression of originality, and is in fact original in the sense that he has thought out for himself the methods and motives of the ancient art by which he is consciously and intentionally influenced.

Finish, it need hardly be said, was not prized by him. It was one of his assumptions that "the better is the enemy of the good," and he preferred the roughness of incompleteness to the suavity of perfect workmanship. He dreaded the suggestion of the machine that lurks in the polished surface and the perfect curve. Nor did he at any time believe in the subdivision of labour by which a workman learns to do one thing with the utmost efficiency, holding that no workman could enjoy such specialised work, and therefore, of course, could not through it give pleasure to others. The following is the creed which, according to his "compact with himself,"

PAINTED WALL DECORATION DESIGNED BY MORRIS

he made it a duty to repeat when he and his fellow-men came together to discuss art:

"We ought to get to understand the value of intelligent work, the work of men's hands guided by their brains, and to take that, though it be rough, rather than the unintelligent work of machines or slaves though it be delicate; to refuse altogether to use machine-made work unless where the nature of the thing compels it, or where the machine does what mere human suffering would otherwise have to do; to have a high standard of excellence in wares and not to accept make-shifts for the real thing, but rather to go without — to have no ornament merely for fashion's sake, but only because we really think it beautiful, otherwise to go without it; not to live in an ugly and squalid place (such as London) for the sake of mere excitement or the like, but only because our duties bind us to it — to treat the natural beauty of the earth as a holy thing not to be rashly dealt with for any consideration; to treat with the utmost care whatever of architecture and the like is left us of the times of art."

Wall-papers were among the earliest staple products of the firm in Red Lion Square, although Morris always regarded them in the light of a compromise; an altogether unsatisfactory substitute for the hand-painting, or tapestry or silk or printed cotton hangings, which he considered the proper covering for the bare walls which, of course, no one not in "an unhealthy state of mind and probably of body also" could endure to leave bare. The first to be designed, the *Trellis* paper, was the combined work of Morris and Webb, the former being responsible for the rose-trellis intended, we may suppose, to bring with it pleasant recollections of gardens in June and inspired by his own sweet garden at Upton, the latter for the birds that cling to the lattice or dart upward among the heavily thorned stems. In the early papers the designs were very simple and direct, often more quaint than beautiful, as in the case of the well-known *Daisy* paper, and depending greatly on the colouring for the attractiveness they possessed. Later came such intricate patterns as the *Pimpernel,* the *Acanthus,* so elaborate as to require a double set of blocks and no less than thirty-two printings, and the paper designed for St. James's Palace, as large and magnificent as the environment in which it was to be placed demanded. It is quite obvious from these designs that Morris did not regard his wall-hangings as backgrounds but as decorations in themselves. As a matter of fact he did not fancy pictures for his walls. After his early burst of enthusiasm over Rossetti's paintings he bought few pictures if any, and they do not seem ever to have entered into his schemes of decoration. The wall of a room was always important to him, and despite his discontent with paper coverings for it, he was anxious to have such coverings as ornamental as possible, admitting them to be useful "as things go," and treating them in considerable detail in his lectures on the decorative arts.

DESIGN FOR ST. JAMES'S PALACE WALL-PAPER

(Reproduced by courtesy of Mr. Bulkley)

He advised making up for the poverty of the material by great thoughtfulness in the design: "The more and the more mysteriously you interweave your sprays and stems, the better for your purpose, as the whole thing has to be pasted flat upon a wall and the cost of all this intricacy will but come out of your own brain and hand." Concerning colour he was equally specific. In his lecture characteristically called *Making the Best of It,* in which with an accent of discouragement he endeavours to show his audience how at the time of his speaking to make a middle-class home "endurable," he lays down certain rules which indicate at one and the same time his mastery of his subject and the incommunicability of right taste in this direction, although many of his ideas may be pondered to great advantage by even the mind untrained in colour schemes. He begins with his usual preliminary statement as to the health of those who disagree with him. "Though we may each have our special preferences," he says, "among the main colours, which we shall do quite right to indulge, it is a sign of disease in an artist to have a prejudice against any particular colour, though such prejudices are common and violent enough among people imperfectly educated in art, or with naturally dull perceptions of it. Still colours have their ways in decoration, so to say, both positively in themselves, and relatively to each man's way of using them. So I may be excused for setting down some things I seem to have noticed about these ways."

After thus establishing friendly relations with his audience, he instructs them that yellow is a colour to be used sparingly and in connection with "gleaming materials" such as silk; that red to be at its finest must be deep and full and between crimson and scarlet; that purple no one in his senses would think of using bright and in masses, and that the best shade of it tends toward russet; green, he continues, must seldom be used both bright and strong. "On the other hand," he adds, "do not fall into the trap of a dingy, bilious-looking yellow-green, a colour to which I have a special and personal hatred, because (if you will excuse my mentioning personal matters) I have been supposed to have somewhat brought it into vogue." Dingy colours were abhorred by him in all cases, and his patience with those customers who demanded them was extremely limited. Blue was his "holiday colour," and "if you duly guard against getting it cold if it tend toward red, or rank if it tends toward green," you "need not be much afraid of its brightness."

From his hatred of mechanical methods grew his preferences among the lesser arts. He once complained that he never could see any scene "with a frame as it were around it," and the less necessity there was for bounding and limiting his design the happier he was in making it. Embroidery he loved, for here the worker had an almost absolutely free hand. There was no "excuse" in embroidery for anything short of striking beauty. "It is not worth

EARLY DESIGN FOR MORRIS WALL-PAPER "DAISY AND COLUMBINE"

CHRYSANTHEMUM DESIGN FOR WALL-PAPER

doing," he said, " unless it is either very copious and rich, or very delicate — or both. For such an art nothing patchy or scrappy, or half-starved should be done." Tapestry-weaving stood next in freedom of method, and this was not only a favourite art with him, but one which he carried to an extraordinary degree of perfection, he and Burne-Jones combining their designs to produce results coming nearer to the old Arras effects than to the work of modern weavers. In tapestry-weaving Morris used the *haute lisse* or " high loom," the weaver holding apart with his left hand the threads of the warp which stands upright before him as with his right hand he works his bobbins in and out, seeing the picture he is making in a mirror placed on the other side of the loom. The interest of Morris in the weaving craft is said to have been first awakened by the sight of a man in the street selling toy models of weaving machines, one of which he promptly bought for experimental purposes. It was many years before he could find a full-sized loom of the kind he wanted, which had become obsolete or nearly so, and which was the only style of loom he would consider using as it was most like the looms on which the splendid fabrics of mediæval times had been woven. By such difficulties he was rarely baffled. In the case of his tapestries the method he proposed to revive had died out in Cromwell's time and there was no working model which could be used as a guide. But there was an old French official handbook that came in his way, from which he was able to pick up the details of the craft and this sufficed. His personal familiarity with his process is apparent in his various discussions of it. He speaks with the authority of a workman whose hand has held the tool. This practical and positive knowledge saved him from the sentimentalism into which his theories might otherwise have led him. He designed his patterns fully aware of the way in which they were going to behave in the process of application. When in 1882 he was called upon to give evidence before the Royal Commission appointed to inquire into the subject of technical instruction, he urged the necessity of this working-knowledge on the part of every designer. "I think it essential," he said, "that a designer should learn the practical way of carrying out the work for which he designs; he ought to be able to weave himself." In all his talk about art he tried to tell people how to do only the things he himself had done, in which he differed widely and wholesomely from his master Ruskin whose teachings were so often on his lips. The activity of his hand was a needed and to a great extent an effective check upon the activity of his sentiment. But—like Ruskin here—he found it hard to stay long away from the moral or emotional significance of the art he was discussing. The art that speaks to the mind he did not completely understand. The art that speaks to the senses he abundantly explained. The amazingly ingenious point of view from which he defends his preoccupation with what he has named "the lesser arts" is displayed in the following passage, beginning with the almost inevitable formula:

"A healthy and sane person being asked with what kind of art he would clothe his walls, might well answer, 'with the best art,' and so end the question. Yet out on it! So complex is human life, that even this seemingly most reasonable answer may turn out to be little better than an evasion. For I suppose the best art to be the pictured representation of men's imaginings: what they have thought has happened to the world before their time, or what they deem they have seen with the eyes of the body or the soul; and the imaginings thus represented are always beautiful indeed, but oftenest stirring to men's passions and aspirations and not seldom sorrowful or even terrible.

"Stories that tell of men's aspirations for more than material life can give them, their struggle for the future welfare of the race, their unselfish love, their unrequited service; things like this are the subjects for the best art; in such subjects there is hope surely, yet the aspect of them is likely to be sorrowful enough: defeat, the seed of victory, and death, the seed of life, will be shown on the face of most of them.

"Take note, too, that in the best art all these solemn and awful things are expressed clearly and without any vagueness, with such life and power that they impress the beholder so deeply that he is brought face to face with the very scenes, and lives among them for a time: so raising his life above the daily tangle of small things that wearies him to the level of the heroism which they represent. This is the best art, and who can deny that it is good for us all that it should be at hand to stir the emotions; yet its very greatness makes it a thing to be handled carefully, for we cannot always be having our emotions deeply stirred: that wearies us body and soul; and man, an animal that longs for rest like other animals, defends himself against that weariness by hardening his heart and refusing to be moved every hour of the day by tragic emotions,—nay, even by beauty that claims his attention overmuch. Such callousness is bad, both for the arts and our own selves, and therefore it is not so good to have the best art forever under our eyes, though it is abundantly good that we should be able to get at it from time to time.

"Meantime, I cannot allow that it is good for any hour of the day to be wholly stripped of life and beauty, therefore we must provide ourselves with lesser (I will not say worse) art with which to surround our common work-a-day or restful times; and for those times I think it will be enough for us to clothe our daily and domestic walls with ornament that reminds us of the outward face of the earth, of the innocent love of animals, or man passing his days between work and rest as he does. I say with ornament that reminds us of these things and sets our

ANEMONE PATTERN FOR SILK AND WOOL CURTAIN MATERIAL

minds and memories at work easily creating them; because scientific representation of them would again involve us in the problems of hard fact and the troubles of life, and so once more destroy our rest for us."

Was ever a craftsman of the ancient guilds so at pains to make clear the propriety and usefulness of his wood-carving or enamelling or niello! Like the early workman, however, he moved with marvellous facility from one branch of his art to another. From wall-papers it was but a step to cotton prints which in a way were the playthings of a mind at leisure. They might be as gay as one chose to make them, and "could not well go wrong so long as they avoided commonplace and kept somewhat on the daylight side of nightmare." From the weaving of hangings to the weaving of carpets was a step as easily taken, and when the impulse seized him to carry on the great but dying art of Persia in this direction, Morris so effectively applied himself to mastering the conditions under which the beautiful Eastern carpets were brought to their perfection as to produce at least one example—that called *The Buller's Wood Carpet*—that fairly competes with the splendour of its prototypes. Stained glass for a time baffled him. "His was not the temperament," says one of his critics, "patiently to study the chemistry of glass colour; or to prove by long experiment the dependence to be placed upon a flux." Although many windows were made by the firm, the larger number of them designed by Burne-Jones, Morris being responsible for the colour, he never seemed to forget that he had come near to being worsted in his fight with the technical difficulties of this most difficult art, and economised his enthusiasm for it accordingly. Hand-painted tiles, however, which he was the first to introduce into England, were favourites with him, and in them he perpetuated some of his attempts at drawing the human figure. Furniture, though an important feature of the work undertaken by the firm, did not appeal to him, and he left it to his associates. His experiments in vegetable dyes produced interesting results, although here also his technical knowledge was not entirely adequate to his task. In connection with his textile work he early felt the imperative necessity of having finer colours than the market offered. To get them as he wanted them he was obliged to go back as far as Pliny, but this was a small matter to one whose mind was always ready to provide him with an Aladdin's carpet. Back to Pliny he went to learn old methods, and in addition he called to his aid ancient herbals and French books of the sixteenth and seventeenth centuries, finally setting up his own vats and becks and very literally plunging in. At first he complained of "looking such a beast," but his enthusiasm soon overcame this rather remarkable display of concern for his personal appearance, and he wrote most joyously of working in sabots and blouse in the dye-house "pretty much

PORTION OF HAMMERSMITH CARPET

all day long." Out of his vats came the blue of his indigo, the red of his madder, the yellow of weld or Persian berry, the rich brown of walnut juice, making beautiful combinations, which, when they faded, changed into paler tints of the same colour and were not unpleasant to look upon. The aniline dyes, which in 1860 were the latest wonder of science, and in a very crude stage of their development, called out his most picturesque invective. Each colour was hideous in itself, crude, livid, cheap, and loathed by every person of taste, the "foul blot of the capitalist dyer." In brief, the invention supposed to be for the benefit of an art "the very existence of which depends upon its producing beauty" was "on the road; and very far advanced on it, towards destroying all beauty in the art." The only thing to do was to turn one's back on the chemical dyes, relegate them to a museum of scientific curiosities, and go back "if not to the days of the Pharaohs yet at least to those of Tintoret." It was highly characteristic of him that he chose the remedy of "going back" in place of progressing with the new material as far as possible.

His work with silks and with wools was naturally greatly enriched by his use of his own full, soft and brilliant colours, and his personal attention to the art of dyeing counted for so much that one of his most accomplished pupils in embroidery is quoted by Mr. Mackail as saying that she promptly felt the difference when Morris ceased to dye with his own hands, that the colours became more monotonous and prosy and the very lustre of the silk was less beautiful. It is, however, difficult to impress yourself upon the public precisely as you are, whatever vigour your personality may have. Morris, with his intense love of bright full hues, has come down as the promoter of the so-called "æsthetic" dulness of colour, and his name has been especially associated with the peacock blue and the "sage-green" to which he had an especial aversion. It was one of his doctrines that a room should be kept cheerful in tone, and how happily he could carry out this doctrine is seen in more than one of the rooms decorated by the firm. A visitor to Stanmore Hall, for example, has noted the delicate tones of the painted ceilings as looking like embroidery on old white silk, giving a bright yet light and aërial effect, and forming with the woodwork of untouched oak an impression of delightful gayety.

That Morris made himself a master of so many crafts and grappled even so successfully as he did with the technical difficulties involved would be somewhat remarkable had he attempted none of the other undertakings in which he gained for himself a name to be remembered. His eagerness to express his ideals in a practical form led him on indefinitely. To the very last a new world to conquer roused his spirit and made him tingle to be off. For a man with the trace of the plodder in him such a career would have been an impossible one, but Morris went blithely from craft to craft by a series of leaps and bounds.

He stayed with each just long enough to understand its working principles and to make himself efficient to teach others its peculiar virtues and demands, and he then passed on. "Each separate enterprise on which he entered," says one of his biographers, "seems for a time to have moved him to extraordinary energy. He thought it out, installed it, set it going, designed for it, trained men and women in the work to be done, and then by degrees, as the work began to run smoothly and could be trusted to go on without him, his interest became less active: a new idea generated in his mind, or an old one burst into bud, and his energies burst out afresh in some new doing." As time went on he had less and less practically to do with the firm of which he was the head and of which he continued to the end to be the consulting adviser. He gathered about him coöperators who not only were sympathetic with his methods but absorbed his style. His distinction as a designer was neither so great nor so personal that it could not to a considerable degree be communicated, and this accounts for the enduring quality of his influence which has been handed down to us through others without too much subtracted from it, with many of the characteristics most to be cherished still present. Greater decorators have existed, indeed, but it may be questioned if anyone has been quite so inspiriting; has had the matter quite so much at heart. He persuaded the multitude from the intensity of his own conviction, and he persuaded them on the whole toward good things and toward beauty. He made other men's ideas his own but he adopted them body and soul. He followed his own fashion, inveighing with vigour and frequently with logic against nearly all the fashions of his time. It is not surprising that he himself became the great fashion of the nineteenth century in matters of decoration. And this certainly was what he wanted, in the sense of wanting everyone in England to see as he did the possibilities of household art and to share in furthering them by turning their backs upon the sham art with which the commercial world was largely occupied. But he made no effort toward gaining the patronage of those unwilling to admit that what he disliked was intolerable. His was never a conciliatory policy. The following passage from his lecture on *The Lesser Arts* reveals his attitude in his own phrasing:

"People say to me often enough: If you want to make your art succeed and flourish, you must make it the fashion: a phrase which I confess annoys me: for they mean by it that I should spend one day over my work to two days in trying to convince rich, and supposed influential people, that they care very much for what they really do not care in the least, so that it may happen according to the proverb: *Bell-wether took the leap and we all went over;* well, such advisers are right if they are content with the thing lasting but a little while: say till you can make a little money, if you don't get pinched by the door shutting too quickly: otherwise they are wrong: the

SOFA DESIGNED BY THE MORRIS CO.
(Reproduced by courtesy of Mr. Bulkley)

SECRETARY DESIGNED BY THE MORRIS CO
(Reproduced by courtesy of Mr. Bulkley)

people they are thinking of have too many strings to their bow, and can turn their backs too easily on a thing that fails, for it to be safe work trusting to their whims: it is not their fault, they cannot help it, but they have no chance of spending time enough over the arts to know anything practical of them, and they must of necessity be in the hands of those who spend their time in pushing fashion this way and that for their own advantage.

"Sirs, there is no help to be got out of these latter, or those who let themselves be led by them: the only real help for the decorative arts must come from those who work in them: nor must they be led, they must lead.

"You whose hands make those things that should be works of art, you must all be artists, and good artists too, before the public at large can take real interest in such things; and when you have become so, I promise you that you shall lead the fashion; fashion shall follow your hands obediently enough."

CHAPTER V.

FROM THE RED HOUSE TO KELMSCOTT.

WHILE Morris was developing the industries of the firm with essential steadiness, despite the rapid transitions from one pursuit to another, he was going through a variety of personal experiences, some of which involved his disappointment in deeply cherished plans. For one thing, and this perhaps the most grievous, he was obliged to give up the Red House upon which so much joyous labour had been spent. Several causes contributed to the unhappy necessity, chief among them an attack of rheumatic fever that made him sensitive to the bleak winds which the exposed situation of the building invited. The distance between London and Upton became also a serious matter after his illness, as he found it almost impossible to make the daily journeys required by his attention to the business. Several compromises were thought of, the most enticing being the removal of the works from Red Lion Square to Upton, and the addition of a wing to the Red House for Burne-Jones and his family; but in the end the beautiful house was sold, Morris, after leaving it, never again setting eyes upon it.

The first move was to Queen Square, London, where Morris and the business became house-mates in the autumn of 1865, remaining together there, with more or less interruption, for seven years. Queen Square is in Bloomsbury, not far from the British Museum, and a part of the ugly London middle-class region for which Morris had so little liking, but as a place to carry on the rapidly increasing work of the firm it possessed great advantages. The number of the house was 26, and adjacent buildings and grounds were used for the workshops. At this time Mr. George Warrington Taylor was made business manager for the company, and Morris gained by his accession much valuable time, not only for designing and experimenting, but for the literary work that again began to claim his attention. He was still, however, a familiar figure in "the shop," acting as salesman, showman, designer, or manual labourer. His aspect as he strode along the streets of the dull neighbourhood must have been refreshing. Those who knew him have repeatedly described him as the image of a sea-captain in general appearance. He wore habitually a suit of navy-blue serge cut in nautical fashion, and his manner was bluff and hearty as that of the proverbial seaman. Mr. Mackail gives a breezy picture of him in his workman's blouse, hatless, with his ruddy complexion and rocking walk, bound for the Faulkners' house where once upon a time a new maid took him for the butcher. To have seen him in these days was to have seen one of his own ideal workmen out of *News from Nowhere.* As a master of men he seems to have been singularly successful, despite the temper which led him at times to commit acts of positive violence. His splendid zest for work must have been stimulating and to a degree contagious. Merely to be in the company of one who thought hearty manual labour so interesting and so pleasant and so heartily to be desired by everyone, must have had its vivifying effect. He was stating the simple truth when he said that he should die of despair and weariness if his daily work were taken from him unless he could at once make something else his daily work, and he is constantly drawing persuasive pictures of the charm of the various handicrafts — that of weaving for example, his description of which would invite the most discontented mind. He does not call the weaver's craft a dull one: "If he be set to doing things which are worth doing — to watch the web growing day by day almost magically, in anticipation of the time when it is to be taken out and one can see it on the right side in all its well-schemed beauty — to make something beautiful that will last out of a few threads of silk and wool, seems to me not an unpleasant way of earning one's livelihood, so long only as one lives and works in a pleasant place, with work-day not too long, and a book or

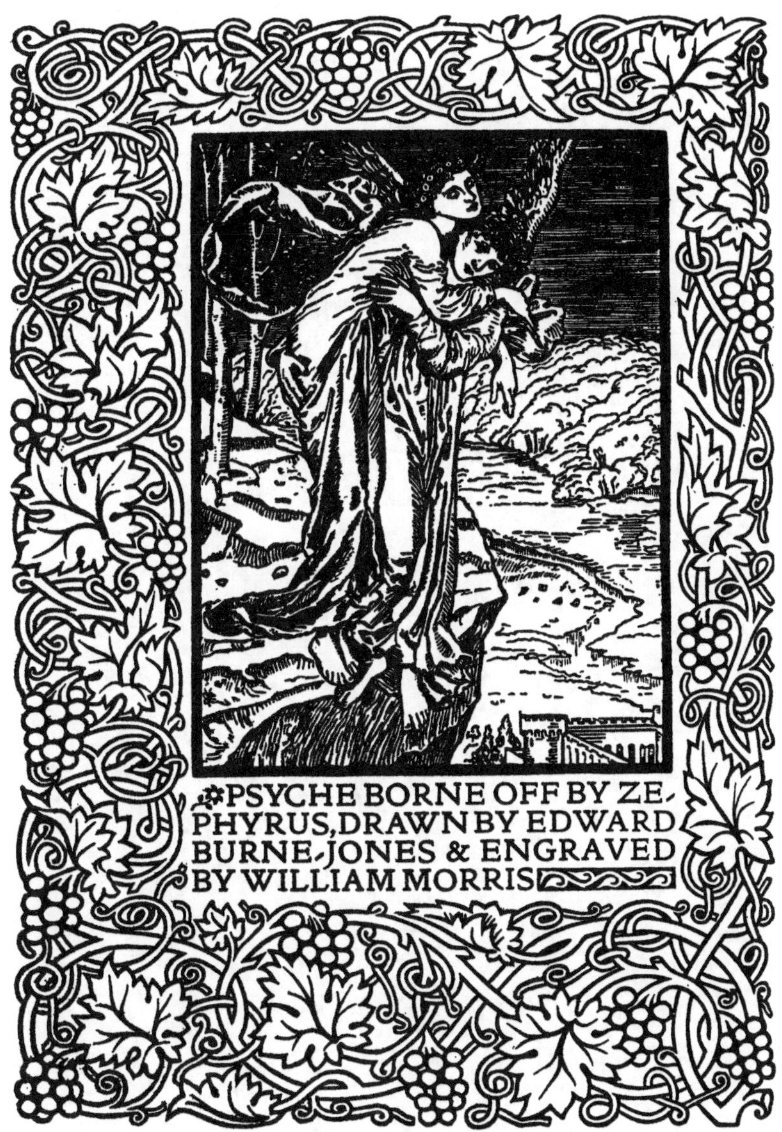

ILLUSTRATION BY BURNE-JONES FOR PROJECTED EDITION OF "THE EARTHLY PARADISE," CUT ON WOOD BY MORRIS HIMSELF

two to be got at." His own weavers were some of them boys trained in the shop from a condition of absolute ignorance of drawing and of the craft to such an efficiency as enabled them to weave the Stanmore tapestry, one panel of which took two years to the making, and which was of the utmost elaboration and magnificence of design. The exigencies of the business presently made it necessary to devote the whole of the premises in Queen Square to the work going on there, and the Morris family removed in 1872 to a small house between Hammersmith and Turnham Green, near Chiswick Lane, Morris retaining a couple of rooms in the Queen Square house for his use when busy there. Even the extended quarters soon proved insufficient, however, and in 1877 rooms were taken in Oxford Street for showing and selling the work of the firm, the manufacturing departments being still ensconced in Queen Square. In 1881 these also were transferred to more suitable premises. The dyeing and cotton-printing demanded workshops by the side of some stream of clear water "fit to dye with," and after much search Morris found an ideal situation on the banks of the little Wandle River, near Wimbledon. There were the ruins of Merton Abbey where the Barons once gave their famous answer "Nolumus leges Angliæ mutari," and there manufactures had been carried on for centuries. In the long low-roofed worksheds on the river's bank his workmen could move about in ample space, practising ancient methods of dyeing, printing, and weaving, seven miles from Charing Cross. It is anything but a typical manufactory that has been depicted by visitors to the Merton Abbey works. We read of an old walled garden gay with old-fashioned flowers and shrubs, of the swift little Wandle River rushing along between the buildings, its trout leaping under the windows, a water-wheel revolving at ease, hanks of yarn, fresh from the vats, drying in the pure air, calico lying "clearing" on the meadow grass in an enclosure made by young poplar trees, a sunlit picture of peaceful work carried on by unharried workers among surroundings of fresh and wholesome charm. Women and men were both employed, some of them old and not all of them competent, but none of them overworked or underpaid. Though Morris had somewhat scant courtesy of manner toward those who worked for and with him, he had at least the undeviating desire to promote their welfare. If he expected work of his work-people, as certainly he did, he expected it only under the most healthful and agreeable conditions. Judging others by himself, he could not conceive anyone as happy in idleness, but neither did he expect anyone to be happy without leisure. In his own business he proved what the nineteenth century found hard to believe, that honest, thorough, and artistic workmanship, accomplished under reasonable exactions by people enjoying their occupation, could be combined with commercial prosperity. That the

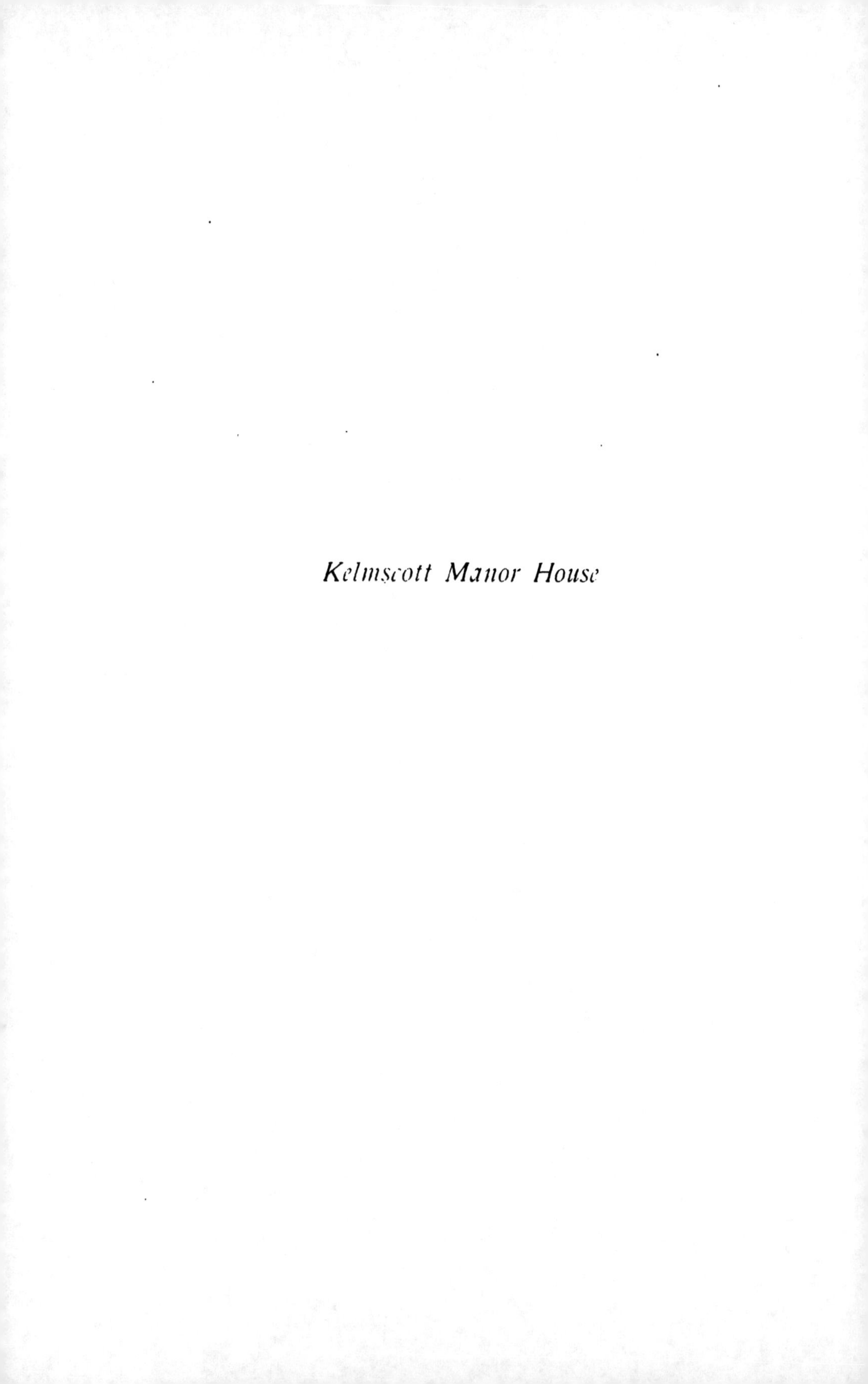

Kelmscott Manor House

products of such labour could not be bought by the poorer classes was due, he argued, to a social order wrong at the root. The time when art could be made "by the people and for the people, as a happiness to the maker and the user," was a far-off dream.

Shortly before Morris abandoned Queen Square as a place of residence, he discovered for himself a "heaven on earth," in which he could spend his vacations from town, and free himself from the contamination of London streets. This was Kelmscott Manor House, which he rented—at first jointly with Rossetti—in 1871, and in which he took infinite satisfaction for the remainder of his life. The beautiful old place was in its way as characteristic of him and of his tastes as the Red House had been, and has become intimately associated with him in the minds of all who knew him during his later years, his passion for places investing those for which he cared with a sentiment not to be ignored or slighted in making up the sum of his interests. For a couple of years Rossetti was an inmate of Kelmscott Manor, and through his letters many vivid glimpses of it are obtained. The village of Kelmscott was at the time no more than a hamlet containing a hundred and seventeen people, and situated two and a half miles from the nearest town, Lechlade, to whose churchyard Shelley lent distinction by writing a poem there. The nearest station-town was Farringdon, so far off that the carrier who brought railway parcels to the occupants of the Manor charged six shillings and sixpence for each trip. "Thus," writes Rossetti, who was chronically short of money, "a good deal of inconvenience tempers the attractions of the place." Nothing, however, unless the presence of Rossetti, who was "unromantically discontented" there, tempered them for Morris. In an article for *The Quest* for November, 1895, he describes the house in the most minute detail, accentuating its charms with a touch of comment for each that falls like a caress. The roofs are covered with the beautiful stone slates of the district, "the most lovely covering which a roof can have." The "battering" or leaning back of the walls is by no means a defect but a beauty, "taking from the building a rigidity which otherwise would mar it," and the stout studded partitions of the entrance passage are "very agreeable to anyone who does not want cabinet work to supplant carpentry." To the building of it all must have gone, he thinks, "some thin thread of tradition, a half-anxious sense of the delight of meadow and acre and wood and river, a certain amount (not too much, let us hope) of common-sense, a liking for making materials serve one's turn, and perhaps at bottom some little grain of sentiment." And from Rossetti we hear of the primitive Kelmscott church "looking just as one fancies chapels in the *Mort d'Arthur,*" of clouds of starlings sinking in the copses "clamourous like mill-waters at wild play," of "mustering rooks innumerable," of a "delicious" garden and meadows leading to the river brink, of apple blos-

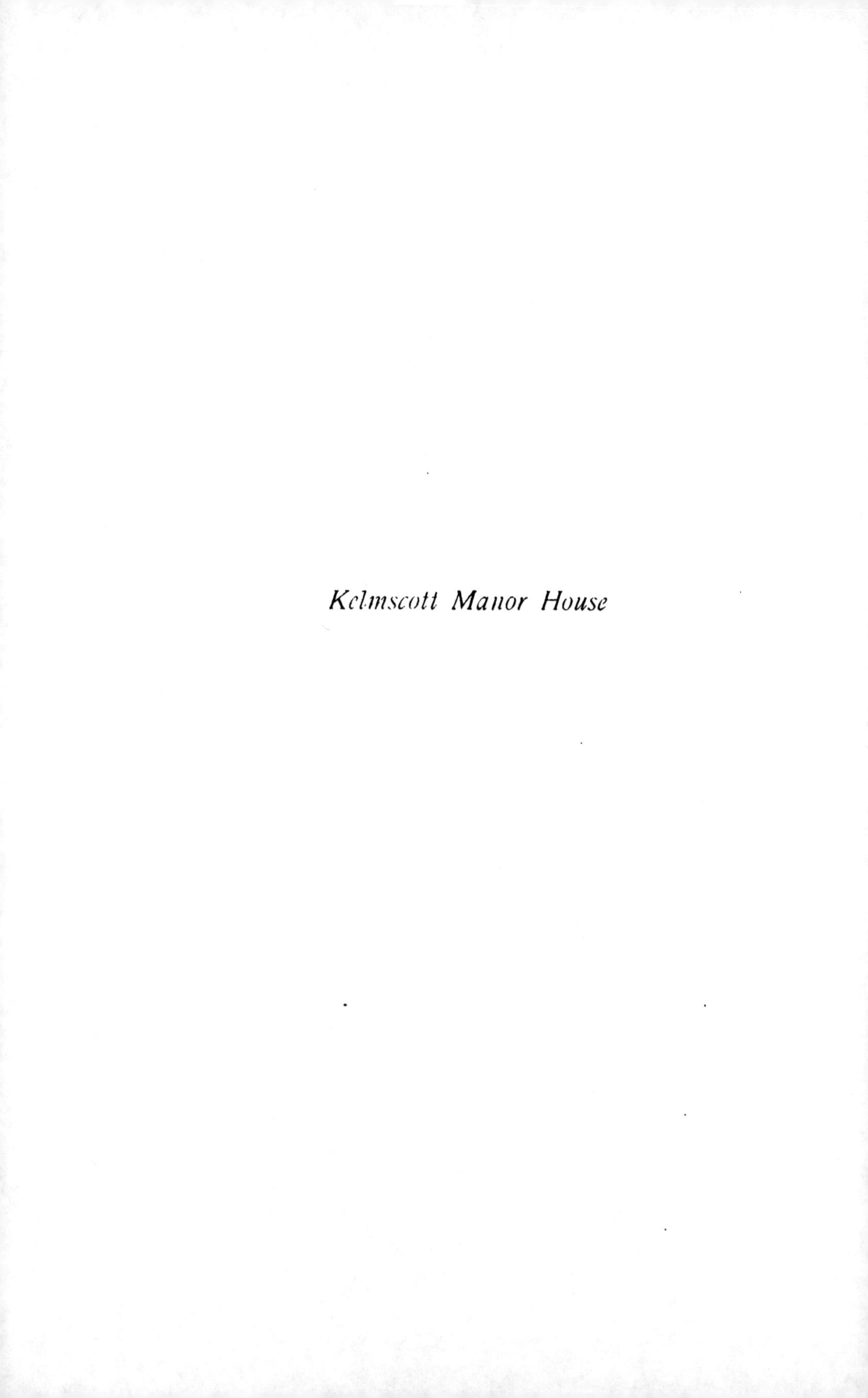

Kelmscott Manor House

soms and marigolds and arrow-heads and white lilies "divinely lovely," of an island by the boat-house rich in wild periwinkles, and of many another exquisite aspect of a place whose unvexed quietness was nevertheless powerless to soothe the turmoil of that tormented soul.

To realise fully how Morris himself felt toward it, one must turn to his description in *News from Nowhere.* There he is supposed to see it through the kindly mist of time, returning to it from a regenerate and beautified world, and his problem is to write of it with the penetrating eloquence and melancholy associated with remembered happiness. It is supremely characteristic of him that he could perfectly strike this note while still living in hale activity upon the spot he is to praise with the tenderness of reminiscence. The great virtue of his temperament lay in this peculiar intensity of realisation. He needed neither loss nor change to spur his sensibility and awaken his recognition of the worth or special quality of what he loved. Vital as few men are, he seems, nevertheless, always to have dwelt in sight of death and to have grasped life as though the next moment he was to be torn from it. The burden of the song which Ogier the Dane hears on a fair May morning:

> Kiss me love! for who knoweth
> What thing cometh after death?

so often quoted in evidence of his fainting and dejected spirit, embodies indeed the sentiment of his attitude toward the pleasures and satisfactions to be drawn from the visible and perishable world, but does not hint at the energy with which he seized those pleasures, the sturdiness with which he filled himself with those satisfactions. When *News from Nowhere* was written, Morris had lived the better part of twenty years in close relation with the Kelmscott house, but custom had not staled for him its infinite variety. This is what he writes of it and of its surroundings in his romance of *An Epoch of Rest:* He and his companions have approached it by way of the river.

"Presently we saw before us a bank of elm trees, which told us of a house amidst them. In a few minutes we had passed through a deep eddying pool into the sharp stream that ran from the ford, and beached our craft on a tiny strand of limestone gravel, and stepped ashore.

"Mounting on the cart-road that ran along the river some feet above the water, I looked round about me. The river came down through a wide meadow on my left, which was grey now with the ripened seeding grasses; the gleaming water was lost presently by a turn of the bank, but over the meadow I could see the gables of a building where I knew the lock must be. A low wooded ridge bounded the river-plain to the south and south-east, whence we had come, and a few low houses lay about its feet and up its slope. I turned a little to my right and through the hawthorn sprays and long shoots of the wild roses could see the flat country spreading out far away under the sun of the calm evening, till something that might be called hills with a look of sheep pastures about them bounded it with a soft blue line. Before one, the elm boughs still hid most of what houses there might be in this river-side dwelling of men; but to the right of the cart-road a few grey buildings of the simplest kind showed here and there.

"I had a mind to say that I did not know the way thither, and that the river-side dwellers should lead: but almost without my will my feet moved on along the road they knew. The raised way led us into a little field bounded by a backwater of the river on one side: on the right hand we could see a cluster of small houses and barns and a wall partly overgrown with ivy, over which a few grey gables showed. The village road ended in the shallow of the aforesaid backwater. We crossed the road, and again almost without my will my hand raised the latch of a door in the wall, and we stood presently on a stone path which led up to the old house to which fate in the shape of Dick had so strangely brought me in this world of men. My companion gave a sigh of pleased surprise and enjoyment, nor did I wonder, for the garden between the wall and the house was redolent of the June flowers, and the roses were rolling over one another with that delicious superabundance of small well-tended gardens which at first sight takes away all thought from the beholder save that of beauty. The blackbirds were singing their loudest, the doves were cooing on the roof-ridge, the rooks in the high elm trees beyond were garrulous among the young leaves, and the swifts wheeled, whining, about the gables. And the house itself was a fit guardian for all the beauty of this heart of summer.

"Once again Ellen echoed my thoughts as she said: 'Yes, friend, this is what I came out to see; this many-gabled old house built by the simple country-folk of the long-past times, regardless of all the turmoil that was going on in cities and courts, is lovely still amidst all the beauty which these latter days have created; and I do not wonder at our friends 'tending it so carefully and making much of it. It seems to me as if it had waited for these happy days, and held in it the gathered crumbs of happiness of the confused and turbulent past.'

"She led me up close to the house and laid her shapely sun-browned hand and arm upon the lichened wall as if to embrace it, and cried out: 'O me! O me! How I love the earth and the seasons and weather, and all the things that deal with it and all that grows out of it,—as this has done!'

"We went in and found no soul in any room as we wandered from room to room—from the rose-covered porch to the strange and quaint garrets amongst the great timbers of the roof, where of old time the tillers and herdsmen of the manor slept, but which a-nights seemed now, by the small size of the beds, and the litter of useless and disregarded matters—

bunches of dying flowers, feathers of birds, shells of starling's eggs, caddis worms in mugs and the like,—seemed to be inhabited for the time by children.

"Everywhere there was but little furniture, and that only the most necessary, and of the simplest forms. The extravagant love of ornament which I had noted in this people elsewhere, seemed here to have given place to the feeling that the house itself and its associations was the ornament of the country life amidst which it had been left stranded from old times, and that to reornament it would but take away its use as a piece of natural beauty.

"We sat down at last in a room over the wall which Ellen had caressed, and which was still hung with old tapestry, originally of no artistic value, but now faded into pleasant grey tones which harmonised thoroughly well with the quiet of the place, and which would have been ill supplanted by brighter and more striking decoration.

"I asked a few questions of Ellen as we sat there, but scarcely listened to her answers, and presently became silent, and then scarce conscious of anything but that I was there in that old room, the doves crooning from the roofs of the barn and dovecot beyond the window opposite."

In 1878 Morris took a London house on the Upper Mall, Hammersmith, which he occupied alternately with Kelmscott Manor. This place, which Mr. Mackail describes as "ugly without being mean," was also on the banks of the river, and Morris gained much satisfaction from the thought that the water flowing by it had come in its due course past the beloved Kelmscott garden. A somewhat inconvenient touch of sentiment caused him to give his Hammersmith home the name of "Kelmscott House" in compliment to the home actually situated at Kelmscott, the latter being distinguished by the title of "Manor," a title that seems to belong to it by courtesy alone.

From the great fondness felt by Morris for these places on which he lavished his art until they spoke more eloquently than his words of the aims and theories so dear to him, the domesticity of his life would naturally be inferred. Nor was he an eager traveller judged by modern standards. Nevertheless, he managed to find time for some extended trips just as he found time for everything that came in his way with an appeal to his liking. The most important of these was a voyage to Iceland, made in company with Faulkner and two other friends during the summer of 1871, just after the acquisition of Kelmscott Manor, in which he left Rossetti. His mind was ripe for the experience. He had already published translations from the Icelandic sagas made in collaboration with Mr. Magnusson, and his interest in the bracing Northern literature was reaching its height. Long years after, Rossetti said of him, "There goes the last of the Vikings!" and his mood in visiting Iceland was not unlike that of a modernised

Viking returning to his home. Thoughts of the country's great past were constantly with him. The boiling geysers, the conventional attraction for tourists who "never heard the names of Sigurd and Brunhild, of Njal, or Gunnar, or Grettir, or Gisli, or Gudrun," were a source of irritation to him. His pilgrimages to the homes of the ancient traditions were the episodes of his journey worth thinking about, and about them he thought much and vigorously, seeing in imagination the figures of the old heroes going about summer and winter, attending to their haymaking and fishing and live stock, eating almost the same food and living on the same ground as the less imposing Norsemen of the present. "Lord!" he writes, "what littleness and helplessness has taken the place of the old passion and violence that had place here once—and all is unforgotten; so that one has no power to pass it by unnoticed." His two months spent among the scenes of the greater sagas left him with an intense impression of a land stern and terrible, of toothed rocks and black slopes and desolate green, a land that intensified his melancholy by its suggestion of short-lived glory and early death, and intensified also his enjoyment of life by the sense of adventure, the rugged riding, and the fresh keen air. One of the important events of the trip was the exploration of the great cave at Surts-hellir, and twenty years after, many of its incidents were embodied in the book called *The Story of the Glittering Plain,* wherein

Hallblithe and the three Seekers make their way through the stony tangle of the wilderness seeing "nought save the wan rocks under the sun."

Two years later he made a still more adventurous journey across the arid tableland occupying the central portion of Iceland and across the northern mountains to the sea. It was highly characteristic of him that for the time he yielded himself utterly to the influence of the strange and awful land upon his imagination, and that for years afterward his writing was flooded by the impressions that continually swept back upon his mind as he reverted to these experiences. Mr. Mackail gives an amusing instance of the way in which the interest uppermost with him became an obsession leading to the most childlike extravagances. During a holiday tour in Belgium he came to a place where neither French nor English was spoken. He therefore "made a desperate effort at making himself understood by haranguing the amazed inn-keeper in Icelandic." His first visit to Italy, made between the first and second visits to Iceland, took faint hold upon him, nor was the second Italian journey, made some years later, and marked by a troublesome attack of gout, notably successful. He was a man of the North as surely as Rossetti was a man of the South, and it would have been a renaissance indeed that could have turned him into a Florentine or a Venetian.

During this middle period of his life, at the height of his great activity, an event occurred involving the

DESIGN BY ROSSETTI FOR WINDOW EXECUTED BY MORRIS & CO.
(THE PARABLE OF THE VINEYARD)

DESIGN BY ROSSETTI FOR STAINED-GLASS WINDOW EXECUTED BY THE MORRIS CO. *(THE PARABLE OF THE VINEYARD)*

element of tragedy, if the breaking of friendships be accounted tragic. In 1875 the firm was dissolved. Following Mr. Mackail's account of the circumstances that led to the dissolution, we find that the business had become one in which Morris supplied practically all the capital, invention, and control. It was also the chief source of his income. On the other hand, his partners might find themselves at any time seriously involved in the liabilities of a business which was rapidly extending. Hence the desirability of the dissolution and reconstitution of the firm. But in connection with this step an embarrassing situation arose. Under the original instrument, each partner had equal rights in the assets of the firm. After the first year or two the profits had never been divided, and the six partners of Morris, for the hundred and twenty pounds by which they were represented in the contributed capital at the beginning, had now claims on the business for some seven or eight thousand pounds. If these claims were insisted upon, Morris would be placed in a position of considerable financial difficulty. Burne-Jones, Webb, and Faulkner refused to accept any consideration. "The other three," says Mr. Mackail, "stood on the strict letter of their legal rights." Naturally the relations between Morris and the latter became grievously strained, and with Rossetti the break was absolute and irremediable. In passing out of Morris's life, as he then did, he certainly left it more serene, but with him went also the vivifying influence of his genius. In considering the very unfortunate part played by him in the conflict among the members of the firm, it is fair to give a certain weight to details emphasised in Mr. William Rossetti's account as modifying—to a slight degree, it is true, but still modifying—the sordid aspect of Rossetti's action. Madox Brown, who was one of the partners wishing not to forego their legal rights, was getting on in years and was a comparatively poor man. He had always counted on the firm "as an important eventual accession to his professional earnings." No one familiar with Rossetti's character can doubt that a desire to stand by his old friend and teacher in such a matter would have a strong influence with him. To his brother's mind, his attitude was throughout "one of conciliation," with the wish "to adjust contending claims had that but been possible." "He himself," says Mr. William Rossetti, "retired from the firm without desiring any compensation for his own benefit. A sum was, however, assigned to him. He laid it apart for the eventual advantage of a member of the Morris family, but, ere his death, circumstances had induced him to trench upon it not a little." It is easy to imagine circumstances trenching upon any sum of money under Rossetti's direct control, and in the absence of any testimony the reader acquainted with his prodigal disposition may very well be pardoned for doubting whether any member of the Morris family became appreciably the richer for his impulse. Nevertheless, it is a reasonable conclusion that he was not actuated by a sordid motive in opposing the essentially just claim made by Morris, but was to his own mind acting in accordance with the demands of a friendship older and closer than that between him and Morris. It must be noted, however, that a reconciliation was effected in the course of time between Morris and Madox Brown, while in Rossetti's case the wound never healed. The outcome of the negotiations was that Madox Brown was bought out, "receiving a handsome sum," says Mr. William Rossetti, and the business went on under the sole management and proprietorship of Morris.

In addition to the annoyance and real trouble of mind caused Morris by these transactions, he had the further anxiety at about this time of a breakdown of a serious and permanent nature in the health of his eldest daughter. This he took deeply to heart, losing spirits to a marked degree, but nothing human had power to stay his fertile brain and busy hand.

CHAPTER VI.

POETRY.

INTENT as he was upon the artistic success of his work in decoration, and ardent in giving time and thought to achieving this success, Morris was far from excluding poetry from the sum of his occupations. The five years following his marriage (1859–1864), indeed, were barren of any important literary work. He had planned, somewhat anticipating the large scale of his later verse, a cycle of twelve poems on the Trojan War, but he completed only six of the twelve, and the project was presently abandoned. After the Red House was sold, however, and he was back in London with the time on his hands saved from the daily journey, he began at once to make poetry of a form entirely different from anything he had previously written. The little sheaf of poems contained in his early volume had been put together by the hand of a boy. The poem published in June, 1867, under the title *The Life and Death of Jason,* was the work of a man in full possession of his faculty. It was simple, certain, musical, and pre-

Morris's Bed, with Hangings designed by himself and embroidered by his Daughter

destined to speedy popularity, even Tennyson, with whom Morris was not a favourite, liking the Jason. It flowed with sustained if monotonous sweetness through seventeen books in rhymed pentameter, occasionally broken by octosyllabic songs. Although published as a separate poem, on account of the length to which it ran, apparently almost in despite of its author's will, it had been intended to form part of the series called *The Earthly Paradise,* the first division of which followed it in 1868. This ambitious work was suggested by Chaucer's *Canterbury Tales,* and consists of no fewer than twenty-four long narrative poems, set in a framework of delicate descriptive verse containing passages that are the very flower of Morris's poetic charm. The scheme of the arrangement is interesting. A little band of Greeks, "the seed of the Ionian race," are found living upon a nameless island in a distant sea. Hither at the end of the fourteenth century—the time of Chaucer—come certain wanderers of Germanic, Norse, and Celtic blood who have set out on a voyage in search of a land that is free from death, driven from their homes by the pestilence sweeping over them. Hospitably received, the wanderers spend their time upon the island entertaining their hosts with the legends current in their day throughout Western Europe, and in turn are entertained with the Hellenic legends which have followed the line of living Greek tradition and are told by the fourteenth-century islanders in the mediæval form and manner proper to them at that time. Among the wanderers are a Breton and a Suabian, and the sources from which the stories are drawn have a wide range. They were at first, indeed, intended to represent the whole stock of the world's legends, but this field was too vast for even the great facility of Morris, and much was set aside. At the end we find *The Lovers of Gudrun,* taken from the Laxdæla Saga of Iceland, and bearing witness in the grimness of its tragedy and the fierceness of its Northern spirit to the powerful influence of the Icelandic literature upon the mind of Morris. It is the only story in the collection which has dominated his dreamy mediævalism and struck fire from his pen.

In *The Earthly Paradise* we have all the qualities that make its author dear to most of his readers. The mind is steeped in the beauty of imagery, and content to have emotion and thought lulled by the long, melancholy swing of lines that seem like the echo of great poetry without its living voice. Such poetry is what Morris wished his decorations to be — the "lesser art" that brings repose from the quickening of soul with which a masterpiece is greeted. The spirit revealed through the fluent murmur of the melodious words is very true to him and lies at the root of all his efforts toward making life fair to the eyes and soothing to the heart. The "unimpassioned grief," the plaintive longing with which he regarded the fleeting and unsatisfying aspects of a world so beautiful and so sorrowful, never found more exquisite expression than in passage after passage of this pellucid and lovely verse. The flight from death and the seeking after eternal life on this material globe constitute a theme that had for him a singular fitness. No one could have rendered with more sensitive appreciation the mood of men who set their life at an unmeasured price. No one could have expressed the dread of dying with more poetic sympathy. The preludes to the stories told on the island are poems addressed to the months of the changing year, and not one is free from the grievous suggestion of loss or the weary burden of fear and dejection. Read without the intervening narratives, they wrap the mind in an atmosphere of foreboding. There is no welcome unaccompanied by the shadow of farewell. There is no leaping of the heart to meet sunshine and fair weather without its corresponding faintness of shrinking from the clouds and darkness certain to follow. With a brave determination to seize exultation on the wing, he cries to March:

> Yea, welcome March! and though I die ere June,
> Yet for the hope of life I give thee praise,
> Striving to swell the burden of the tune
> That even now I hear thy brown birds raise,
> Unmindful of the past or coming days;
> Who sing: "O joy! a new year is begun:
> What happiness to look upon the sun!"

But what follows? The sure reminder of the silence that shall come after the singing:

> Ah, what begetteth all this storm of bliss
> But Death himself, who crying solemnly,

E'en from the heart of sweet Forgetfulness,
Bids us " Rejoice, lest pleasureless ye die.
Within a little time must ye go by.
Stretch forth your open hands, and while ye live
Take all the gifts that Death and Life may give."

And in the stanzas for October, written, Mr. Mackail tells us, in memory of a happy autumn holiday, we have the most poignant note of which he was capable:

Come down, O Love; may not our hands still meet,
Since still we live to-day, forgetting June,
Forgetting May, deeming October sweet—
—O hearken, hearken! through the afternoon,
The grey tower sings a strange old tinkling tune!
Sweet, sweet, and sad, the toiling year's last breath,
Too satiate of life to strive with death.

And we too—will it not be soft and kind,
That rest from life, from patience and from pain;
That rest from bliss we know not when we find;
That rest from Love which ne'er the end can gain ?—
Hark, how the tune swells, that erewhile did wane ?
Look up, Love!—ah, cling close and never move!
How can I have enough of life and love ?

June, the high tide of the year, he selects as the fitting month in which to tell of something sad:

Sad, because though a glorious end it tells,
Yet on the end of glorious life it dwells.

In February he asks:

Shalt thou not hope for joy new born again,
Since no grief ever born can ever die
Through changeless change of seasons passing by ?

Kelmscott Manor House from the Orchard

Thus across the charming images of French romance, Hellenic legend, and Norse drama, falls the suggestion of his own personality, and it is due to this pervading personal mood or sentiment that *The Earthly Paradise* has a power to stir the imagination almost wholly lacking to his later work. It cannot be said that even here he is able to awaken a strong emotion. But the human element is felt. A warm intelligence of sympathy creeps in among dreams and shadows, the reader is aware of a living presence near him and responds to the appeal of human weakness and depression. It is because Morris in the languid cadences of *The Earthly Paradise* spoke with his own voice and took his readers into the confidence of his hopeless thoughts, that the book will remain for the multitude the chief among his works, the only one that portrays for us in its most characteristic form the inmost quality of his temperament. Nor does he seem to have had for any other book of his making quite the intimate affection he so frankly bestowed upon this. The final stanzas in which the well-known message is sent to "my Master, Geoffrey Chaucer," confide the autobiographic vein in which it was written. Says the Book of its maker:

> I have beheld him tremble oft enough
> At things he could not choose but trust to me,
> Although he knew the world was wise and rough:
> And never did he fail to let me see
> His love,—his folly and faithlessness, maybe;

And still in turn I gave him voice to pray
Such prayers as cling about an empty day.

Thou, keen-eyed, reading me, mayst read him through,
For surely little is there left behind;
No power great deeds unnameable to do;
No knowledge for which words he may not find;
No love of things as vague as autumn wind—
Earth of the earth lies hidden by my clay,
The idle singer of an empty day.

Written at great speed, one day being marked by a product of seven hundred lines, the last of *The Earthly Paradise* was in the hands of the printers by the end of 1870, and Morris was free for his Icelandic journey and new interests.

He was no sooner home from Iceland than he set to work upon a curious literary experiment—a dramatic poem of very complicated construction, called *Love is Enough, or the Freeing of Pharamond: A Morality,* the intricate metrical design of which is interestingly explained by Mr. Mackail. Rossetti and Coventry Patmore both spoke in terms of enthusiasm of its unusual beauty. The story is that of a king, Pharamond, who has been gallant on the field and wise on the throne, but is haunted by visions of an ideal love sapping his energy and driving peace from his heart. He deserts his people, and with his henchman, Oliver, wanders through the world until he encounters Azalais, a low-born maiden, who satisfies his dream. He returns to find that his people have become estranged from him and he abdicates at once, to retire into obscurity with his love. There

Portrait of Edward Burne-Jones

By Watts

has been an obvious struggle on the part of the poet to obtain a strong emotional effect, and certain passages have indeed the "passionate lyric quality" ascribed to them by Rossetti; but as a drama it hardly carries conviction. The songs written to be sung between the scenes have nevertheless much of the haunting beauty soon to be lost from his work, and of these the following is a felicitous example:

Love is enough: it grew up without heeding
    In the days when ye knew not its name nor its measure,
    And its leaflets untrodden by the light feet of pleasure
Had no boast of the blossom, no sign of the seeding,
    As the morning and evening passed over its treasure.

And what do ye say then?—that Spring long departed
    Has brought forth no child to the softness and showers;
    That we slept and we dreamed through the Summer of
        flowers;
We dreamed of the Winter, and waking dead-hearted
    Found Winter upon us and waste of dull hours.

Nay, Spring was o'er happy and knew not the reason,
    And Summer dreamed sadly, for she thought all was ended
    In her fulness of wealth that might not be amended,
But this is the harvest and the garnering season,
    And the leaf and the blossom in the ripe fruit are blended.

It sprang without sowing, it grew without heeding,
    Ye knew not its name and ye knew not its measure,
    Ye noted it not 'mid your hope and your pleasure;
There was pain in its blossom, despair in its seeding,
    But daylong your bosom now nurseth its treasure.

Although Morris planned a beautifully decorated edition of the poem which was highly valued by him, its failure to impress itself upon the public was no great grief to him, and he put it cheerfully out of mind to devote himself to translation and to Icelandic literature.

The surprising task to which he first turned was a verse translation of Virgil's *Æneid,* in which he attempted to give the closest possible rendering of the Latin and to emphasise the romantic side of Virgil's genius. He followed with an almost word-for-word accuracy the lines and periods of the original using, and he threw over the poem a glamour of romance, but Mr. Mackail says truly that he had taken his life in his hands in essaying a classic subject with his inadequate training and unclassic taste. The same authority, who on this subject, certainly, is not to be disputed by the lay reader, considers the result a success from Morris's own point of view, declaring that he "vindicated the claim of the romantic school to a joint ownership with the classicists in the poem which is not only the crowning achievement of classical Latin, but the fountain-head of romanticism in European literature." The opposing critics are fairly represented by Mr. Andrew Lang, who, in this case as in many another, is an ideal intermediary between scholar and general reader.

"There is no more literal verse-translation of any classic poem in English," he says, "but Mr. Morris's manner and method appear to me to be mistaken. Virgil's great charm is his perfection of style and the exquisite harmony of his numbers. These are not represented by the singularly rude measures and archaistic language of Mr. Morris. Like Mr. Morris, Virgil was a learned antiquarian, and perhaps very accomplished scholars may detect traces of voluntary archaism in his language and style. But these, if they exist, certainly do not thrust themselves on the notice of most readers of the *Æneid*. Mr. Morris's phrases would almost seem uncouth in a rendering of Ennius. For example, take

> 'manet alta mente repostum
> Judicium Paridis, spretæque injuria formæ.'

This is rendered in a prose version by a fine and versatile scholar, 'deep in her soul lies stored the judgment of Paris, the insult of her slighted beauty.' Mr. Morris translates:

> 'her inmost heart still sorely did enfold
> That grief of body set at naught by Paris' doomful deed.'

Can anything be much less Virgilian? Is it even intelligible without the Latin? What modern poet would naturally speak of 'grief of body set at naught,' or call the judgment of Paris 'Paris' doomful deed'? Then 'manet alta mente repostum' is strangely rendered by 'her inmost heart still sorely did enfold.' This is an example of the translation at its worst, but defects of the sort illustrated are so common as to leave an impression of wilful ruggedness, and even obscurity, than which what can be less like Virgil? Where Virgil describes the death of Troilus, 'et versa pulvis inscribitus hasta' ('and his reversed spear scores the dust'), Mr. Morris has 'his wrested spear a-writing in the dust,' and Troilus has just been 'a-fleeing weaponless.' Our doomful deed, is that to be a-translating thus is to write with wrested pen, and to give a rendering of Virgil as unsatisfactory as it is technically literal. In short, Mr. Morris's *Æneid* seems on a par with Mr. Browning's *Agamemnon*. But this," Mr. Lang is careful to add, "is a purely personal verdict: better scholars and better critics have expressed a far higher opinion of Mr. Morris's translation of Virgil."

Mr. Lang's whimsical despair over the affectations of language which abound in the translation of the *Æneid* with less pertinence than in many other writings of Morris where also they abound, recalls the remonstrance that Stevenson could not resist writing out in the form of a letter although it was never sent on its mission. Acknowledging his debt to Morris for many "unforgettable poems," the younger writer and more accomplished student of language protests against the indiscriminate use of the word *whereas* in the translations from the sagas. "For surely, Master," he says, "that tongue that we write, and that you have illustrated so nobly, is yet alive. She has her rights and laws, and is our mother, our queen, and our instrument. Now in that living tongue, *where* has one sense, *whereas* another."

The translation of the *Æneid* was published under the title of *The Æneids,* in the autumn of 1875. Morris had written a good part of it in the course of his trips back and forth on the Underground Railway, using for these first drafts a stiff-covered copy-book, which was his constant companion. In the summer of the same year he had brought out a volume of the translations from the Icelandic which he was making in collaboration with Mr. Magnusson, calling it *Three Northern Love-Stories and Other Tales.* He had still, he declared "but few converts to Saga-ism," and he regarded his translating from the Icelandic as a pure luxury, adopting it for a Sunday amusement. During the winter of 1875–76, however, he was embarked on a cognate enterprise of the utmost importance to him, although he thought, and with truth, that his public would be indifferent to it. This was the epic poem which he called *The Story of Sigurd the Volsung,* based on the Volsunga Saga, the story of the great Northern heroes told and re-told from generation to generation, polished and perfected until the final form, in which it preserves the traditions of the people who cherish it, is the noblest attained in the Icelandic legends. Morris had published a prose translation of the saga in 1870, and the following passage from his preface shows how deeply his emotions were stirred by his subject:

"As to the literary quality of this work we might say much," he writes, "but we think we may well trust the reader of poetic insight to break through whatever entanglement of strange manners or unused element may at first trouble him, and to meet the nature and beauty with which it is filled: we cannot doubt that such a reader will be intensely touched by finding amidst all its wildness and remoteness such startling realism, such subtlety, such close sympathy with all the passions that may move himself to-day. In conclusion, we must again say how strange it seems to us, that this Volsung Tale, which is in fact an unversified poem, should never before have been translated into English. For this is the Great Story of the North, which should be to all our race what the tale of Troy was to the Greeks—to all our race first, and afterwards, when the change of the world has made our race nothing more than a name of what has been—a story too—then should it be to those that come after us no less than the Tale of Troy has been to us."

In the course of the following six years, during which he was constantly increasing his intimacy with the literature of the North, an impulse not unlike that which tempted Tennyson toward the *Idylls of the King* led him to try the winning of a wider audience for the tale of great deeds and elemental passions by which he himself had been so much inspired. In the prose translation he had given the Volsunga Saga to the public as it had been created for an earlier public of more savage tastes and fiercer tendencies. Now he proposed to divest it of some of the childish and ugly details that formed a stumbling block to the modern reader (though plausible and interesting enough to those for whom they were invented), and to add to the "unversified poem" rhyme and metre, emphasising the essential points and such characteristics of the actors as most appealed to him. A comparison of the saga with the poem will show that in his effort to preserve the heroic character of the antique conception by accentuating everything pleasing, leaving out much of the rudeness and cruelty, and adorning it with copious descriptive passages, he robs the story of a great part of the wild life stirring in its ancient forms, and more or less confuses and involves it. The modern poem really requires for its right understanding a mind more instructed in its subject than the prose translation of the old saga, and readers to whom the latter is unfamiliar may find a plain outline of the story not superfluous.

In the translation, the origin of the noble Volsung race, of which Sigurd is the flower and crown, is traced to Sigi, called the son of Odin, and sent out from his father's land for killing a thrall. He is fortunate in war, marries a noble wife, and rules over the land of the Huns. His son is named Rerir. Volsung is the son of Rerir, and thus the great-grandson of Odin himself. He marries the daughter of a giant, and the ten sons and one daughter of this union are strong in sinew and huge in size, the Volsung race having the fame of being "great men and high-minded and far above the most of men both in cunning and in prowess and all things high and mighty." Volsung becomes in his turn king over Hunland, and builds for himself a noble Hall in the centre of which grows an oak-tree whose limbs "blossom fair out over the roof of the hall," and the trunk of which is called Branstock.

The poem opens with the description of a wedding-feast held in this Hall for Signy, King Volsung's daughter, who has been sought in marriage by Siggeir, King of the Goths, a smaller and meaner race than the Volsungs. Signy is not content with her fate, but her father has deemed the match to be a wise one, and, eminent in filial obedience as in all things else, she yields. From this point for some distance saga and poem march together save for certain minor changes intended to increase Signy's charm. During the feasting a one-eyed stranger enters the Hall and thrusts his sword up to its hilt into the tree-trunk, saying that who should draw the sword from the trunk should have it for his own and find it the best he had ever borne in his hand. This, of course, is Odin. Siggeir tries to draw the sword, and after him his nobles, and then the sons of King Volsung, but none succeeds until Sigmund, the twin of Signy, draws it lightly forth as an easy task. Siggeir is wroth and offers to buy the sword for thrice its weight in gold, but Sigmund will not part with it, and Siggeir sets sail for home in dudgeon, though concealing his feelings from the Volsungs and inviting them cordially to visit him in Gothland. Signy reads the future, and implores her father to undo the marriage and let Siggeir depart without her. (In the poem Morris has her offer herself as a sacrifice if her father will but remain in his kingdom and decline

Siggeir's invitation.) King Volsung, however, insists on keeping his troth, and Signy and Siggeir depart, followed in due time by King Volsung and his sons and nobles in response to Siggeir's request. What Signy prophesied comes to pass and King Volsung falls at the hands of the Goths while his ten sons are taken captive. Now Signy prays her husband that her brothers be put for a time in the stocks, since home to her mind comes "the saw that says *Sweet to eye while seen.*" Siggeir is delighted to consent though he deems her "mad and witless" to wish longer suffering for her brothers. Here the poem departs from the original in that Morris puts the idea of the stocks into the mind of Siggeir in answer to Signy's suggestion that her brothers be spared for a little time. Sigmund and the rest of the brothers are taken to the wildwood, and a beam is placed on their feet, and night by night for nine nights a she-wolf comes to devour one of them. (In the poem Morris hastens matters somewhat by having two wolves appear each night to despatch the brothers two at a time.) Each morning Signy sends a messenger to the wildwood who brings back the woeful news. Finally she thinks of a ruse, and on the tenth night the messenger is sent to smear the face of Sigmund, now the sole remaining brother, with honey, putting some also into his mouth. When the wolf comes she licks his face, and then puts her tongue into his mouth to get the last delicious drop. Sigmund promptly closes his teeth upon her tongue and in the struggle that ensues Sigmund's bonds are burst and the wolf escapes, leaving her tongue between his teeth. This incident was probably not sufficiently heroic to please Morris, and in the poem no mention is made of Signy's clever device, Sigmund gaining his freedom in a more dignified fashion and the details being slurred over lightly, with a vague and general allusion to snapping "with greedy teeth." Sigmund dwells in the wildwood in hiding, and Signy sends to him in turn her two sons by King Siggeir, that he may test their fitness to help avenge the fate of her family. Here again Morris mitigates the stern temper of Signy for a more womanly type. In the saga when Signy finds that the boys are not stout enough of heart to accomplish her purpose she bids Sigmund kill them at once: "Why should such as they live longer?" In the poem, however, when Signy sends her son to Sigmund he is delivered with the diplomatic message that if his heart avail not he may "wend the ways of his fate," and when it is found that his heart does not avail, he is returned in safety to his mother, Sigmund awaiting the slow coming of the competent one.

The story of the birth of Sinfjotli, in whose veins runs unmixed the blood of the Volsungs, is given a certain dignity not accorded it in Wagner's familiar version of the legend as Mr. Buxton Forman, Morris's most devoted critic, has pointed out, but true to the account in the original saga. The saga is followed, also, in the burning of Siggeir's Hall by

William Morris

From painting by Watts

Sigmund and Sinfjotli, but the Signy who kisses her brother in "soft and sweet" farewell certainly fails to recall to the mind the vengeful creature of the original. Sigmund returns to the Hall of the Volsungs with Sinfjotli, and marries Borghild. Presently Sinfjotli sails abroad with the brother of Queen Borghild, Gudrod by name, and kills him for reason — as given in the translation — of their rivalry in loving "an exceeding fair woman." In the poem, however, Morris records a shabby trick played upon Sinfjotli by Gudrod in the dividing of their spoils of battle, making this the cause of the duel in which Gudrod was killed. Sinfjotli returns to his home with the news of Gudrod's death, and Borghild in revenge poisons him. Sigmund then sends her away and takes for his wife fair Hiordis, meeting his death at the hand of Odin himself, who appears to him in battle and shatters the sword he had drawn in his youth from the Volsung Branstock. As he lies dying he tells Hiordis that she must take good care of their child, who is to carry on the Volsung tradition, and must guard well the shards of Odin's sword for him. Then comes the carrying away of Hiordis by a sea-king to his kingdom in Denmark, and here ends, rightly speaking, the epic of Sigmund's career, which, as Mr. Mackail has said, is a separate story neither subordinate to nor coherent with the later epic of Sigurd, but which Morris could not forbear uniting to it. Sigurd the Volsung, the golden-haired, the shining one, the symbol of the sun, is born of

Hiordis in the home of King Elf, and fostered by Regin, an aged man and "deft in every cunning save the dealings of the sword." When Sigurd has grown to be a boy of high mind and stout heart, Regin urges him to ask of King Elf a horse. This he does, and is sent to choose one for himself. He chooses the best horse in the world and names him, Greyfell in the poem, Grani in the prose. Regin now presses him to attack Fafnir the "ling-worm," or dragon, who guards a vast hoard of treasure in the desert. According to the saga, Sigurd is not ashamed to own to a slight hesitation in attacking a creature of whose size and malignity he has heard much, but in the poem he is ready for the deed, merely hinting that "the wary foot is the surest and the hasty oft turns back." Thereupon follows the tale of the treasure told by Regin with great directness in the prose, and with much circumlocution in the poem.

When Sigurd learns that Fafnir is the brother of Regin, and is keeping him out of his share of treasure belonging to them both, on which, however, a curse is laid, he pities Regin, and promises that if he will make him a sword worthy of the deed he will kill Fafnir for him. This Regin attempts to do and fails until Sigurd brings him the shards of Odin's mighty sword, his inheritance from his father Sigmund. With a sword forged from the shards and named by him "the Wrath," Sigurd sets out on Greyfell, accompanied by Regin, to attack the dragon. The description in the poem of the ride across the desert is rich in the fruits of Morris's own experience, and reflects very closely his impressions of the mournful place of "short-lived eagerness and glory." Sigurd and Regin ride to the westward.

. . . and huge were the mountains grown
And the floor of heaven was mingled with that tossing world of stone;
And they rode till the moon was forgotten and the sun was waxen low,
And they tarried not though he perished, and the world grew dark below.
Then they rode a mighty desert, a glimmering place and wide,
And into a narrow pass high-walled on either side
By the blackness of the mountains, and barred aback and in face
By the empty night of the shadow; a windless silent place:
But the white moon shone o'erhead mid the small sharp stars and pale,
And each as a man alone they rode on the highway of bale.

So ever they wended upward, and the midnight hour was o'er,
And the stars grew pale and paler, and failed from the heaven's floor,
And the moon was a long while dead, but where was the promise of day?
No change came over the darkness, no streak of the dawning grey;
No sound of the wind's uprising adown the night there ran:
It was blind as the Gaping Gulf ere the first of the worlds began.

The fight with the dragon, the roasting of the dragon's heart, the tasting of the blood by Sigurd, and his instant knowledge of the hearts of men and beasts and of the speech of birds, follow with close adherence of poem to saga, the most marked divergence being the substitution of eagles for the woodpeckers who sing to Sigurd of his future. Through his new accomplishment Sigurd is able to read Regin's heart, and sees therein a traitorous intent, therefore he kills Regin, loads Greyfell with the treasure, and rides to the mountain where Brynhild, the warrior maiden struck with slumber by Odin in punishment for disobedience to him, is lying in her armour guarded by flames. Sigurd wins through the fire, and awakens her, and they hold loving converse together on the mountain, Brynhild teaching him wisdom in runes and in the saga, bringing him beer in a beaker, "the drink of love," although in the poem this hospitable ceremony is omitted. After a time they part, plighting troth, and later, when they meet at the home of Brynhild in Lymdale, they again exchange vows of faith.

Then Sigurd rides to a realm south of the Rhine, where dwell the Niblung brothers with their sister Gudrun and their fierce-hearted mother, Grimhild, who brews for Sigurd a philter that makes him forget the vows he exchanged with Brynhild and become enamoured of Gudrun. Completely under the power of the charm, he weds the latter and undertakes to woo and win Brynhild for her brother Gunnar. This he does by assuming Gunnar's semblance, and riding once more through the fire that guards Brynhild, reminding her of her oath to marry whomever should perform this feat, and returning to his own form after gaining her promise for Gunnar. This ruse is made known to Brynhild (after she has wedded Gunnar) by Gudrun, who is not averse to marring the peace of the greatest of women, and Brynhild makes the air ring with her wailing over the woeful fact that Gudrun has the braver man for her husband. In the saga she is a very outspoken lady and in a wild temper, and even in the poem her grief fails in noble and dignified expression. At her instigation Sigurd is killed by Gunnar and his brethren. The vengeance brings no happiness, however, and Brynhild pierces her breast with a sword that she and Sigurd may lie on one funeral pyre! Lovers of Wagner opera will remember that the story as there told ends with this climax, but Morris carries it on to Gudrun's marriage with King Atli, Brynhild's brother, and to the struggle between him and the Niblungs for the fatal treasure, which results in the murder of the Niblungs (Gudrun's brothers) and the irrevocable loss of the treasure. Although Gudrun has approved Atli's deed, she finds she can no longer abide with him after it has been accomplished, and accordingly sets fire to his house and throws herself into the sea. Morris omits the grewsome incident of the supper prepared for Atli by Gudrun from the roasted hearts of their children whom she had killed, and also leaves out the subsequent account of the bringing ashore of Gudrun and the wedding and slaying of Swanhild, her daughter by Sigurd.

To the poetic and symbolic elements of this strange old saga, Morris has been abundantly sensitive. The curse attending the desire for gold, which is the pointed moral of the saga, is brought out, not dramatically, but by allusions and suggestions, not always apparent at a casual reading. The conception of Sigurd as the sun-god destroying the powers of darkness and illuminating a shadowy world is constantly hinted at, as when he threatens Regin with the light he sheds on good and ill, and when Regin, looking toward him as he sits on Greyfell, sees that the light of his presence blazes as the glory of the sun. The heroism of Sigurd, his rôle as the ideal lover and warrior and spiritual saviour of his race, is perhaps over-emphasised. As King Arthur certainly lost in interest by Tennyson's re-creation of him, so Sigurd is more lovely and fair and golden and glorious in the poem than in the saga, and considerably less human and attractive withal. In fact, none of the characters in the poem—all so intensely alive to Morris himself—lives in quite a like degree for his readers. His power to probe beneath externals and rouse emotions of spiritual force was curiously limited. There are indications in his biography that his business with crafts and "word-spinning," as he called it, served him as a kind of armour, protecting him from the wounds of feelings too poignant to handle freely, too deadly to invite. We read of his agony of apprehension, for example, when in Iceland he did not hear from his home for a considerable period. "Why does not one drop down or faint or do something of that sort when it comes to the uttermost in such matters!" he exclaims. But in his writing it is mainly the surface of the earth and the surface of the mind with which he deals. It is in the nature of his genius, says one of his most accomplished critics, to dispense with those deeper thoughts of life which for Chaucer and for Shakespeare were "the very air breathed by the persons living in their verse." Nevertheless, his service to English literature, in translating the Northern sagas as none but a poet could have translated them, was very great, and his *Story of Sigurd* is in many respects a splendid performance. In writing it he endeavoured to infuse into his style the energy and passion of the literature from which he drew his material, and to brace it with the sturdy fibre of the Icelandic tongue. His efforts to de-Latinise his sentences had already lent his translations a vigour lacking in his earlier work. He had captured something of the Northern freshness corresponding very truly to his external aspect if not to the workings of his brain. The chief defect from which his story of Sigurd suffers lies in the extreme garrulity of the narrative. A single passage, set by the side of the translation, will suffice to show the manner in which a direct statement is smothered and amplified until the reader's brain is dull with repetition, and the episode or description is extended to three or four times its original length. Thus in the saga we are told that after Sigurd had eaten of the dragon's heart "he leapt on his horse and rode along the trail of the worm Fafnir, and so right unto his abiding-place; and he found it open, and beheld all the doors and the gear of them that they were wrought of iron; yea, and all the beams of the house; and it was dug down deep into the earth: there found Sigurd gold exceeding plenteous, and the sword Rotti; and thence he took the Helm of Awe, and the Gold Byrny, and many things fair and good. So much gold he found there, that he thought verily that scarce might two horses, or three belike, bear it thence. So he took all the gold and laid it in two great chests, and set them on the horse Grani, and took the reins of him, but nowise will he stir, neither will he abide smiting. Then Sigurd knows the mind of the horse, and leaps on the back of him, and smites spurs into him, and off the horse goes even as if he were unladen."

From this comparatively unvarnished tale Morris evolves the following:

Now Sigurd eats of the heart that once in the Dwarf-king lay,
The hoard of the wisdom begrudged, the might of the earlier
 day.
Then wise of heart was he waxen, but longing in him grew
To sow the seed he had gotten, and till the field he knew.
So he leapeth aback of Greyfell, and rideth the desert bare,
And the hollow slot of Fafnir that led to the Serpent's lair.
Then long he rode adown it, and the ernes flew overhead,
And tidings great and glorious of that Treasure of old they said,
So far o'er the waste he wended, and when the night was
 come
He saw the earth-old dwelling, the dread Gold-wallowers
 home.
On the skirts of the Heath it was builded by a tumbled stony
 bent;
High went that house to the heavens, down 'neath the earth it
 went,

Of unwrought iron fashioned for the heart of a greedy king:
'T was a mountain, blind without, and within was its plenishing
But the Hoard of Andvari the ancient, and the sleeping Curse unseen,
The Gold of the Gods that spared not and the greedy that have been.
Through the door strode Sigurd the Volsung, and the grey moon and the sword
Fell in on the tawny gold-heaps of the ancient hapless Hoard:
Gold gear of hosts unburied, and the coin of cities dead,
Great spoil of the ages of battle, lay there on the Serpent's bed:
Huge blocks from mid-earth quarried, where none but the Dwarfs have mined,
Wide sands of the golden rivers no foot of man may find,
Lay 'neath the spoils of the mighty and the ruddy rings of yore:
But amidst was the Helm of Aweing that the Fear of earth-folk bore,
And there gleamed a wonder beside it, the Hauberk all of gold,
Whose like is not in the heavens nor has earth of its fellow told:
There Sigurd seeth moreover Andvari's Ring of Gain,
The hope of Loki's finger, the Ransom's utmost grain;
For it shone on the midmost gold-heap like the first star set in the sky,
In the yellow space of even when the moon-rise draweth anigh.
Then laughed the Son of Sigmund, and stooped to the golden land,
And gathered that first of the harvest and set it on his hand;
And he did on the Helm of Aweing, and the Hauberk all of gold,—
Whose like is not in the heavens nor has earth of its fellow told:
Then he praised the day of the Volsungs amid the yellow light,
And he set his hand to the labour and put forth his kingly might;
He dragged forth gold to the moon, on the desert's face he laid
The innermost earth's adornment, and rings for the nameless made;

He toiled and loaded Greyfell, and the cloudy war-steed shone,
And the gear of Sigurd rattled in the flood of moonlight wan;
There he toiled and loaded Greyfell, and the Volsung's armour rang
'Mid the yellow bed of the Serpent — but without the eagles sang:

"Bind the red rings, O Sigurd! let the gold shine free and clear!
For what hath the Son of the Volsungs the ancient Curse to fear?

"Bind the red rings, O Sigurd! for thy tale is well begun,
And the world shall be good and gladdened by the Gold lit up by the sun.

"Bind the red rings, O Sigurd! and gladden all thine heart!
For the world shall make thee merry ere thou and she depart.

"Bind the red rings, O Sigurd! for the ways go green below,
Go green to the dwelling of Kings, and the halls that the Queen-folk know.

"Bind the red rings, O Sigurd! for what is there bides by the way,
Save the joy of folk to awaken, and the dawn of the merry day?

"Bind the red rings, O Sigurd! for the strife awaits thine hand
And a plenteous war-field's reaping, and the praise of many a land.

"Bind the red rings, O Sigurd! but how shall storehouse hold
That glory of thy winning and the tidings to be told?"

Now the moon was dead and the star-worlds were great on the heavenly plain,
When the steed was fully laden; then Sigurd taketh the rein
And turns to the ruined rock-wall that the lair was built beneath,
For there he deemed was the gate and the door of the Glittering Heath,
But not a whit moved Greyfell for aught that the King might do;

Then Sigurd pondered awhile, till the heart of the beast he knew,
And clad in all his war-gear he leaped to the saddle-stead,
And with pride and mirth neighed Greyfell and tossed aloft his head,
And sprang unspurred o'er the waste, and light and swift he went,
And breasted the broken rampart, the stony tumbled bent;
And over the brow he clomb, and there beyond was the world,
A place of many mountains and great crags together hurled.
So down to the west he wendeth, and goeth swift and light,
And the stars are beginning to wane, and the day is mingled with night;
For full fain was the sun to arise and look on the Gold set free,
And the Dwarf-wrought rings of the Treasure and the gifts from the floor of the sea.

Beautiful and full of poetic spirit and suggestion as this phraseology is, a reader may be forgiven if it recalls the reply of Hamlet when asked by Polonius what it is he reads. Compared with the swift dramatic method employed by Wagner to make the heroes and heroines of this same saga live for our time, it must be admitted that the latter drives home with the greater energy and conviction. Morris himself, however, was "not much interested" in anything Wagner did, looking upon it "as nothing short of desecration to bring such a tremendous and world-wide subject under the gaslights of an opera, the most rococo and degraded of all forms of art."

To the group of translations and adaptations already described must be added one other ambitious effort which belongs to it, properly speaking, although separated from it in time by more than ten years.

In 1887 Morris published a translation of the *Odyssey,* written in anapæstic couplets, and rendered as literally as by the prose crib of which he made frank use. Mr. Watts-Dunton finds in this translation the Homeric eagerness, although the Homeric dignity is lacking. The majority of competent critics were against it, however, nor is a high degree of classical training necessary to perceive in it an incoherence and clumsiness of diction impossible to associate with the lucid images of the Greeks. Compare, for example, Morris's account of the recognition of Ulysses by Argus with Bryant's limpid rendering of the same episode, and the tortured style of the former is obvious at once. Bryant's translation reads:

There lay
Argus, devoured with vermin. As he saw
Ulysses drawing near, he wagged his tail
And dropped his ears, but found that he could come
No nearer to his master. Seeing this
Ulysses wiped away a tear unmark'd
By the good swineherd whom he questioned thus:
"Eumæus, this I marvel at,—this dog
That lies upon the dunghill, beautiful
In form, but whether in the chase as fleet
As he is fairly shaped I cannot tell.
Worthless, perchance, as house-dogs often are
Whose masters keep them for the sake of show."

And thus, Eumæus, thou didst make reply:

"The dog belongs to one who died afar.
Had he the power of limb which once he had
For feats of hunting when Ulysses sailed
For Troy and left him, thou wouldst be amazed
Both at his swiftness and his strength. No beast

In the thick forest depths which once he saw,
Or even tracked by footprints, could escape.
And now he is a sufferer, since his lord
Has perished far from his own land. No more
The careless women heed the creature's wants;
For, when the master is no longer near,
The servants cease from their appointed tasks,
And on the day that one becomes a slave
The Thunderer, Jove takes half his worth away."

He spake, and, entering that fair dwelling-place,
Passed through to where the illustrious suitors sat,
While over Argus the black night of death
Came suddenly as soon as he had seen
Ulysses, absent now for twenty years.

And here is the description by Morris of the infinitely touching scene:

There then did the woodhound Argus all full of ticks abide;
But now so soon as he noted Odysseus drawing anear
He wagged his tail, and fawning he laid down either ear,
But had no might to drag him nigher from where he lay
To his master, who beheld him and wiped a tear away
That he lightly hid from Eumæus, unto whom he spake and said:

"Eumæus, much I marvel at the dog on the dung-heap laid;
Fair-shapen is his body, but nought I know indeed
If unto this his fairness he hath good running speed,
Or is but like unto some — men's table-dogs I mean,
Which but because of their fairness lords cherish to be seen."

Then thou, O swineherd Eumæus, didst speak and answer thus:

"Yea, this is the hound of the man that hath died aloof from us;
And if yet to do and to look on he were even such an one
As Odysseus left behind him when to Troy he gat him gone
Then wouldest thou wonder beholding his speed and hardihood,
For no monster that he followed through the depths of the tangled wood

Would he blench from, and well he wotted of their trail and
where it led.
But now ill he hath, since his master in an alien land is dead,
And no care of him have the women, that are heedless here
and light;
Since thralls whenso they are missing their masters' rule and
might.
No longer are they willing to do the thing that should be;
For Zeus, the loud-voiced, taketh half a man's valiancy
Whenso the day of thralldom hath hold of him at last."

So saying into the homestead of the happy place he passed
And straight to the hall he wended 'mid the Wooers overbold.
But the murky doom of the death-day of Argus now took hold
When he had looked on Odysseus in this the twentieth year.

The decade between the publication of *The Earthly Paradise* and *Sigurd the Volsung* had been one of sustained literary effort varied, as we have seen, but hardly interrupted by the work in decoration. The latter Morris called his "bread-and-cheese work," the former his "pleasure work of books." The time had not yet come for a complete union between the two, although it was foreshadowed by the illuminated manuscripts made for friends during these years. A selection from his own poems, a translation of the *Eyrbyggja Saga,* a copy of Fitzgerald's *Rubaiyat of Omar Khayyam*, and the *Æneid* of Virgil were among the works that Morris undertook to transcribe with his own hand on vellum, with decorative margins with results of great beauty. He had now long been happy in work calling out all this enthusiasm, but the world was going on without, to use his own words, "beautiful and strange and dreadful and worshipful." He was approaching the time when his conscience would no longer let him rest in the thought that he was "not born to set the crooked straight."

CHAPTER VII.

PUBLIC LIFE AND SOCIALISM.

IN the autumn of 1876, just after the publication of *Sigurd the Volsung,* Morris took his first dip in the ocean of public affairs, the waves of which were presently almost to submerge him. He was forty-two years of age, and had thus far managed to keep well within the range of his individual interests and away from the political and social questions that none the less stirred in his mind from time to time, and pricked him to random assertions that he would have nothing to do with them, that his business was with dreams, and that he would remain "the idle singer of an empty day." He was roused to action, however, by the barbarous massacre on the part of the Mussulman soldiery of men, women, and children in Bulgaria, the news of which moved the heart of England to a frenzy of indignation. When Russia intervened, the possibility that England might take up arms on the side of Turkey in order to erect a barrier against Russian aggression was intolerable to him, and he wrote to the *Daily News* in eloquent protestation. "I who am writing this," he said, with a just appreciation of his ordinary attitude toward political matters, "am one of a large class of men — quiet men, who usually go about their own business, heeding public matters less than they ought, and afraid to speak in such a huge concourse as the English nation, however much they may feel, but who are now stung into bitterness by thinking how helpless they are in a public matter that touches them so closely. "I appeal," he continued, "to the workingmen, and pray them to look to it that if this shame falls upon them they will certainly remember it and be burdened by it when their day clears for them and they attain all and more than all they are now striving for." Again in the spring of 1877, when war seemed imminent, Morris appealed "to the workingmen of England," issuing a manifesto which was practically his first Socialist document and heralded the long series of lectures and addresses, poems, articles, and treatises, presently to take the place of romances and epics in his literary life. After declaring that the people who were bringing on the war were "greedy gamblers on the Stock Exchange, idle officers of the army and navy (poor fellows!), worn-out mockers of the clubs, desperate purveyors of exciting war-news for the comfortable breakfast-tables of those who have nothing to lose by war, and lastly, in the place of honour, the Tory Rump, that we fools, weary of peace, reason, and justice, chose at the last election to represent us," he added a passage that reads like the outcome of many a heated discussion with brethren of his own social class.

"Workingmen of England, one word of warning yet," he said: "I doubt if you know the bitterness of hatred against freedom and progress that lies at the hearts of a certain part of the richer classes in this country; their newspapers veil it in a kind of decent language, but do but hear them talking amongst themselves, as I have often, and I know not whether scorn or anger would prevail in you at their folly and insolence. These men cannot speak of your order, of its aims, of its leaders, without a sneer or an insult; these men, if they had the power (may England perish rather!) would thwart your just aspirations, would silence you, would deliver you bound hand and foot forever to irresponsible capital. Fellow-citizens, look to it, and if you have any wrongs to be redressed, if you cherish your most worthy hope of raising your whole order peacefully and solidly, if you thirst for leisure and knowledge, if you long to lessen these inequalities which have been our stumbling-block since the beginning of the world, then cast aside sloth and cry out against an Unjust War, and urge us of the middle classes to do no less."

By this time he was treasurer of the Eastern Question Association, and working with all his might against the principles of the war party in England, contributing to the general agitation the political ballad called *Wake, London Lads!* which was sung

Picture by Rossetti in which the Children's Faces are Portraits of May Morris

with much enthusiasm at one of the meetings to the appropriate air, *The Hardy Norseman's Home of Yore,* and was afterwards freely distributed in the form of a leaflet among the mechanics of London. It was during this period of political activity that J. R. Green wrote of him to E. A. Freeman: "I rejoiced to see the poet Morris—whom Oliphant setteth even above you for his un-Latinisms—brought to grief by being prayed to draw up a circular on certain Eastern matters, and gravelled to find 'English words.' I insidiously persuaded him that the literary committee had fixed on him to write one of a series of pamphlets which Gladstone wants brought out for the public enlightenment, and that the subject assigned him was 'The Results of the Incidence of Direct Taxation on the Christian Rayah,' but that he was forbidden to speak of the 'onfall of straight geld,' or other such 'English' forms. I left him musing and miserable." Musing and miserable he may well have been at finding that his duty, as he conceived it, was leading him into such unlovely paths, but the English of his polemical writings was unmistakable enough and unconfused by any affectations, Saxon or Latin. In declining to stand for the Professorship of Poetry at Oxford on the occasion of Matthew Arnold's withdrawal from it, he had confessed to a peculiar inaptitude for expressing himself except in the one way in which his gift lay, and it was true that his mind was singularly inept outside its natural course. He had not a reasoning mind.

His opinions, dictated as they were chiefly by sentiment, were not worked out by the careful processes dear to genuine thinkers. But he was before all things a believer. No man was ever more certain of the absolute rectitude of his views, and by this sincerity of conviction they were driven home to his public. He was so eager to make others feel as he felt that he spent his utmost skill upon the delivery of his message, using the simple and downright phrases that could be understood by the least cultivated of his hearers. It was impossible to listen to him, says one of his friends, not a convert to his views, without for the time at least agreeing with him. Thus he conquered the "peculiar inaptitude" of which he speaks by the force of his great integrity, and although he complained that "the cursed words" went to water between his fingers, they accomplished their object.

"When the crisis in the East was past," says Mr. Mackail, "it left Morris thoroughly in touch with the Radical leaders of the working class in London, and well acquainted with the social and economic ideas which, under the influence of widening education and of the international movement among the working classes, were beginning to transform their political creed from an individualist Radicalism into a more or less definite doctrine of State Socialism." This contact was sufficient to kindle into activity the ideas implanted in his own mind during his college days. Carlyle had then thundered forth his amazing anathemas against modern civilisation and had declaimed that Gurth born thrall of Cedric, with a brass collar round his neck, was happy in comparison with the poor of to-day enjoying their "liberty to die by starvation," no displeasing gospel to a young mediævalist; while Ruskin had preached with vociferous eloquence the doctrine that happiness in labour is the end and aim of life. From the beginning of his work in decorative art Morris had shown the influence of these beliefs in peace. He was now to let them lead him into war.

Before he wrote himself down a Socialist, however, he set on foot a movement not so important in the eyes of the public, but much more characteristic of his personal mission in the world of life and art. He had long before learned from Ruskin that the so-called restoration of public monuments meant "the most total destruction which a building can suffer: a destruction out of which no remnants can be gathered: a destruction accompanied with false description of the thing destroyed." Whatever his feeling may have been concerning the destructive restoration, of which he must have seen manifold examples before this period of his middle age, he seems to have awakened rather suddenly to the necessity of taking some active measure to check the ravages of the restorer. Goaded, finally, by the sight of alterations going on in one of the beautiful parish churches near Kelmscott, he conceived the idea of forming a society of protest. Early in 1877 the impending fate of the Abbey Church at Tewkesbury, under the devastating hands of Sir Gilbert Scott, prompted him to put the idea at once before the public, and he wrote to the *Athenæum* a letter in which he went straight to the heart of his subject with clearness and simplicity.

"My eye just now caught the word 'restoration' in the morning paper," he wrote, "and on looking closer, I saw that this time it is nothing less than the Minster of Tewkesbury that is to be destroyed by Sir Gilbert Scott. Is it altogether too late to do something to save it,—it and whatever else of beautiful and historical is still left us on the sites of the ancient buildings we were once so famous for? Would it not be of some use once for all, and with the least delay possible, to set on foot an association for the purpose of watching over and protecting these relics which, scanty as they are now become, are still wonderful treasures, all the more priceless in this age of the world, when the newly-invented study of living history is the chief joy of so many of our lives?

"Your paper has so steadily and courageously opposed itself to these acts of barbarism which the modern architect, parson, and squire call 'restoration,' that it would be waste of words here to enlarge on the ruin that has been wrought by their hands; but, for the saving of what is left, I think I may write you a word of encouragement, and say that you by no means stand alone in the matter, and that there are many thoughtful people who would be glad to sacrifice time, money, and comfort in defence of those ancient monuments; besides, though I admit that the architects are, with very few exceptions, hopeless, because interest, habit, and an ignorance yet grosser, bind them; still there must be many people whose ignorance is accidental rather than inveterate, whose good sense could surely be touched if it were clearly put to them that they were destroying what they, or more surely still, their sons and sons' sons would one day fervently long for, and which no wealth or energy could ever buy again for them.

"What I wish for, therefore, is that an association should be set on foot to keep a watch on old monuments, to protest against all 'restoration' that means more than keeping out wind and weather, and, by all means, literary and other, to awaken a feeling that our ancient buildings are not mere ecclesiastical toys, but sacred monuments of the nation's growth and hope."

In less than a month the association was formed under the title of the "Society for Protection of Ancient Buildings," abbreviated by Morris to the "Anti-Scrape Society," in cheerful reference to the pernicious scraping and pointing indulged in by the restorers. Morris was made secretary of the Society, and, as long as he lived, worked loyally in its behalf, giving, in addition to time and money, the labour, which to him was grievous, of lecturing for it. He wrote a prospectus that was translated into French, German, Italian, and Dutch, and among the more important of his protests were those against the demolition of some of the most beautiful portions of St. Mark's at Venice, and the "bedizening" of the interior of Westminster Abbey.

For the sentiment which inspired him, the inextinguishable love in his heart toward every example however humble of the art he reverenced, we may turn to one of the most eloquently reasonable passages of his numerous lectures. Closing his account of pattern designing with a reference to the creation of modern or Gothic art, he says: "Never until the time of that death or cataleptic sleep of the so-called Renaissance did it forget its origin, or fail altogether in fulfilling its mission of turning the ancient curse of labour into something more like a blessing."

"As to the way in which it did its work," he continues, "as I have no time, so also I have but little need to speak, since there is none of us but has seen and felt some portion of the glory which it left behind, but has shared some portion of that most kind gift it gave the world; for even in this our turbulent island, the home of rough and homely men, so far away from the centres of art and thought which I have been speaking of, did simple folk labour for those that shall come after them. Here in the land we yet love they built their homes and temples; if not so majestically as many peoples have done, yet in such sweet accord with the familiar nature amidst which they dwelt, that when by some happy chance we come across the work they wrought, untouched by any but natural change, it fills us with a satisfying untroubled happiness that few things else could bring us. Must our necessities destroy, must our restless ambition mar, the sources of this innocent pleasure, which rich and poor may share alike—this communion with the very hearts of the departed men? Must we sweep away these touching memories of our stout forefathers and their troublous days that won our present peace and liberties?

"If our necessities compel us to it, I say we are an unhappy people; if our vanity lure us into it, I say we are a foolish and light-minded people, who have not the wits to take a little trouble to avoid spoiling our own goods. Our own goods? Yes, the goods of the people of England, now and in time to come: we who are now alive are but life-renters of them. Any of us who pretend to any culture know well that in destroying or injuring one of these buildings we are destroying the pleasure, the culture—in a word, the humanity—of unborn generations. It is speaking very mildly to say that we have no right to do this for our temporary convenience. It is speaking too mildly. I say any such destruction is an act of brutal dishonesty. . . . It is in the interest of living art and living history that I oppose 'restoration.' What history can there be in a building bedaubed with ornament, which cannot at best be anything but a hopeless and lifeless imitation of the hope and vigour of the earlier world? As to the art that is concerned in it, a strange folly it seems to me for us who live among these bricken masses of hideousness, to waste the energies of our short lives in feebly trying to add new beauty to what is already beautiful. Is that all the surgery we have for the curing of England's spreading sore? Don't let us vex ourselves to cure the antepenultimate blunders of the world, but fall to on our own blunders. Let us leave the dead alone, and, ourselves living, build for the living and those that shall live. Meantime, my plea for our Society is this, that since it is disputed whether restoration be good or not, and since we are confessedly living in a time when architecture has come on the one hand to Jerry building, and on the other to experimental designing (good, very good experiments some of them), let us take breath and wait; let us sedulously repair our ancient buildings, and watch every stone of them as if they were built of jewels (as indeed they are), but otherwise let the dispute rest till we have once more learned architecture, till we once more have among us a reasonable, noble, and universally used style. Then let the dispute be settled. I am not afraid of the issue. If that day ever comes, we shall know what beauty, romance, and history mean, and the technical meaning of the word 'restoration' will be forgotten.

"Is not this a reasonable plea? It means prudence. If the buildings are not worth anything they are not worth restoring; if they are worth anything they are at least worth treating with common sense and prudence.

"Come now, I invite you to support the most prudent Society in all England."

It is easy to understand from such examples as this how Morris gained his popularity as a lecturer. In the printed sentences you read the eager, persuasive accent, so convincing because so convinced. On the platform he stood, say his friends, like a conqueror, stalwart and sturdy, his good grey eyes flashing or twinkling, his voice deepening with feeling, his gesture and speech sudden and spontaneous, his aspect that of an insurgent, a fighter against custom and orthodoxy.

It was not long after the formation of the Society for the Protection of Ancient Buildings that he began to show himself a rebel in more than words against existing social laws. The steps by which he reached his membership in the Democratic Federation in the year 1883 are not very easily traced. Comments on the distressing gulf between rich and poor and on the conditions under which the modern workingman did his task became more frequent in his letters and addresses. His mind seemed to be gradually adjusting itself to the thought that the only hope for obtaining ideal conditions in which — this was always the ultimate goal — art might be constantly associated with handicraft, was perhaps to let art go for the time being, and upset society and all its conventions in preparation for a new earth.

"Art must go under," he wrote in one of his private letters "where or however it may come up again." But it was always the fate of art that concerned him. He never really understood what Socialism technically and economically speaking meant. He read its books with labour and sorrow, and struggled with its theories in support of his antagonism to the commercial methods of modern business, but he gained no firm grasp of any underlying political principle. In most of his later addresses he talked pure sentiment concerning social questions, characteristically declaring it to be the purest reason. His avowed belief was that "workmen should be artists and artists workmen," and this, he felt, could only be attained under the freest conditions. A workman should not be clothed in shabby garments, should not be wretchedly housed, overworked, or underfed. But neither will it profit him much if he wear good clothes, and keep short hours, and eat wholesome food, and contribute to the ugliness of the wares turned out by commerce. The idea that a man works only to earn leisure in which he does no work was shocking to him as it had been to Ruskin. Pleasant work to do, leisure for other work of a different pleasantness, this was what the workingman really wanted if only he knew it. It was clear to Morris that he himself worked "not the least in the world for the sake of earning leisure by it," but "partly driven by the fear of starvation and disgrace," and partly because he loved the work itself;

and while he was ready to confess that he spent a part of his leisure "as a dog does" in contemplation, and liked it well enough, he also spent part of it in work which gave him as much pleasure as his bread-earning work, neither more nor less. Obviously if there are men with whom such is not the case it is because they have not the right kind of work to do, and are not doing it in the right way, and it is equally obvious that the wrong work and the wrong way of doing it are forced upon them. Left to themselves they are bound to do what pleases them and what will please others of right minds. The ideal handicraftsman developing under an ideal social order "shall put his own individual intelligence and enthusiasm into the goods he fashions. So far from his labour being 'divided,' which is the technical phrase for his always doing one minute piece of work and never being allowed to think of any other, so far from that, he must know all about the ware he is making and its relation to similar wares; he must have a natural aptitude for his work so strong that no education can force him away from his special bent. He must be allowed to think of what he is doing and to vary his work as the circumstances of it vary, and his own moods. He must be forever stirring to make the piece he is at work at better than the last. He must refuse at anybody's bidding to turn out, I won't say a bad, but even an indifferent piece of work, whatever the public want or think they want. He must have a voice, and a voice worth listening to in the whole affair."

This attitude is almost identical with that of Ruskin. To see how the theories of master and pupil coincide one has only to read *The Stones of Venice* and compare with the passage quoted above the famous chapter on *The Nature of the Gothic.*

"It is verily this degradation of the operative into a machine," says Ruskin, "which, more than any other evil of the times, is leading the mass of the nations everywhere into vain, incoherent, destructive struggling for a freedom of which they cannot explain the nature to themselves. Their universal outcry against wealth and against nobility is not forced from them either by the pressure of famine or the sting of mortified pride. These do much, and have done much in all ages; but the foundations of society were never yet shaken as they are at this day. It is not that men are ill-fed, but that they have no pleasure in the work by which they make their bread, and therefore look to wealth as the only means of pleasure. It is not that men are pained by the scorn of the upper classes, but they cannot endure their own; for they feel that the kind of labour to which they are condemned is verily a degrading one, and makes them less than men. . . . We have much studied and much perfected, of late, the great civilised invention of the division of labour; only we give it a false name. It is not, truly speaking, the labour that is divided; but the men — divided into mere segments of men — broken into small fragments and crumbs of life, so that all the little piece of intelligence that is left in a man is not enough to make a pin or a nail, but exhausts itself in making the point of a pin, or the head of a nail. . . . And the great cry that rises from all our manufacturing cities, louder than their furnace blast, is all in very deed for this, — that we manufacture everything there except men. . . . And all the evil to which that cry is urging our myriads can be met only . . . by a right understanding on the part of all classes, of what kinds of labour are good for men, raising them and making them happy; by a determined sacrifice of such convenience, or beauty, or cheapness as is to be got only by the degradation of the workman." But Ruskin was altogether too much of an aristocrat, too much of an egoist, to root out classes. We can hardly imagine him preaching as Morris finally came to preach a revolution which should make it impossible for him to condescend. He could devote seven thousand pounds of his own money to establishing a St. George Society, but it would probably never have occurred to him to head a riot in Trafalgar Square.

When Morris, under the influence of old theories and new associations, came to consider not only the desirability but the possibility of establishing a social order in which men could work quite happily and art could get loose from handcuffs welded and locked by commercialism, it was a necessity of his temperament that he should turn his back on half-way methods and urge drastic reforms. His way was not the way of compromise, and he seriously believed that if "civilisation" could be swept out of the path by a revolution which should destroy all class distinctions and all machinery and machine-made goods, which should do away with commercialism and strip the world to its bare bones, so that men could start afresh, all equal and all freed from the superfluities of life, there would grow up a charming communism in which kind hearts would take the place of coronets, and cheerful labour the place of hopeless toil. We find him writing in a private letter — madly, yet with the downright force that kindled where it struck — that he has "faith more than a grain of mustard seed in the future history of civilisation," that he now knows it to be doomed to destruction, and that it is a consolation and joy to him to think of barbarism once more flooding the world, "and real feelings and passions, however rudimentary, taking the place of our wretched hypocrisies." It was thus he thought, or felt, about the new field of labour upon which he was entering, and it is from this point of view that he must be defended against the slurs that have been cast at him as a "Capitalist-Socialist." He did not ignore the ideal of renunciation which had tempted him in his youth, and which he again thought of in his middle age — though less tempted, perhaps. But he reasoned, logically enough, that for one man or a few

HONEYSUCKLE DESIGN FOR LINEN

men to divide his or their wealth with the poor would not advance the world by a furlong or a foot toward the state of things which he had at heart to bring about. It might raise the beneficiaries a little higher in the ranks—in other words, bring them a little closer to the dangerous middle-class, from which came the worst of their troubles, and it might also have the effect of making them a trifle more content with existing conditions. Neither effect was desirable in his eyes. A divine discontent to be spread throughout all classes was the end and aim of such Socialism as he accepted. Nothing could be done except through the antagonism of classes, which seemed in itself to provide a remedy. In *News from Nowhere*, his best known Socialistic romance, the name of which was perhaps suggested by Kingsley's Utopian and anagrammatic *Erewhon*, he puts into the mouth of an old man who is himself a survival from the days of "class slavery," a description of the imaginary change to an ideal Communism. Toward the end of the nineteenth century, it is assumed, a federation of labour made it possible for the workmen or "slaves" to establish from time to time important strikes that would sometimes stop an industry altogether for a while, and to impose upon their "masters" other restrictions that seriously interfered with the systematic conduct of commerce. The resulting "bad times" reached a crisis in the year 1952, when the "Combined Workers" determined upon the bold step of demanding a practical reversal of classes, by which they should have the management of the whole natural resources of the country, together with the machinery for using them. The upper classes resisting, riots ensued, then the "Great Strike." "The railways did not run," the old man recalls; "the telegraph wires were unserved; flesh, fish, and green stuff brought to market was allowed to lie there still packed and perishing; the thousands of middle-class families, who were utterly dependent for the next meal on the workers, made frantic efforts through their more energetic members to cater for the needs of the day, and amongst those of them who could not throw off the fear of what was to follow, there was, I am told, a certain enjoyment of this unexpected picnic—a forecast of the days to come in which all labour grew pleasant." Out of all this came civil war, with destruction of wares and machinery and also the destruction of the spirit of commercialism. With the removal of the spur of competition it is admitted that there was a temporary danger of making men dull by giving them too much time for thought or idle musing. How was this danger overcome? By a growing interest in art, to be sure. The people, all workmen now, and providing very simply for their simple needs, "no longer driven desperately to painful and terrible overwork," began to wish to make the work they had in hand as attractive as possible, and rudely and awkwardly to ornament the wares they produced.

"Thus at last and by slow degrees," the old man concludes, "we got pleasure into our work; then we became conscious of that pleasure, and cultivated it, and took care that we had our fill of it, and then all was gained and we were happy."

There is little here to charm the logically constructive mind, acquainted with human nature, and in the lectures setting forth in more detail and with more attempt at practical teaching the methods by which society could be enlightened and raised to his standard of excellence, Morris boldly invites the scorn of the political economist by the wholly visionary character of his pathetically "reasonable" views. Nevertheless, he was not without an instinct for distinguishing social evils and suggesting right remedies. Strip his doctrines of their exaggerated conclusions from false premises, and it is possible to find in them the seeds of many reforms that have come about to the inestimable benefit of the modern world. In his lecture on *Useful Work versus Useless Toil*, the very title of which is a flash of genius, he advocates the kind of education that is directed toward finding out what different people are fit for, and helping them along the road which they are inclined to take. He would have young people taught "such handicrafts as they had a turn for as a part of their education, the discipline of their minds and bodies; and adults would also have opportunities of learning in the same schools." He preaches the necessity of agreeable surroundings, claiming that science duly applied would get rid of the smoke, stench, and noise of factories, and that factories and buildings in which work is carried on should be made decent, convenient, and beautiful, while workers should be given opportunities of living in quiet country homes, in small towns, or in industrial colleges, instead of being obliged to "pig together" in close city quarters. Not one of these considerations is ignored by the organisations now endeavouring in the name of civilisation to raise the standard of the community. Manual training schools, free kindergartens, health protective associations, model tenement societies, have all arisen to meet in their own ways the needs to which Morris was so keenly alive. It was not the word reform, however, but the word revolution, that he constantly reiterated, and declined to relinquish in favour of any milder term. His friend William Clarke has summed up in a single paragraph the substance of many conversations held with him on the subject of social progress. "Existing society is, he thinks, gradually, but with increasing momentum, disintegrating through its own rottenness. The capitalist system of production is breaking down fast and is compelled to exploit new regions in Africa and other parts, where, he thinks, its term will be short. Economically, socially, morally, politically, religiously, civilisation is becoming bankrupt. Meanwhile it is for the Socialist to take advantage of this disintegration by spreading discontent, by preaching economic truths, and by any kind of demonstration which may harass the authorities and develop among the people an *esprit de corps*. By these means the people will, in some way or other, be ready to take up the industry of the world when the capitalist class is no longer able to direct or control it."

The expression "in some way or other" very well indicates the essential vagueness underlying Morris's definite speech. He had no idea of the means by which the people could be educated to the assumption of unfamiliar control. The utmost that he could suggest was that they should be awakened to the beauty of life as he saw it in his dreams. This beauty he continually set before them in phrases as simple and as eloquent as he could make them. Nor did he shirk the responsibilities raised by his extreme point of view. Nothing testifies more truly to his fidelity of nature and devotion to his ideal than his readiness to put aside the pursuits he loved with his whole heart and take up activities detested by him for many years of that gifted, interesting life of his, in the hope of bringing about, for people whom he really cared for only in the mass, who did not understand him and whom he did not very well understand, an order of things which should in time, but not in his time, make them—so he thought—quite happy. The extent to which he renounced was not slight.

Now indeed was the time when his friends might

justly lament that he was being kept labouring at what he could not do, with work all round that he could do so well. First he joined the Democratic Federation and was promptly put on its executive committee. We find him writing that it is naturally harder to understand the subject of Socialism in detail as he gets alongside of it, and that he often gets beaten in argument even when he knows he is right, which only drives him to more desperate attempts to justify his theories by the study of other people's arguments. While he was a member of the Federation (a definitely Socialist body at the time) he delivered a lecture at Oxford with the effect of rousing consternation in the University despite the fact that he had taken pains to inform the authorities of his position as an active Socialist. They did not understand the extent of his activity, and when he wound up an agreeable talk by frankly appealing to the undergraduates of the Russell Club, at whose invitation he was speaking, to join the Democratic Federation, the Master of University was brought to his feet to explain that nothing of the kind had been foreseen when Mr. Morris was asked to express there "his opinion on art under a democracy."

Besides his lecturing, which went on in London, or at Manchester, Leeds, Blackburn, Leicester, Glasgow, and anywhere else where a hopeful opportunity afforded, he was writing for the weekly paper of the Federation, the little sheet called *Justice*, and also writing pamphlets for distribution among the people. The measures urged in *Justice* for immediate adoption as remedies for the evils of existing society were:

Free Compulsory Education for all classes, together with the provision of at least one wholesome meal a day in each school.

Eight Hours or less to be the normal Working day in all trades.

Cumulative Taxation upon all incomes above a fixed minimum not exceeding £300 a year.

State Appropriation of Railways, with or without compensation.

The Establishment of National Banks, which shall absorb all private institutions that derive a profit from operations in money or credit.

Rapid Extinction of the National Debt.

Nationalisation of the Land and organisation of agricultural and industrial armies under State control on Coöperative principles.

The objects of the Federation were: "To unite the various Associations of Democrats and Workers throughout Great Britain and Ireland for the purpose of securing equal rights for all, and forming a permanent centre of organisation; to agitate for the ultimate adoption of the programme of the Federation; to aid all Social and political movements in the direction of these reforms." Morris believed himself to be in full sympathy with the fundamental principles of the Federation, and faithfully resented the assumption of a kindly intentioned critic who stated that his imperfect sympathy with them must in charity be supposed. To the implication that he cared only for art and not for the other side of the social questions he had been writing about, he responded: "Much as I love art and ornament, I value it chiefly as a token of the happiness of the people, and I would rather it were all swept away from the world than that the mass of the people should suffer oppression"; but he continued with the familiar challenge, opportunity to utter which was seldom lost, "At the same time, Sir, I will beg you earnestly to consider if my contention is not true, that genuine Art is always an expression of pleasure in Labour?" In explaining his point of view to the public before whom he placed his little collection of Socialist lectures, he expressed his conviction that all the ugliness and vulgarity of civilisation, which his own work had forced him to look upon with grief and pain are "but the outward expression of the innate moral baseness into which we are forced by our present form of society." The ethical and practical sides of the problem he was trying to face honestly, grew up in his mind as he dwelt upon its artistic side, and he made noble efforts to evolve schemes of practical expediency. In his reasonableness he went so far as to admit the possible usefulness of machinery in the new order toward which he was directing the attention of his followers; but he is swift to add, "for the consolation of the artists," that this usefulness will probably be but temporary; that a state of social order would lead, at first, perhaps, to a great development of machinery for really useful purposes, "because people will still be anxious about getting through the work necessary to holding society together"; but after a while they will find that there is not so much work to do as they expected and will have leisure to reconsider the whole subject, and then "if it seems to them that a certain industry would be carried on more pleasantly as regards the worker, and more effectually as regards the goods, by using hand-work rather than machinery they will certainly get rid of their machinery, because it will be possible for them to do so." "It is n't possible now," he adds; "we are not at liberty to do so; we are slaves to the monsters we have created. And I have a kind of hope that the very elaboration of machinery in a society whose purpose is not the multiplication of labour, as it now is, but the carrying on of a pleasant life, as it would be under social order, — that the elaboration of machinery, I say, will lead to the simplification of life, and so once more to the limitation of machinery."

Although the discussion of methods and external forms was entirely foreign to Morris's habit of mind, he was not averse to discussing the history of society. He was not much more an historian than he was an economist in the strict sense. He ignored, idealised, and blackened at will, always perfectly certain that he was setting forth the contrast between the past and the present in its true light; but his delight in the mediæval past, which was the only past to which he gave much attention, lends to his pictures of it a charm most appealing to those who have not too prodding a prejudice in favour of historical accuracy. He is at his best when he breaks from his grapple with the subject of the commercial classes and their development to evoke the visions which neither history nor economics could obscure in his mind. "Not seldom I please myself with trying to realise the face of mediæval England," he says to the motley audience gathering at a street corner or in some dingy little hall or shed to listen to him, "the many chases and great woods, the stretches of common tillage and common pasture quite unenclosed; the rough husbandry of the tilled parts, the unimproved breeds of cattle, sheep, and swine; especially the latter, so lank and long and lathy, looking so strange to us; the strings of packhorses along the bridle-roads; of the scantiness of the wheel-roads, scarce any except those left by the Romans, and those made from monastery to monastery; the scarcity of bridges, and people using ferries instead, or fords where they could; the little towns, well bechurched, often walled; the villages just where they are now (except for those that have nothing but the church left to tell of them), but better and more populous; their churches, some big and handsome, some small and curious, but all crowded with altars and furniture, and gay with pictures and ornament; the many religious houses, with their glorious architecture; the beautiful manor-houses, some of them castles once, and survivals from an earlier period; some new and elegant; some out of all proportion small for the importance of their lords. How strange it would be to us if we could be landed in fourteenth-century England; unless we saw the crest of some familiar hill like that which yet bears upon it a symbol of an English tribe, and from which, looking down on the plain where Alfred was born, I once had many such ponderings, we should not know into what country of the world we were come: the name is left, scarce a thing else."

CHAPTER VIII.

PUBLIC LIFE AND SOCIALISM *(Continued).*

BY the latter part of 1884 the political agitations and internal differences in the Federation, now called The Social Democratic Federation, became so violent as to force Morris to leave the association in which he had had no desire to be a leader, but had been unable to keep the position of acquiescent follower. In his connection with this and other public organisations, the underlying gentleness and real humility of his nature was clearly to be seen. He learned patience through his conflict with unsympathetic minds. From the weary experience of working in constant intercourse with men whose temper and practice and many of whose theories were directly antagonistic to his own, although identified with them in the public mind by a common responsibility, he learned to subdue those elements of his temperament that worked against the success of what he had most loyally at heart. From self-confidence, a critical habit, an overbearing positiveness of assertion, he

MERTON ABBEY WORKS

WASHING CLOTH AT THE MERTON ABBEY WORKS

passed to comparative reticence, tolerance, even docility. To his equals it was painful to see ignorant men assign to him his task, but he never failed to comply instantly with their orders.

It could not, however, have been an education in which he could take conscious pleasure, and at this juncture he doubtless would have been happy indeed could he have gone quietly back to the weaving and dyeing and writing of poetry with which his new preoccupation had seriously interfered. His conscience, however, was too deeply involved to permit a desertion, which would, he said, be dastardly. The question now constantly in his mind was how he would have felt against the system under which he lived had he himself been poor. He was convinced that he would have found it unendurable. Therefore, with a longing glance at his chintz bleaching in the sunlight and pure air of Merton Abbey, he put his shoulder to the wheel again, and, gathering together a few of his sympathisers, inaugurated a new party, the Socialist League, with the famous little *Commonweal* for its organ, a monthly paper now the joy of collectors on account of the beautiful headings of Walter Crane and the remarkable quality of the contributions by Morris himself. In this new society, for which he was primarily responsible, Morris found his work redoubled. He was editor of the *Commonweal* as well as contributor to it. He continued his lecturing, often under the most depressing conditions, speaking to small and indifferent audiences in small and miserable quarters. At Hammersmith he instituted a branch of the League in the room previously given up to his carpet-weaving, and there he gave Sunday evening addresses. On Saturday afternoons and Sunday mornings he spoke at the outdoor meetings which were to be the insidious foes of his health, and which more than once brought him into personal notoriety of a disagreeable kind.

The first of these occasions was on the 21st of September, 1885, when a number of people were arrested for gathering together that Sunday morning at the corner of Dod Street and Burdett Road against orders from the authorities to the effect that meetings at that place — a favourite spot with open-air speakers — must be stopped. Morris, with other members of the League, was present in court when the prisoners were brought up, and joined in the hisses and cries of "Shame!" when one prisoner was sentenced to two months' hard labour and the others were fined. Morris was arrested, subjected to a little questioning from the magistrate, and dismissed. The following Sunday another meeting, comprising many thousands of people, was held on the forbidden corner; nothing occurred, and they dispersed victoriously. The next year a Sunday-morning meeting in a street off Edgeware Road was interfered with by the police, and Morris was summoned to the police court and fined a shilling and costs for the offence of obstructing the highway.

Out of these experiences resulted, we may very well imagine, the farce entitled: *The Tables Turned; or, Nupkins Awakened,* given at an entertainment in the Hall of the Socialist League, at Farringdon Road, on October 15, 1887. Copies of it are still in existence—sorry little pamphlets in blue wrappers, bearing no kinship to the aristocratic products of the Kelmscott Press so soon to follow, but extremely entertaining as showing Morris in his least conventional and most aggressive public mood. As the pamphlet is quite rare, a brief description of its contents is not, perhaps, superfluous, although its literary merit amounts to as little as possible considering its authorship. It opens with a scene in a court of justice, Justice Nupkins presiding, in which a Mr. La-di-da is found guilty of swindling and of robbing the widow and the orphan. He is sentenced to imprisonment for the space of one calendar month. Next Mary Pinch, a poor woman (the part was taken by Morris's daughter May), is accused of stealing three loaves of bread, and, after absurd and contradictory testimony by witnesses for the prosecution (constables and sergeants), is sentenced to eighteen months of hard labour. Next, John Freeman, a Socialist, is accused of conspiracy, sedition, and obstruction of the highway. The Archbishop of Canterbury (this rôle enacted by Morris), Lord Tennyson, and Professor Tyndall are called as witnesses and give testimony, the manner and speech of the renowned originals being somewhat rudely parodied.

After contradictory evidence by these witnesses and the former ones, the prisoner is sentenced to six years' penal servitude with a fine of one hundred pounds, his offence having been an open-air speech advocating the principles of Socialism. As his sentence is pronounced the *Marseillaise* is heard, and a Socialist ensign enters with news that the Revolution has begun.

It is in the second part that the tables are turned upon Nupkins. The scene this time is laid in the fields near a country village, with a copse close by. The time is after the Revolution. Justice Nupkins is found skulking in the copse, half mad with fear at the reversal of social conditions, his past cruelty giving him small reason to hope for gentle treatment at the hands of the former "lower classes," who are now running affairs to suit themselves. He meets Mary Pinch, who pities his deplorable aspect and invites him to her house, now a pleasant and prosperous home. He cannot believe in the sincerity of her apparent kindness, and flees from her in a panic, only to meet other of his former victims who further alarm him by pretending to arrest him and give him a mock trial, during which he thinks he is to be sentenced to death. He learns at last that under the beautiful new order he is free to do what he pleases, and may dig potatoes and earn his own living by such tilling of the soil. The citizens dance about him singing the following words to the tune of the *Carmagnole:*

What 's this that the days and the days have done?
Man's lordship over man hath gone.

How fares it, then, with high and low?
Equal on earth they thrive and grow.
Bright is the sun for everyone;
Dance we, dance we the Carmagnole.

How deal ye, then, with pleasure and pain?
Alike we share and bear the twain.

And what 's the craft whereby ye live?
Earth and man's work to all men give.

How crown ye excellence of worth?
With leave to serve all men on earth.

What gain that lordship's past and done?
World's wealth for all and everyone.

This somewhat childlike but not too bland revenge on the powers of the law met with an enthusiastic reception at the Hall of the Socialist League; Mr. Bernard Shaw, who was present, declaring that there had been no such successful "first night" within living memory.

The year 1887 was marked, however, by events much more serious than the acting of a little farce. On the 13th of November,—"Bloody Sunday" it was called,—the efforts of the Government to check open-air speaking culminated in an organised riot on the part of the Socialists in alliance with the extreme Radicals. Sir Charles Warren had prohibited by proclamation the holding of any meeting in Trafalgar Square,—a meeting having been announced to take place there to protest against the Irish policy of the Government. Thereupon it was agreed by the Socialist League, the Social Democratic Federation, the Irish National League, and certain Radical clubs that their members should assemble at various centres and march toward Trafalgar Square. Morris put himself at the head of the Clerkenwell contingent, first delivering a short speech mounted on a cart in company with Mrs. Besant and others. He declared that wherever it was attempted to put down free speech it was a bounden duty to resist the attempt by every possible means, and told his audience that he thought their business was to get to the Square by some means or other; that he intended to do his best to get there, whatever the consequences might be, and that they must press on like orderly people and good citizens. Thus pressing on, with flags flying and bands playing, they were met at the Bloomsbury end of St. Martin's Lane by the police, mounted and on foot, who charged in among them, striking right and left, and causing complete disorder in the ranks. The triumph of law and order over the various columns of the demonstrators was soon complete, and the outcome consisted of the arrest of three hundred men or more (many of whom were sent to prison and a few condemned to penal servitude) and the killing of three. The first to die was Alfred Linnell, for whom a public funeral was given —great masses of men marching in perfect and solemn order to Bow Cemetery, where he was buried, the service at the grave being read by the light of a lantern. Such an event would inevitably stir Morris to sympathetic rage, and the dirge written by him to be sung as poor Linnell was buried has an inflammatory sound despite the obvious effort at restraint:

> We asked them for a life of toilsome earning,
> They bade us bide their leisure for our bread;
> We craved to speak to tell our woful learning,
> We came back speechless, bearing back our dead!

Thus time was spent. Sometimes Morris was heading processions "with the face of a Crusader," says Joseph Pennell, describing one occasion on which he led a crowd, "among the red flags, singing with all his might the *Marseillaise*"—into Westminster Abbey to attend the Sunday services. Sometimes he was bailing out his friends who had been "run in" by the police. Sometimes he was tramping, whatever the weather, at the head of the workless workers of Hammersmith to interview the Guardians of the Poor. Sometimes he was delivering his lectures among woful hovels in tumble-down sheds to a score or so of people of whose comprehension he felt most doubtful. Always he was preaching "Education toward Revolution," but with an ever-increasing consciousness that a vast amount of education was needed before revolution could be effectively reforming. His imagination had formed great ideals and had pictured those ideals in triumphant practice, but his practical sense was sufficient to show him the futility of unintelligent action. He had spent much money, not in profit-sharing among his workmen (although this obtained to a certain extent in his business), but in bearing the various and heavy expenses imposed by the publication of the organs of Socialism, which he supported almost as largely by his purse as by his pen, and by a thousand other needs of the cause to which in 1882 he had also sacrificed the greater part of his valuable library. He had spent much time, which, to one so deeply interested in pursuits for which any one life is far too short, meant infinitely more than the expenditure of money or the relinquishing of property that, after all, may be got back again. And he had worked against the grain with all sorts and conditions of companions, from whom he was as widely separated as the east is from the west — never more widely than when he was marching by their side toward a goal that neither could see clearly. He was now longing more and more to get back to his own life and away from a life so foreign. As he had said in the first flush of his enthusiasm, "Art must go under," he was now prepared "to see all organised Socialism run into the sand for a while." It is not surprising that he "somehow did not seem to care much" when the Socialist League became disintegrated and insolvent. He had done his best for it, but its strongest members had drifted away from it, the executive control had been gained by a group of Anarchists, and Morris had been by these deposed from the editorship of the *Commonweal.* Before the society reached its lowest depths he resigned, giving expression in the *Commonweal* for the 15th of November, 1890, to his feeling in the form it then took toward the movement which so long had carried him out of his course and kept him in turbulent waters. This movement had then been going on for about seven years. Those concerned in it had made, he thought, "about as many mistakes as any other party in a similar space of time." When he first joined it he hoped that some leaders would turn up among the workingmen who "would push aside all middle-class help and become great historical figures." This hope he had pretty well relinquished. In the beginning there had been little said about anything save the great ideals of Socialism, but as the Socialist idea had become more and more impressed upon the epoch a somewhat vulgarised and partial realisation of these ideals had pressed upon the friends of the cause. They began to think of methods, and mostly of "methods of impatience," as Morris from his ripened and moderated point of view now designated them. "There are two tendencies in this matter of methods," he said; "on the one hand is our old acquaintance, palliation, elevated now into vastly greater importance than it used to have, because of the growing discontent, and the obvious advance of Socialism; on the other is the method of partial, necessarily futile, inconsequent revolt, or riot rather, against the authorities, who are our absolute masters, and can easily put it down.

"With both these methods I disagree; and that the more because the palliatives have to be clamoured for, and the riots carried out by men who do not know what Socialism is, and have no idea what their next step is to be, if, contrary to all calculation, they should happen to be successful. Therefore, at the best, our masters would be our masters still, because there would be nothing to take their place. *We are not ready for such a change as that!*" The time was favourable, he thought, for preaching the simple principles of Socialism regardless of the policy of the passing hour, nor was any more active work desirable. "I say, for us *to make Socialists,*" he concluded, "is *the* business at present, and at present I do not think we can have any other useful business. Those who are not really Socialists—who are Trades Unionists, disturbance-breeders, or what not—will do what they are impelled to do, and we cannot help it. At the worst there will be some good in what they do; but we need not and cannot heartily work with them, when we know that their methods are beside the right way.

"Our business, I repeat, is the making of Socialists, *i.e.,* convincing people that Socialism is good for them and is possible. When we have enough people of that way of thinking, *they* will find out what action is necessary for putting their principles in practice. Therefore, I say, make Socialists. We Socialists can do nothing else that is useful."

This was practically the end of militant Socialism for Morris. Together with a handful of his true followers and sympathisers he did organise or reorganise under very simple rules a little society named the Hammersmith Socialist Society, which took the place of the Hammersmith Branch of the Socialist League. The manifesto explained that the separation had been made because the members of the new society did not hold the Anarchistic views of the majority of the old society's members, and would be likely to waste in bickering time "which should be spent in attacking capitalism." The business of the Hammersmith Society was to spread the principles of Socialism, the method so warmly recommended by Morris in his *Commonweal* article. But it was obvious that his interest was no longer keen in even this passive mode of advancing the cause for which he had laboured so long and, on the whole, so thanklessly. He set himself dutifully to work at writing the manifesto, but complained, "I would so much rather go on with my Saga work."

It cannot be said, however, that he was inconsistent. He had gone into militant Socialism as he went into everything, with a superabundant energy that must work itself off in activity. But there was more vehemence than narrowness in his partisanship. When his party forsook the principles for the sake of which he had joined it, he forsook the party. He learned of human nature much that was discouraging during his efforts to make many of his fellows work together in harmony, but he brought out of the fiery experience an unharmed ideal. And among the clashing of creeds and the warring of minds he played the part of peacemaker to an extent remarkable in so impulsive a nature. "It seemed as though he wanted to have all his own way," says one of his acquaintances, "yet put him in the chair at a meeting and he was as patient as the mildest of us." His inmost belief was much the same at the end as at the beginning, — matured by study and tempered by practical failures, but holding to the fundamental idea that art is the great source of pleasure in human life as well as pleasure's best result, and must be made possible for everyone to practise with a free mind and a body unwearied by hopeless toil. The letter to the *Daily Chronicle* of the 10th of November, 1893, on "Help for the Miners, the Deeper Meaning of the Struggle," sounds the familiar note as positively as ever, and contains all that is required to represent the creed of his later years. "I hold firmly to the opinion," he says in this letter, "that all worthy schools of art must be in the future, as they have been in the past, the outcome of the aspirations of the people towards the beauty and true pleasure of life. And, further, now that democracy is building up a new order, which is slowly emerging from the confusion of the commercial period, these aspirations of the people towards beauty can only be born from a condition of practical equality, of economical condition amongst the whole population. Lastly, I am so confident that this equality will be gained that I am prepared to accept, as a consequence of the process of that gain, the apparent disappearance of what art is now left us, because I am sure that that will be but a temporary loss, to be followed by a genuine new birth of art which will be the spontaneous expression of the pleasure of life innate in the whole people. This, I say, is the art which I look forward to, not as a vague dream, but as a practical certainty, founded on the general well-being of the people. It is true that the blossom of it I shall not see; therefore I may be excused if, in common with other artists, I try to express myself through the art of to-day, which seems to us to be only a survival of the organic art of the past, in which the people shared, whatever the other drawbacks of their condition might have been. . . . Yet if we shall not (those of us who are as old as I am) see the New Art, the expression of the general pleasure of life, we are even now seeing the seed of it beginning to germinate. For if genuine art be impossible without the help of the useful classes, how can these turn their attention to it if they are living amidst sordid cares which press upon them day in, day out? The first step, therefore, towards the new birth of art must be a definite rise in the condition of the workers; their livelihood must (to say the least of it) be less niggardly and less precarious, and their hours of labour shorter; and this improvement must be a general one and confirmed against the chances of the market by legislation. But, again, this change for the better can only be realised by the efforts of the workers themselves. 'By us, and not for us,' must be their motto. . . . What these staunch miners have been doing in the face of such tremendous odds other workmen can and will do; and when life is easier and fuller of pleasure people will have time to look around them and find out what they desire in the matter of art, and will also have time to compass their desires."

Just why Morris with his extreme independence stopped short of Anarchism is difficult to see unless it be attributed to an instinct for order inherited from the sturdy stock to which he belonged. The necessity of a public rule of action was always, however, quite clear to him. He contended that you have a right to do as you like so long as you do not interfere with your neighbour's right to do as he likes, a contention which not even a fairly conservative mind finds very difficult to uphold: he was not willing to admit the right of an individual to act "unsocially." Indeed all the charm of his pictures of the ideal life derives from the atmosphere of loving-kindness and mutual helpfulness with which he surrounds them. The Golden Rule was always in his mind as he built up in his imagination his Paradise on earth. He possessed the optimism of the kind-hearted, the faith in his fellow men that made him sure of their right acting could they only start afresh with a field clear of injury and abuse. He never dreamed in all his dreaming that these would again grow up and destroy the beautiful fabric of his new Society, so bright and unspotted in his mind. Of course there would be a social conscience "which, being social, is common to every man." Without that there could be no society; and "Man without society is not only impossible but inconceivable." Thus he argued and thus he believed. His militant Socialism had, while it lasted, a very dangerous side. His Socialist "principles" are easily torn to ribbons by the political economist in possession of facts showing the increasing prosperity of the working classes and their increasing interest under existing conditions in the arts and in education; but regarding his views merely as representing one aspect of his impressive personality, it is easy to find them attractive. To quote what the *Pall Mall Gazette* said of the Sunday evenings at the Hammersmith Hall, "They are patches of bright colour in the great drab, dreary, dull, and dirty world." They bring with them such thoughts as Arnold had of the repose that has fled "for ever the course of the river of Time." The spirit breathed through them in strong contrast to the spirit of many of his co-workers, ennobles all efforts toward true reform, diffuses the love of humanity among a cold people, and makes for the innocent and exquisite happiness which our human nature is so apt paradoxically to deny us. In Morris's world we should all be very happy if we were like Morris. He was not very happy in our world, yet perhaps he managed to get out of it as much of the joy of doing as it can be made to yield to any one man. His Socialism, from one point of view, was certainly a tremendous failure, but no other side of his life visible to the public at large showed so plainly his moral virtues, his generosity, his sincerity, his power of self-sacrifice, his effort toward self-control. It was significant that when, with a last rally of his forces to active work for the cause, he joined in a concerted effort to unite all Socialists into a single party, he was chosen as the best man for the purpose, all the societies having "a deep regard and respect for him." It is even more significant that his own employees in his large business also esteemed him highly, feeling the sincerity with which he tried to make his practices accord with his theories. If his business was a successful one it was not because he tried to get from his workmen the utmost he could claim in time and labour. The eight-hour working-day was in practice in the Merton factory, and the wages paid were the highest known in the trade. He was free from the self-complacency that gives to justice the name of charity, and he was not distinguished for civility toward the people under his direction, but he was, they said in their emphatic and expressive vernacular, "the sort of bloke you always could depend upon."

Toward the end of his activity for the cause of Socialism he became connected with a society which perhaps would not have existed without his influence, although he was not directly responsible for its formation. This was the Arts and Crafts Exhibition Society [founded in 1888], the aims of which were described by one of its members in the following words: "To assert the possibilities of Art in design, applied even to the least pretentious purpose and in every kind of handicraft; to protest against the absolute subjection of Art in its applied form to the interests of that extravagant waste of human energy which is called economic production; to claim for the artist or handicraftsman, whose identity it has been the rule to hide and whose artistic impulse it has been the custom to curb (until he was really in danger of becoming, in fact as in name, a mere hand), some recognition and some measure of appreciation; to try and discover whether the public cared at all, or could be brought to care, for the Art which, good or bad, is continually under their eyes; and whether there might not be, in association with manufacture, or apart from it, if that were out of the question, some scope for handicraft, some hope for Art."

Morris's point of view is apparent in these aims, and the society was composed chiefly of young men who, says Mr. Mackail, "without following his principles to their logical issues or joining any Socialist organisation, were profoundly permeated with his ideas on their most fruitful side,—that of the regeneration, by continued and combined individual effort, of the decaying arts of life." The Art Workers' Guild, dating from 1884, was the source from which the new society sprang, the immediate purpose of the latter being to get the work of men who combined art with handicraft before the public by means of exhibitions, the committees of the Royal Academy and kindred associations refusing to accept examples of applied art for the exhibitions which they devoted to what they called "fine art proper." Mr. Mackail calls attention to the fact that Morris at this stage of his life was so thoroughly imbued with the idea that the general public were ignorant of and indifferent to decorative art, as to feel more sceptical of the success of the exhibitions than was justified by their outcome. He lent his aid, however, with his customary energy, guaranteeing a considerable sum of money, and contributing some valuable papers and lectures, the exhibitions being combined with instruction by acknowledged masters of handicraft. In 1891 he was elected President of the Society, holding that office until the time of his death, when he was succeeded by Walter Crane. He was a member of the Art Workers' Guild as well, and was elected Master of the Guild in 1892. He also belonged to the Bibliographical Society formed in that year, and in 1894 was elected a Fellow of the Society of Antiquaries of London. The societies were all directly concerned with questions in which Morris had all his life been interested, and his connection with them was not only natural but almost inevitable. He was not a man to whom public business made a strong appeal. He undertook it with reluctance and relinquished it with delight. Nor did he care for the labels of distinction for which most men, even among the greatly distinguished, have a measure of regard. He was, however, gratified when, in 1882, he was unanimously elected Honorary Fellow of Exeter College at Oxford, an honour which is rarely conferred, and is generally reserved, says Mr. Mackail, "for old members who have attained the highest official rank in their profession."

CHAPTER IX.

LITERATURE OF THE SOCIALIST PERIOD.

DESPITE the large amount of time and comparatively unproductive thought given by Morris to his Socialism, the period of his greatest activity in this direction was not without result in the field of pure literature. The years from 1884 to 1890 were crowded with pamphlets, leaflets, newspaper articles, manifestoes, and treatises, all with the one object—the making of Socialists. Many of these were more or less works of art—but of art in fetters; in the main they bore sad witness to the havoc made in the æsthetic life of their author by his propagandising policy, and in their deadly dulness betrayed the unwillingness of his mind to labour in a field so foreign to it. Not even the overwhelming tasks imposed upon him sufficed, however, to subdue entirely his restless imagination. From time to time in the arid desert of his writings for "the cause" a poem of romance appeared of a quality to show that the sap still ran in the products of his mind. Between the first issue of *The Commonweal* and the inauguration of the Kelmscott Press he wrote in the following order: *The Pilgrims of Hope, A Dream of John Ball, The House of the Wolfings, The Roots of the Mountains,* and *News from Nowhere.*

Each is interesting as throwing a varied yet steady light upon his mental processes, and the first is especially interesting despite its conspicuous defects, as one of the very few examples of its author's style when treating a subject belonging to the actual present, not to the past or future. In it the reader leaves dreamland and is confronted by modern problems and situations set forth in plain modern English. A garden is no longer a garth, a dwelling-place is no longer a stead, the writer no longer wots and meseems. So violent a change in vocabulary could hardly be accomplished with entire success; at all events it was not, and much of the phraseology is an affliction to the ear, showing a peculiarly deficient taste in the use of a style uninspired by mediæval tradition. Yet, withal, *The Pilgrims of Hope* is touched with life, as many of Morris's more artful compositions are not. The old bottles will not always serve for the new wine, Lowell warns us, and there is a noticeably quickening element in this wine poured from the bottle of the day. It is mentioned in Mr. Mackail's biography that Morris once began to write a modern novel, but left it unfinished. The fabric of *The Pilgrims of Hope* is that of a modern novel, and the characters and incidents are such as Morris might easily have found in his daily path. A country couple leading a life of peaceful simplicity go down to London, and among the sordid influences of the town become converts to Socialism. Much that follows may be considered a record of Morris's personal experience. The husband in the poem tries, as Morris tried, to learn the grounds of the Socialist faith, and takes up, as he did, the burden of spreading it among an indifferent people. The following description might very well have been culled from the diary kept by Morris during a part of his period of militant Socialism, but it must be confessed that the balance of poetic charm is all in favour of the account in the diary.

I read day after day
Whatever books I could handle, and heard about and about
What talk was going amongst them ; and I burned up doubt after doubt,
Until it befell at last that to others I needs must speak
(Indeed, they pressed me to that while yet I was weaker than weak).
So I began the business, and in street-corners I spake
To knots of men. Indeed, that made my very heart ache,
So hopeless it seemed, for some stood by like men of wood.
And some, though fain to listen, but a few words understood;
And some but hooted and jeered: but whiles across some I came
Who were keen and eager to hear; as in dry flax the flame
So the quick thought flickered amongst them: and that indeed was a feast.
So about the streets I went, and the work on my hands increased;
And to say the very truth, betwixt the smooth and the rough
It was work, and hope went with it, and I liked it well enough.

A similar passage, also showing the style at its worst, renders the actual scene encountered by Morris at many a lecture, and contains a careful portrait of himself as he appeared in his own eyes on such occasions. For the sake of its accuracy its touch of self-consciousness may well be forgiven. Not a conceited man, and curiously averse to mirrors, Morris was not in the habit of using their psychological counterparts, and it is impossible to surprise him in the act of posing to himself in becoming attitudes. There is, therefore, no irritation to the mind in his occasional frank assumption of interest in himself as a feature of the landscape, so to speak. Here he is on the Socialist platform as the Pilgrim of Hope beholds him, the Pilgrim explaining how it happened that he got upon his track.

This is how it befell: a workman of mine had heard
Some bitter speech in my mouth, and he took me up at the word,
And said: "Come over to-morrow to our Radical spouting-place;
For there, if we hear nothing new, at least we shall see a new face;
He is one of those Communist chaps, and 't is like that you two may agree."
So we went, and the street was as dull and as common as aught you could see.
Dull and dirty the room. Just over the chairman's chair
Was a bust, a Quaker's face with nose cocked up in the air.
There were common prints on the walls of the heads of the party fray,
And Mazzini dark and lean amidst them gone astray.

Some thirty men we were of the kind that I knew full well,
Listless, rubbed down to the type of our easy-going hell.
My heart sank down as I entered, and wearily there I sat
While the chairman strove to end his maunder of this and that.

And partly shy he seemed, and partly indeed ashamed
Of the grizzled man beside him as his name to us he named;
He rose, thickset and short, and dressed in shabby blue,
And even as he began it seemed as though I knew
The thing he was going to say, though I never heard it before.
He spoke, were it well, were it ill, as though a message he bore.
A word that he could not refrain from many a million of men.
Nor aught seemed the sordid room and the few that were listening then
Save the hall of the labouring earth and the world which was to be,
Bitter to many the message, but sweet indeed unto me,
And every soul rejoicing in the sweet and bitter of life:
Of peace and good-will he told, and I knew that in faith he spake,
But his words were my very thoughts, and I saw the battle awake,
And I followed from end to end! and triumph grew in my heart
As he called on each that heard him to arise and play his part
In the tale of the new-told gospel, lest as slaves they should live and die.

He ceased, and I thought the hearers would rise up with one cry,
And bid him straight enroll them; but they, they applauded indeed,
For the man was grown full eager, and had made them hearken and heed.
But they sat and made no sign, and two of the glibber kind
Stood up to jeer and to carp his fiery words to blind.

I did not listen to them, but failed not his voice to hear

When he rose to answer the carpers, striving to make more clear
That which was clear already; not overwell, I knew
He answered the sneers and the silence, so hot and eager he grew;
But my hope full well he answered, and when he called again
On men to band together lest they live and die in vain,
In fear lest he should escape me, I rose ere the meeting was done,
And gave him my name and my faith — and I was the only one.
He smiled as he heard the jeers, and there was a shake of the hand,
He spoke like a friend long known; and lo! I was one of the band.

There is nothing impressive in such rhyming save its message, the form costing little trouble and awakening little interest. Here, obviously, Morris, like Dante, would rather his readers should find his doctrine sweet than his verses. Parts of the poem are, however, upon a much higher plane of accomplishment. The first section, called *The Message of the March Wind,* contains exquisite images and moves to a fresh elastic measure; a world both real and lovely being evoked by the opening stanzas:

Fair now is the springtide, now earth lies beholding
  With the eyes of a lover the face of the sun;
Long lasteth the daylight, and hope is enfolding
  The green-growing acres with increase begun.

Now sweet, sweet it is through the land to be straying
  'Mid the birds and the blossoms and the beasts of the fields;
Love mingles with love and no evil is weighing
  On thy heart or mine, where all sorrow is healed.

From township to township, o'er down and by tillage
  Fair, far have we wandered and long was the day,
But now cometh eve at the end of the village,
  Where o'er the grey wall the church riseth grey.

There is wind in the twilight; in the white road before us
  The straw from the ox-yard is blowing about;
The moon's rim is rising, a star glitters o'er us,
  And the vane on the spire-top is swinging in doubt.

Down there dips the highway, toward the bridge crossing over
  The brook that runs on to the Thames and the sea.
Draw closer, my sweet, we are lover and lover;
  This eve art thou given to gladness and me.

In the course of the poem the Pilgrims are called to Paris by the voice of the Revolution, and there the wife is killed. Interwoven with the main incidents is the domestic tragedy most familiar to fiction, the alienation of the wife's affections by one of the husband's friends. Morris in his treatment of this situation shows a peculiarly fine and tender quality, sufficiently rare in life itself and seldom to be found in pictures of life. He preserves the dignity of his unhappy characters by a delicate sincerity in their attitude toward one another and by an immeasurable gentleness and self-forgetfulness on the part of the one most wronged. A similar situation in *News from Nowhere* is made trivial and consequently revolting by the impression it gives that it was created to illustrate a theory. In no place does *The Pilgrims of Hope* give such an impression. It is a drawing from life, clumsy and summary enough in outline,

Portrait of Mrs. Morris

By Rossetti

yet firm and expressive of the thing seen, and with power to convey a genuine emotion.

The Pilgrims of Hope appeared serially in *The Commonweal* during 1885–1886. It was soon followed by a romance called *The Dream of John Ball.* This subject with its mediæval setting suited Morris well, and was treated by him in his ripest and strongest vein. Although the story opens in a lightly facetious manner, never a particularly happy one with him, its tone as it proceeds is that of subdued and stately pathos. The writer dreams himself in a village of Kent, where men are hanging upon the words of that poor tutor of Oxford, the "Mad Priest," preaching the equality of gentle and villein on the text

When Adam dalf, and Eve span
Who was thanne a gentilman?

Apparently the dream is the result of a mournfully retrospective mood. The dreamer hears the plain and stirring speech of John Ball, listens to his eager appeal to the men of Kent that they help their brethren of Essex cast off the yoke placed upon them by bailiff and lord, and to his prophecies that in the days to come, when they are free from masters, "man shall help man, and the saints in heaven shall be glad, because men no more fear each other . . . and fellowship shall be established in heaven and on the earth." But knowledge of the later time penetrates the dream, and the dreamer ponders "how men fight and lose the battle, and the thing that they fought for comes about in spite of their defeat, and when it comes it turns out not to be what they meant, and other men have to fight for what they meant under another name." At this time Morris was realising in some bitterness of heart that the thing for which he had fought was turning out to be not what he had meant, and the talk between John Ball and the dreamer concerning the future, of which the latter can reveal the secret, is eloquent of sober and noble resignation. The reformer of the earlier age receives with serenity the assurance that his sacrifice will count only as failure in the eyes of the coming generations, since with it goes the further assurance that men will continue to seek a remedy for their wrongs. But we read in the conception the author's foreboding that his own efforts toward the reconstitution of society are also doomed. The dreamer meditates, with an insight born of personal experience and disappointment, upon the darkness of our vision and the difficulty of directing our steps toward our actual goal. Morris obviously traced in John Ball's action a parallel to his own. What happened to the one was what might happen to the other. The hope that inspired the one was the same as inspired the other. The mistakes of the one were akin to the mistakes of the other. Thus, this prose romance, of all that Morris wrote, is warmest and most personal. The historical setting is an aid, not an obstacle, to the imagination. The pathos of the real life touched upon, the knowledge that the hopeful spirit of the preacher was once alive in the land, and that the response of the men of Kent was given in truth and with the might of angry, living hearts, lends a certain solidity and vitality to the figures and inspires Morris to a sturdier treatment of his material than legends could force from him. Had some of the marvellous activity that later went toward the making of purely imaginary situations and characters been spent upon realising for us the individual lives of more of the mediæval workers and thinkers, so vivid to Morris and so dim to most of us, the result might not have been history, but it would have been literature of a rare and felicitous type.

In April, 1888, *The Dream of John Ball* was reprinted from *The Commonweal* in one volume, together with a short story based on the life of Matthias Corvinus, King of Hungary, and called *A King's Lesson*. This also had appeared in *The Commonweal* under the title of "An Old Story Retold."

Hard upon this little volume followed *The House of the Wolfings*, a war-story of the early Middle Ages, and significant as forming, with its immediate successor, a link between old interests and new, marking its author's return to the writing of pure romance, and also his first awakening to an active interest in the typography of his books. The subject is derived from the ancient literature, half myth, half history, in which he had long been steeped, but in its treatment lurks a suggestion of the great moral excitement of the Socialist campaign. Thiodulf, the hero, beloved by a goddess, is the war-duke of a Gothic host and, on the verge of battle with Roman legionaries, is deceived into wearing a hauberk wrought by the dwarfs, the peculiar quality of which lies in its power to preserve the wearer's life at the cost of defeat for his army. Learning of this, Thiodulf removes the magic armour in time to gain his victory, but in the moment of triumph he is killed. His exaltation of mood in thus renouncing life suggests a spiritual ambition different from that commonly associated with the gods and heroes of the early world, and conveys the message by which Morris was at once burdened and inspired: that individual life may cheerfully be sacrificed if the life of the many is saved or elevated thereby. How far a war-duke of the Goths would have felt the compensatory sense that he was gaining immortality through the effect of his deeds on the destiny of his people was probably not in his mind. He himself, despite his constitutional horror of death, would perhaps not have been sorry at this time to lay off his hauberk if he could have been certain of the victory. Throughout the history of Thiodulf runs an elevated ethical intention absent from Morris's later romances. The dignity and seriousness of the women, the nobility of the men, the social unity of the Marksmen, and the high standard of thought and action maintained by them as a community place the interest on a high plane. The shadow of an idealised Socialism intensifies the relations of the characters to one another, and the reader familiar with the course of the author's life interprets the narrative as an expression of personal feeling and moral conviction not wihout pathos in its contrast to the actual world in which Morris was moving and in which he found what he conceived to be his duty so repugnant to his tastes.

Indirectly the book was to open the way for his escape by filling his mind with an enthusiasm along the natural line of his gifts, a zest for further accomplishment in the field he loved that was not to be withstood. It was printed at the Chiswick Press, and owing to a new interest in fine printing due to his intercourse with Mr. Emery Walker, Morris chose for it a quaint and little-known fount of type cut by Howard half a century before, and gave much attention to the details of its appearance. With all his familiarity with mediæval books, and his delight in illustration and illumination, he was still ignorant of the art of spacing and type designing. He had characteristically concentrated his attention on the special feature in which he was interested,— in the case of the old books, the woodcuts and ornaments,— and had passed over even the most marked characteristics which later were to absorb his whole attention. An anecdote told by Mr. Buxton Forman shows the extent to which he subordinated all other questions to the now supreme problem of a handsome page, and also the adaptability of his mind, never at a loss to meet an emergency. Mr. Forman had run across him at the Chiswick Press, whither he had repaired to settle some final points concerning his title-page. Presently down came the proof of the page. "It did not read quite as now," says Mr. Forman; "the difference, I think, was in the fourth and fifth lines where the words stood 'written in prose and verse by William Morris.' Now unhappily the words and the type did not so accord as to come up to Morris's standard of decorativeness. The line wanted tightening up; there was a three-cornered consultation between the Author, the Manager, and myself. The word *in* was to be inserted — 'written in prose and in verse' — to gain the necessary fulness of line. I mildly protested that the former reading was the better sense and that it should not be sacrificed to avoid a slight excess of white that no one would notice. 'Ha!' said Morris, 'now what would you say if I told you that the verses on the title-page were written just to fill up the great white lower half? Well, that was what happened!'" The verses thus produced to fill a purely decorative need were the following, as delicate and filled with tender sentiment as any written by Morris under the most genuine inspiration — if one may assume that any inspiration was more genuine with him than the spur of a problem in decoration:

Whiles in the early winter eve
We pass amid the gathering night
Some homestead that we had to leave
Years past; and see its candles bright

Shine in the room beside the door
Where we were merry years agone
But now must never enter more,
As still the dark road drives us on.
E'en so the world of men may turn
At even of some hurried day
And see the ancient glimmer burn
Across the waste that hath no way;
Then with that faint light in its eyes
Awhile I bid it linger near
And nurse in wavering memories
The bitter-sweet of days that were.

In glee over the fine appearance of *The House of the Wolfings* as it came from the press, Morris passed on to his next book, *The Roots of the Mountains,* also a romance suggesting the saga literature, but without the mythological element. The setting hints at history without belonging to any especial time or place. The plan is quite complicated in incident, and the love-story involved has a modern tinge. Gold-mane, a chieftain of Burgdale, is betrothed to a damsel somewhat prematurely named the Bride. By a magic spell he is drawn through the woods to the Shadowy Vale where he meets a daughter of the Kindred of the Wolf, called Sunbeam, with whom he falls in love. It is a touch characteristic of Morris that makes Gold-mane in describing his old love to the new loyally give the former all the credit of her charm. " Each day she groweth fairer," he says to the maiden who is already her rival in his affections; " there is no man's son and no daughter of woman that does not love her ; yea, the very beasts of field and fold love her." Presently an alliance is formed between the men of Burgdale and the Kindred of the Wolf for the purpose of attacking their common enemy, the Dusky Men, who belong to a race of Huns. Attached to the allied forces is a band of Amazons, and the two brave ladies, the Sunbeam and the Bride, show themselves valorous in battle. The attack on the Dusky Men is victorious, and peace returns to the valleys. In the meantime Gold-mane has firmly, though with gentle words, told the Bride of his intention of breaking his pledge to her, and the Sunbeam's brother, Folkmight, has been moved by compassion and finally by love for the deserted maiden, who consents to be his wife. It is quite in accord with the ideal established by Morris in his works of fiction, as indeed in his life, that sincerity takes the leading place among the virtues of his characters. It requires a certain defiance of the conventional modern mood to tolerate Gold-mane, the deserter, as he deals out cold comfort to the Bride, yet the downright frankness of all these people is a quality so native to their author as to pierce their unreality and give them the touch of nature without which they would be made wholly of dreams.

The Roots of the Mountains was written rapidly and issued with unrelaxed attention to typographical problems. Its title-page was made even more satisfactory than that of its predecessor, and the device of introducing a little poem to fill up the ugly white space in the centre was again employed. The lines in this case have nothing to do with the contents of the book, though forced into a relation with the author's purpose of providing "rest" for the reader. They were, in fact, founded upon an incident of a railway trip when the train passed through meadows in which hay-making was going on. Mr. Emery Walker was with Morris, and as they saw the hay-cocks defrauded by the summer breeze he exclaimed, "A subject for your title-page!" "Aye," said Morris, and jotted it down in his manuscript book.

The Roots of the Mountains was a favourite with Morris, and he planned for it an edition on Whatman paper and bound in two patterns of Morris and Company's chintz. Some of the paper ordered for this edition was left over, and eventually was used by Morris for the first little post-quarto catalogues and prospectuses printed at Hammersmith. Thus the book formed a material link between the Chiswick Press and the Kelmscott Press.

Before the establishment of the latter, however, Morris gave one more book to Socialism. His *News from Nowhere* was the last of his works to appear in *The Commonweal* and was almost immediately reprinted from its pages by an American publisher. It is an account of the civilised world as it might be made, according to Morris's belief, by the application of his principles of Socialism to life in general and in particular. In 1889 he had reviewed for *The Commonweal* Mr. Bellamy's *Looking Backward,* with how much approbation may readily be imagined.

As an expression of the temperament of its author he considered it interesting, but as a reconstructive theory unsafe and misleading. "I believe," he said, "that the ideal of the future does not point to the lessening of man's energy by the reduction of *labour* to a minimum, but rather to the reduction of *pain in labour* to a minimum so small that it will cease to be pain; a gain to humanity which can only be dreamed of till men are more completely equal than Mr. Bellamy's Utopia would allow them to be, but which will most assuredly come about when men are really equal in condition; although it is probable that much of our so-called 'refinement,' our luxury,—in short, our civilisation,—will have to be sacrificed to it." Early in 1890 appeared the first instalment of *News from Nowhere,* in which Morris set himself the task of correcting the impression produced by Mr. Bellamy's views of the future by substituting his own picture of a reconstructed society, from which all the machinery that in *Looking Backward* was brought to so high a degree of efficiency is banished, and the natural energies of man are employed to his complete satisfaction. Homer's *Odyssey,* which Morris at this time was translating by way of refreshment and amusement, may well have served as a partial inspiration for the brilliant, delicate descriptions of handicrafts practised by the art-loving people of Nowhere. We read in both of lovely embroideries; of fine woven stuffs, soft and pliant in texture, and deeply dyed in rich forgotten colours of antiquity; of the quaint elaboration and charm of metals wrought into intricate designs; of all beautiful ornament to be gained from the zeal of skilled and sensitive fingers. The image is before us in *News from Nowhere* of a life as busy and as bright as that of the ancient Greeks, whose cunning hands could do everything save divide use from beauty. As a natural consequence of happy labour, the inhabitants of Nowhere have also the superb health and personal beauty of the Greeks. Their women of forty and fifty have smooth skins and fresh colour, bright eyes and a free walk. Their men have no knowledge of wrinkles and grey hairs. Everywhere is the freshness and sparkle of the morning. The pleasant homes nestle in peaceful security among the lavish fruits of the earth. The water of the Thames flows clean and clear between its banks; the fragrance of flowers pervades the pages and suggests a perpetual summer; athletic sports are mingled with athletic occupations. There is little studying. History is sad and often shameful—why then study it? Knowledge of geography is not important; it comes to those who care to travel. Languages one naturally picks up from intercourse with the people of other countries. Political economy? When one practises good fellowship what need of theories? Mathematics? They would wrinkle the brow; moreover, one learns all that is necessary of them by building houses and bridges and putting things together in the right way. It is not surprising that in this buoyant life filled with active interests, the religion of which is good-will and mutual helpfulness, the thought of death is not a welcome one. A dweller in Nowhere admits that in the autumn he almost believes in death; but no one entertains such a belief longer than he must. Thus we get in this fair idyll the purely visible side of the society depicted. The depths of the human heart and of the human soul are left unsounded. To have what they desire, what is claimed by their hands, by their eyes, by their senses, is the aim of the people. Renunciation, like mathematics, would wrinkle the brow. Arbitrary restraint is not to be considered. Nothing is binding, neither marriage vow nor labour contract, or, to speak more precisely, neither marriage vow nor contract for labour exists. The people live, as we are told, as some of the so-called savages in the South Seas really do live,—in a state of interdependence so perfect that if an individual lays down an obligation the community takes it up. For the fading of life, for the death that may not delay till autumn to thrust itself upon the attention, for the development of spiritual strength to meet an enemy against whom art and beauty will not avail, for the battle with those temptations of the flesh that are not averted by health and comeliness, no provision is made. The author's philosophy is that work, under pleasant conditions will do away with all the evils of both soul and body.

As a document for active Socialists *News from Nowhere* is not effective. Absolutely without any basis of economic generalisation, it is merely the fabric of a vision. At the time of writing it Morris was cutting the last threads that bound him to conventional Socialist bodies. He was making ready to live again, so far as modernity would let him, the life he loved. "No work that cannot be done with pleasure in the doing is worth doing," was a maxim counted by him of the first importance, and assuredly he had not found pleasure in the management of Socialist organisations. His last Socialist book rings with the joy of his release. On its title-page it appears as *Some Chapters from a Utopian Romance,* and it is interesting to see how he regarded the original *Utopia,* to Ralph Robinson's translation of which he wrote a preface, issuing it from his own press in 1893. His interpretation of Sir Thomas More's attitude is not the conventional one, and is inspired chiefly by his own attitude toward the great social question which he continued to ponder, insisting still upon his hope for a new earth.

"Ralph Robinson's translation of More's *Utopia,*" he says, "would not need any foreword if it were to be looked upon merely as a beautiful book embodying the curious fancies of a great writer and thinker of the period of the Renaissance. No doubt till within the last few years it has been considered by the moderns as nothing more serious than a charming literary exercise, spiced with the interest given to it by the allusions to the history of the time, and by our knowledge of the career of its author. But the change of ideas concerning 'the best state of a publique weale,' which I will venture to say is the great event of the end of this century, has thrown a fresh light upon the book; so that now to some it seems not so much a regret for days which might have been, as (in its essence) a prediction of a state of society which will be. In short this work of the scholar and Catholic, of the man who resisted what has seemed to most the progressive movement of his own time, has in our days become a Socialist tract familiar to the meetings and debating rooms of the political party which was but lately like 'the cloud as big as a man's hand.' Doubtless the *Utopia* is a necessary part of a Socialist's library; yet it seems to me that its value as a book for the study of sociology is rather historic than prophetic, and that we Socialists should look upon it as a link between the surviving Communism of the Middle Ages (become hopeless in More's time, and doomed to be soon wholly effaced by the advancing wave of Commercial Bureaucracy), and the hopeful and practical progressive movement of to-day. In fact I think More must be looked upon rather as the last of the old than the first of the new.

"Apart from what was yet alive in him of mediæval Communist tradition, the spirit of association, which amongst other things produced the Gilds, and which was strong in the mediæval

Catholic Church itself, other influences were at work to make him take up his parable against the new spirit of his age. The action of the period of transition from mediæval to commercial society, with all its brutalities, was before his eyes; and though he was not alone in his time in condemning the injustice and cruelty of the revolution which destroyed the peasant life of England and turned it into a grazing farm for the moneyed gentry; creating withal at one stroke the propertyless wage-earner and the masterless vagrant (hodie 'pauper'), yet he saw deeper into its root-causes than many other men of his own day, and left us little to add to his views on this point except a reasonable hope that those 'causes' will yield to a better form of society before long.

"Moreover the spirit of the Renaissance, itself the intellectual side of the very movement which he strove against, was strong in him, and doubtless helped to create his Utopia by means of the contrast which it put before his eyes of the ideal free nations of the ancients, and the sordid welter of the struggle for power in the days of dying feudalism, of which he himself was a witness. This Renaissance enthusiasm has supplanted in him the chivalry feeling of the age just passing away. To him war is no longer a delight of the well-born, but rather an ugly necessity to be carried on, if so it must be, by ugly means. Hunting and hawking are no longer the choice pleasures of knight and lady, but are jeered at by him as foolish and unreasonable pieces of butchery; his pleasures are in the main the reasonable ones of learning and music. With all this, his imaginations of the past he must needs read into his ideal vision, together with his own experiences of his time and people. Not only are there bond slaves and a king, and priests almost adored, and cruel punishments for the breach of marriage contract, in that happy island, but there is throughout an atmosphere of asceticism which has a curiously blended savour of Cato the Censor and a mediæval monk.

"On the subject of war, on capital punishment, the responsibility to the public of kings and other official personages, and such-like matters, More speaks words that would not be out of place in the mouth of an eighteenth-century Jacobin, and at first sight this seems rather to show sympathy with what is now mere Whigism than with Communism; but it must be remembered that opinions which have become (in words) the mere commonplace of ordinary bourgeoise politicians were then looked on as a piece of startlingly new and advanced thought, and do not put him on the same plane with the mere radical life of the last generation.

"In More, then, are met together the man naturally sympathetic with the Communistic side of mediæval society, the protestor against the ugly brutality of the earliest period of commercialism, the enthusiast of the Renaissance, ever looking toward his idealised ancient society as the type and example of all really

Study of Mrs. Morris

Made by Rossetti for pictures called "The Day Dream"

intelligent human life; the man tinged with the asceticism at once of the classical philosopher and of the monk, an asceticism, indeed, which he puts forward not so much as a duty but rather as a kind of stern adornment of life. These are, we may say, the moods of the man who created *Utopia* for us; and all are tempered and harmonised by a sensitive clearness and delicate beauty of style, which make the book a living work of art.

"But lastly, we Socialists cannot forget that these qualities and excellences meet to produce a steady expression of the longing for a society of equality of condition; a society in which the individual man can scarcely conceive of his existence apart from the commonwealth of which he forms a portion. This, which is the essence of his book, is the essence also of the struggle in which we are engaged. Though, doubtless, it was the pressure of circumstances in his own days that made More what he was, yet that pressure forced him to give us, not a vision of the triumph of the new-born capitalistic society, the element in which lived the new learning and the freedom of thought of his epoch, but a picture (his own indeed, not ours) of the real New Birth which many men before him had desired; and which now indeed we may well hope is drawing near to realisation, though after such a long series of events which at the time of their happening seemed to nullify his hopes completely."[1]

[1] When the *Utopia* appeared with this introduction an Eton master who had ordered forty copies in advance, intending the books to be used as prizes for the

Morris's own hope was never completely nullified; nor was he ever indifferent to the questions which for nearly a decade had absorbed his energy. But there was to be little more writing for the sake of Socialism, save as some public incident called out a public letter. What he had done covered a wide field. Beside the works already mentioned he had collaborated with Mr. E. Belfort Bax in a history of the growth and outcome of Socialism, first published in the *Commonweal* under the title of *Socialism from the Root Up,* had written a series of poems called *Chants for Socialists,* and a series of lectures for "the cause" later published as *Signs of Change,* and had produced numerous short addresses to be scattered abroad in the form of penny leaflets that must have been typographical eyesores to him even before the rise of his enthusiasm for typography of the finer sort. In addition his bibliographer has to take into account any number of ephemeral contributions to the press and "forewords" as he liked to call them, to the works of others, a feature rarely present in his own books. In the spring of 1890 he wrote the romance entitled, *The Story of the Glittering Plain* for the *English Illustrated Magazine.* When it was brought out in book form the following year, it was printed at his own press.

boys in his school, withdrew his order, Young England not being allowed at that time to keep such Socialistic company.

CHAPTER X.

THE KELMSCOTT PRESS.

ALTHOUGH Morris turned with what seemed a sudden inspiration to the study of typography, it was, as we have already seen, no less than his other occupations a direct outcome of his early tastes. As long before as 1866 he had planned a folio edition of *The Earthly Paradise* with woodcut illustrations to be designed by Burne-Jones, and printed in a more or less mediæval fashion. Burne-Jones made a large number of drawings for the projected edition, and some thirty-five of those intended for the story of Cupid and Psyche were cut on wood by Morris himself. Specimen pages were set up, but the result was not technically satisfying and the idea was allowed to drop. Later, as we have seen, he had in mind an illustrated and sumptuous edition of *Love is Enough,* which also came to nothing, although a number of marginal decorations were drawn and engraved for it. After that, however, he apparently had been content to have his books printed in the usual way on machine-made paper with the modern effeminate type, without further remonstrance than emphatic denunciation of modern methods in printing as in other handicrafts. About 1888 or 1889, his Hammersmith neighbour, Mr. Emery Walker, whose love of fine printing was combined with practical knowledge of methods and processes, awakened in him a desire for conquest in this field also. He began again collecting mediæval books, this time with the purpose of studying their type and form. Among his acquisitions were a copy of Leonard of Arezzo's *History of Florence,* printed by Jacobus Rubens in 1476, in a Roman type, and a copy of Jensen's *Pliny* of the same year. Parts of these books Morris had enlarged by the hated process of photography, which in this case aided and abetted him to some purpose. He could thus study the individual letters and master the underlying principles of their design. He then proceeded to design a fount of type for himself with the aim of producing letters fine and generous in form, solid in line, without "preposterous thicks and thins," and not compressed laterally, "as all later type has grown to be owing to commercial exigencies." After he had drawn his letters on a large scale he had them reduced by photography to the working size and revised them carefully before submitting them to the typecutter. How minute was his attention to detail is shown in the little reproduction of one of his corrected letters with the accompanying notes. This first type of his, having been founded on the old Roman letters, is of course

While on her hearth lay blazing many a piece
Of sandal-wood, rare gums and cinnamon;
Men scarcely know how beautiful fire is;
Each flame of it is as a precious stone
Dissolved in ever-moving light, and this
Belongs to each and all who gaze upon.
The Witch beheld it not, for in her hand
She held a woof that dimmed the burning brand.

This is the Golden type.

NOW es the rede knyghte slayne,
Lefte dede in the playne,
The childe gone his mere mayne
After the stede;
The stede was swifter than the mere,
For he hade nothynge to bere
But his sadille and his gere,
Fro hym thofe he yede.

This is the Chaucer type.

I dreste me forth, and happede to mete anone
Right a faire lady, I you ensure;
And she come riding by hirself alone,
Al in white; with semblaunce ful demure
I salued hir, and bad hir good aventure
Might hir bifal, as I coude most humbly;
And she answerede: My doughter, gramercy!

This is the Troy type.

KELMSCOTT TYPES

Roman in character and is very clear and beautiful in form. The strong broad letters designed on "something like a square" make easy reading, and there is nothing about the appearance of the attractive page to suggest archaism. The fount, consisting of eighty-one designs including stops, figures, and tied letters, was completed about the beginning of 1891, and on the 12th of January in that year, a cottage was taken at number 16 Upper Mall, near the Kelmscott House, a compositor and a pressman were engaged, and the Kelmscott Press began its career. The new type, which Morris called the "regenerate" or "Jenson-Morris" type, received its formal name, "Golden type," from Caxton's *Golden Legend,* which Morris had intended to reprint as the first work of the Press, and which was undertaken as soon as *The Glittering Plain* was out of the way. Caxton's first edition of 1483 was borrowed from the Cambridge University Library for the purpose and transcribed for the Press by the daughter of Morris's old friend and publisher, F. S. Ellis. No paper in the market was good enough for the great venture, and Morris took down to Mr. Batchelor at Little Chart a model dating back to the fifteenth century and had especially designed from it an unbleached linen paper, thin and tough, and somewhat transparent, made on wire moulds woven by hand for the sake of the slight irregularities thus caused in the texture, and "pleasing not only to the eye, but to the hand also; having something of the clean crisp quality of a new bank-note." For the three different sizes Morris designed three watermarks, an apple, a daisy, and a perch with a spray in its mouth. To print his strong type upon this handmade paper it was necessary to dampen the latter and use a hand-press, the ink being applied by pelt balls, insuring an equable covering of the surface of the type and a rich black impression. The quality of the ink was naturally of great importance and Morris yearned to manufacture his own, but for the time contented himself with some that he procured from Hanover and with which he produced excellent results. One of his happiest convictions in regard to his materials was that heavy paper was entirely unfit for small books.

Concerning spacing and the placing of the matter on the page he had pronounced theories derived from his study of ancient books, but directed by his own sound taste. He held that there should be no more white space between the words than just clearly cuts them off from one another, and that "leads" (strips of metal used to increase the space between the lines of type) should be sparingly employed. The two pages of a book, facing each other as it is opened, should be considered a unit, the edge of the margin that is bound in should be the smallest of the four edges, the top should be somewhat wider, and the front edge wider still, and the tail widest of all. The respective measurements of the most important of the Kelmscott books are, one inch for the inner margin, one and three-

HERE BEGINNETH THE TALES OF CANTERBURY AND FIRST THE PROLOGUE THEREOF

WHAN THAT Aprille with his shoures soote
The droghte of March hath perced to the roote,
And bathed every veyne in swich licour.
Of which vertu engendred is the flour;
Whan Zephirus eek with his swete breeth
Inspired hath in every holt and heeth
The tendre croppes, and the yonge sonne
Hath in the Ram his halfe cours yronne,
And smale foweles maken melodye,
That slepen al the nyght with open eye,
So priketh hem nature in hir corages;
Thanne longen folk to goon on pilgrimages,
And palmeres for to seken straunge strondes,
To ferne halwes, kowthe in sondry londes;
And specially, from every shires ende
Of Engelond, to Caunterbury they wende,
The hooly blisful martir for to seke,
That hem hath holpen whan that they were seeke.

BIFIL that in that seson on a day,
In Southwerk at the Tabard as I lay,
Redy to wenden on my pilgrymage
To Caunterbury with ful devout corage,
At nyght were come into that hostelrye
Wel nyne and twenty in a compaignye,
Of sondry folk, by aventure yfalle
In felaweshipe, and pilgrimes were they alle,
That toward Caunterbury wolden ryde.

PAGE FROM KELMSCOTT "CHAUCER." ILLUSTRATION BY BURNE-JONES. BORDER AND INITIAL LETTER BY MORRIS

eighths inches for the head margin, two and three-quarter inches for the fore edge, and four inches for the tail. "I go so far as to say," wrote Morris, "that any book in which the page is properly put on the paper is tolerable to look at, however poor the type may be (always so long as there is no 'ornament' which may spoil the whole thing), whereas any book in which the page is wrongly set on the paper is intolerable to look at, however good the type and ornaments may be."

The Golden Legend, with its ornamented borders, its handsome initials, its woodcuts, and its twelve hundred and eighty-six pages, kept the one press busy until the middle of September, 1892. Before it was completed Morris had designed another fount of type greatly more pleasing to him than the first. This was called the Troy type from Caxton's *Historyes of Troye,* the first book to be issued in its larger size, and was the outcome of careful study of the beautiful types of Peter Schoeffer of Mainz, Gunther Zainer of Augsburg, and Anthony Koburger of Nuremberg. It was Gothic in character, but Morris strove to redeem it from the charge of unreadableness by using the short form of the small *s*, by diminishing the number of tied letters, and abolishing the abbreviations to be found in mediæval books. How far he succeeded is a disputed question, certainly not so far as to make it as easy reading for modern eyes as the Golden type. As time went on, however, the use of the Golden type at the Kelmscott Press became less and less frequent, giving place in the case of most of the more important books to either the Troy type or the Chaucer type, the latter being similar to the former, save that it is Great Pica instead of Primer size.

Morris's success in the mechanical application of his theories was surprising, or would have been surprising had he not constantly proven his genius for success. Mr. De Vinne quotes a prominent American typefounder as declaring after a close scrutiny of his cuts of type that he had triumphantly passed the pitfalls that beset all tyros and had made types that in lining, fitting, and adjustment show the skill of the expert. "A printer of the old school may dislike many of his mannerisms of composition and make-up," adds Mr. De Vinne, "but he will cheerfully admit that his types and decorations and initials are in admirable accord: that the evenness of colour he maintains on his rough paper is remarkable, and that his registry of black with red is unexceptionable. No one can examine a book made by Morris without the conviction that it shows the hand of a master."

Upon the artistic side it was natural that he should excel. His long practice in and love of design, his close study of the best models, and his exacting taste were promising of extraordinary results. None the less there is perhaps more room for criticism of his book decoration than of his plain bookmaking. He was convinced, as one would expect him to be,

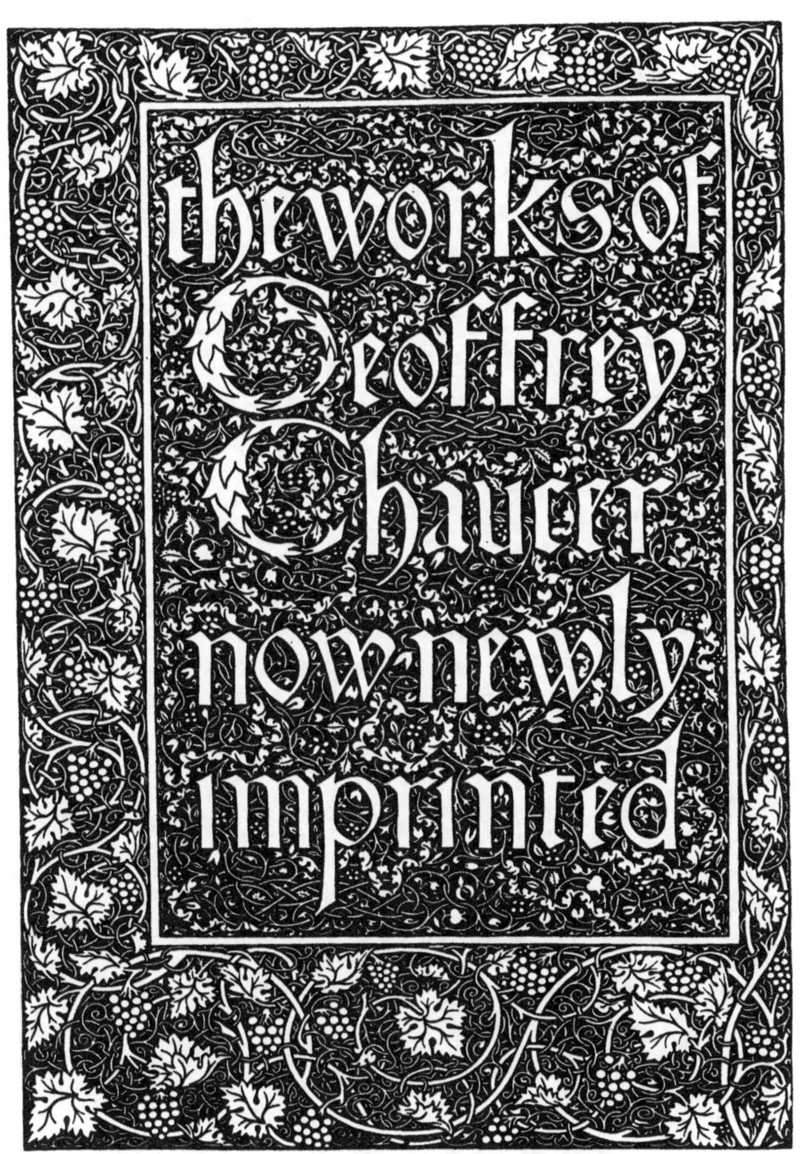

TITLE-PAGE OF THE KELMSCOTT "CHAUCER"

that modern methods of illustrating and decorating a book were entirely wrong, and he argued with indisputable logic for the unity of impression to be gained from ornaments and pictures forming part of the page, in other words, being made in line as readily printed as the type itself and corresponding to it in size and degree of blackness. He argued that the ornament to be ornament must submit to certain limitations and become "architectural," and also that it should be used with exuberance or restraint according to the matter of the book decorated. Thus "a work on differential calculus," he says, "a medical work, a dictionary, a collection of a statesman's speeches, or a treatise on manures, such books, though they might be handsomely and well printed, would scarcely receive ornament with the same exuberance as a volume of lyrical poems, or a standard classic, or such like. A work on Art, I think, bears less of ornament than any other kind of book *(non bis in idem* is a good motto); again, a book that *must* have *illustrations,* more or less utilitarian, should, I think, have no actual *ornament* at all, because the ornament and the illustration must almost certainly fight." He designed all his ornaments with his own hand, from the minute leaves and flowers which took the place of periods on his page, to the full-page borders, titles, and elaborate initials. He drew with a brush, on a sheet of paper from the Press marked with ruled lines, showing the exact position to be occupied by the design. "It was most usual during the last few years of his life," says Mr. Vallance, "to find him thus engaged, with his Indian ink and Chinese white in little saucers before him upon the table, its boards bare of any cloth covering, but littered with books and papers and sheets of MS. He did not place any value on the original drawings, regarding them as just temporary instruments, only fit, as soon as engraved, to be thrown away." Time and trouble counted for nothing with him in gaining the desired result. But though his ornament was always handsome, and occasionally exquisite, he not infrequently overloaded his page with it, and — preaching vigorously the necessity of restraint — allowed his fancy to lead him into garrulous profusion. Despite his mediæval proclivities, his designs for the borders of his pages are intensely modern. Compare them with the early books by which they were inspired, and their flowing elaboration, so free from unexpectedness, so impersonal, so inexpressive, suggests the fatal defect of all imitative work and fails in distinction. But he was individual enough in temper if not in execution, and he brooked no conventional restriction that interfered with his doing what pleased him. For example, the notion of making the border ornaments agree in spirit with the subject matter of the page was not to be entertained for a moment when he had in mind a fine design of grapes hanging ripe from their vines and a page of Chaucer's description of April to adorn.

During the life of the Kelmscott Press, a period of some half dozen years, Morris made six hundred and forty-four designs. The illustrations proper, all of them woodcuts harmonising in their strong black line with the ornaments and type, were made, with few exceptions, by Burne-Jones. His designs were nearly always drawn in pencil, a medium in which his most characteristic effects were obtained. They were then redrawn in ink by another hand, revised by Burne-Jones, and finally transferred to the block again by that useful Cinderella of the Kelmscott Press, photography. It is obvious that the Kelmscott books, whatever fault may be found with them, could not be other than remarkable creations with Morris and Burne-Jones uniting their gifts to make each of them such a picture-book as Morris declared at the height of his ardour was "one of the very worthiest things toward the production of which reasonable men should strive."

The list of works selected to be issued from the Press is interesting, indicating as it does a line of taste somewhat narrow and tangential to the popular taste of the time. Before the three volumes of *The Golden Legend* ("the Interminable" it was called) were out of his hands, Morris had bought a second large press and had engaged more workmen with an idea in mind of printing all his own works beginning with *Sigurd the Volsung*. He had already, during 1891, printed in addition to *The Glittering Plain*, a volume of his collected verse entitled *Poems by the Way*, the final long poem of which, *Goldilocks and Goldilocks,* he wrote on the spur of the moment, after the book was set up in type, to "plump it out a bit" as it seemed rather scant. During the following year, before the appearance of *The Golden Legend,* were issued a volume of poems by Wilfrid Blunt, who was one of his personal friends; the chapter from Ruskin's *Stones of Venice* on "The Nature of the Gothic," with which he had such early and such close associations, and two more of his own works, *The Defence of Guenevere* and *The Dream of John Ball.* In the case of the four books written by himself he issued in addition to the paper copies a few on vellum. All these early books were small quartos and bound in vellum covers. Immediately following *The Golden Legend* came the *Historyes of Troye,* two volumes in the new type, Mackail's *Biblia Innocentium,* and Caxton's *Reynarde the Foxe* in large quarto size and printed in the Troy type. The year 1893 began with a comparatively modern book, Shakespeare's *Poems,* followed in rapid succession by Caxton's translation of *The Order of Chivalry,* in one volume with *The Ordination of Knighthood,* translated by Morris himself from a twelfth-century French poem; Cavendish's *Life of Cardinal Wolsey;* Caxton's history of Godefrey of Boloyne; Ralph Robinson's translation of Sir Thomas More's *Utopia;* Tennyson's *Maud;* a lecture by Morris on *Gothic Architecture,* forty-five copies of which he printed on vellum; and Lady Wilde's translation of *Sidonia the Sorceress* from the German

THE SMALLER KELMSCOTT PRESS-MARK

THE LARGER KELMSCOTT PRESS-MARK

note the different shape of
write in corrected letter

Seriffs perhaps
a little too fat

kind of
buttress or
lean-to to look
of the round
member.

h

this flatten
curve to the
notes and
followed

a tendency to make everything a little
too rigid & square is noticeable: Can this
be remedied

DRAWING BY MORRIS OF THE LETTER "h" FOR KELMSCOTT TYPE, WITH NOTES AND CORRECTIONS

of William Meinhold, a book for which both Morris and Rossetti had a positive passion, Morris considering it without a rival of its kind, and an almost faultless reproduction of the life of the past. The year ended with two volumes of Rossetti's *Ballads and Narrative Poems,* and *The Tale of King Florus and Fair Jehane,* translated by Morris from the French of a little volume that forty years before had served to introduce him to mediæval French romance and had been treasured by him ever since.

"After this continuous torrent of production," says Mr. Mackail, "the Press for a time slackened off a little," but the output in 1894 consisted of ten books as against the eleven of the previous year. The first was a large quarto edition of *The Glittering Plain,* printed this time in the Troy type and illustrated with twenty-three pictures by Walter Crane. Next came another little volume of mediæval romance, the story of *Amis and Amile,* translated in a day and a quarter; and after this, Keats's *Poems.*

In July of the same year the bust of Keats, executed by the American sculptor, Miss Anne Whitney, was unveiled in the Parish Church of Hampstead, the first memorial to Keats on English ground. The scheme for such a memorial had been promoted in America, Lowell being one of the earliest to encourage it, and a little notice of the ceremony was printed at the Kelmscott Press with the card of invitation. Swinburne's *Atalanta in Calydon* followed *Keats* in a large quarto edition. Next came the third volume of the French romances containing *The Tale of the Emperor Constans* and *The History of Oversea.* At this point Morris returned again to the printing of his own works, and the next book to be issued from the Press was *The Wood beyond the World,* with a lovely frontispiece by Burne-Jones representing "the Maid," the heroine of the romance, and one of the most charming of the visionary women created by Morris. *The Book of Wisdom and Lies,* a Georgian story-book of the eighteenth century, written by Sulkhan-Saba Orbeliani, and translated by Oliver Wardrop, was the next stranger to come from the Press, and after it was issued the first of a set of Shelley's *Poems.* A rhymed version of *The Penitential Psalms* found in a manuscript of *The Hours of Our Lady,* written in the fifteenth century, followed it, and *The Epistola de Contemptu Mundi,* a letter in Italian by Savonarola, the autograph original of which belonged to Mr. Fairfax Murray, completed the list of this prolific year. The year 1895 produced only five volumes, the first of them the *Tale of Beowulf,* which Morris with characteristic daring had translated into verse by the aid of a prose translation made for him by Mr. A. J. Wyatt. Not himself an Anglo-Saxon scholar, Morris was unable to give such a rendering of this chief epic of the Germanic races as would appeal to the scholarly mind, and his zeal for literal translation led him to employ a phraseology nothing short of outlandish. At the end of the book he printed a list of "words not commonly used now," but his constructions were even more obstructive than his uncommon words. In the following passage, for example, which opens the section describing the coming of Beowulf to the land of the Danes, only the word "nithing" is defined in the index, yet certainly the average reader may be expected to pause for the meaning:

So care that was time-long the kinsman of Healfdene
Still seethed without ceasing, nor might the wise warrior
Wend otherwhere woe, for o'er strong was the strife
All loathly so longsome late laid on the people,
Need-wrack and grim nithing, of night-bales the greatest.

Morris himself found his interest wane before the work was completed, but he made a handsome quarto volume of it, with fine marginal decorations, and an exceptionally well-designed title-page. A reprint of *Syr Percyvelle of Gales* after the edition printed by J. O. Halliwell from the MS. in the library of Lincoln Cathedral, a large quarto edition of *The Life and Death of Jason;* two 16mo volumes of a new romance entitled, *Child Christopher and Goldilands the Fair;* and Rossetti's *Hand and Soul,* reprinted from the *Germ,* brought the Press to its great year 1896. This year was to see the completion of the folio *Chaucer,* which since early in 1892 had been in preparation, and had filled the heart of Morris with anxiety, anticipation, and joy. Before it came from the press three other books were issued. Herrick's *Poems* came first. Then a selection of thirteen poems from Coleridge, "a muddle-brained metaphysician, who by some strange freak of fortune turned out a few real poems amongst the dreary flood of inanity which was his wont!"

The poems chosen were, *Christabel, Kubla Khan, The Rime of the Ancient Mariner, Love, A Fragment of a Sexton's Tale, The Ballad of the Dark Ladie, Names, Youth and Age, The Improvisatore, Work without Hope, The Garden of Boccaccio, The Knight's Tomb,* and *Alice du Clos.* The first four were the only ones, however, concerning which Morris would own to feeling any interest. The Coleridge volume was followed by the large quarto edition of Morris's latest romance, *The Well at the World's End* in two volumes, and then appeared the *Chaucer,* the mere printing of which had occupied a year and nine months. The first two copies were brought home from the binders on the second of June, in a season of "lots of sun" and plentiful apple-blossoms, during which Morris was beginning to realise that the end of his delight in seasons and in books was fast approaching.

Mr. Ellis has declared the Kelmscott *Chaucer* to be, "for typography, ornament, and illustration combined, the grandest book that has been issued from the press since the invention of typography." Morris lavished upon it the utmost wealth of his invention. The drawing of the title-page alone occupied a fortnight, and the splendid initial letters were each an elaborate work of art. The ornament indeed was too profuse to be wholly satisfactory, especially as much of it was repeated; nevertheless, the book was one of great magnificence and the glee with which Morris beheld it is not to be wondered at. The Chaucer type had been specially designed for it, and Burne-Jones had made for it eighty-seven drawings, while Morris himself designed for it the white pigskin binding with silver clasps, executed at the Doves Bindery for those purchasers who desired their elaborate and costly volume in a more suitable garb than the ordinary half holland covers which gave it the appearance of a silken garment under a calico apron.

During the remainder of the year 1896 the Press issued the first volumes of the Kelmscott edition of *The Earthly Paradise,* a volume of Latin poems *(Laudes Beatae Mariae Virginis),* the first Kelmscott book to be printed in three colours, the quotation heading each stanza being in red, the initial letter in pale blue, and the remaining text in black: *The Floure and the Leafe* and *The Shepherde's Calender.* Before *The Shepherde's Calender* reached its completion, however, Morris was dead, and the subsequent work of the Press was merely the clearing up of a few books already advertised. The first of these to appear was the prose romance by Morris entitled *The Water of the Wondrous Isles:* this was issued on the first day of April, 1897, with borders and ornaments designed entirely by Morris save for a couple of initial words completed from his unfinished designs by R. Catterson-Smith. To this year belong also the two trial pages made for the intended folio edition of *Froissart,* the heraldic borders of which far surpass any of the *Chaucer* ornaments, and the two old English romances, *Sire Degravaunt* and *Syr Ysambrace.* In 1898 came a large quarto volume of German woodcuts, and three more works by Morris, a small folio edition of *Sigurd the Volsung,* which was to have been a large folio with twenty-five woodcuts by Burne-Jones; *The Sundering Flood,* the last romance written by Morris, and a large quarto edition of *Love is Enough.* These were followed by a "Note" written by Morris himself on his aims in starting the Kelmscott Press, accompanied with facts concerning the Press, and an annotated list of all the books there printed, compiled by Mr. S. C. Cockerell, who, since July, 1894, had been secretary to the Press. This was the end.[1]

Although Morris not only neglected commercial considerations in printing his books, lavishing their price many times over in valuable time and labour and the actual expenditure of money to secure some inconspicuous detail; but defied commercial methods openly in the character of his type, the quality of his materials, and the slowness of his processes, the Kelmscott Press testified, as most of his enterprises did testify, to the practical worth of his ideals. Quite content to make just enough by his books to continue printing them in the most conscientious and desirable way he knew, he gradually obtained from them a considerable profit. The Press had early been

[1] The trustees are now publishing the remainder of Morris's own works in the type of the Kelmscott Press, though without the ornaments, that a uniform edition may be had.

Specimen Page from the Kelmscott "Froissart"
(Projected Edition)

HERE BEGYNNETH THE PROLOGE OF SYR JOHAN FROISSART OF THE CHRONICLES OF FRAUNCE, INGLANDE, AND OTHER PLACES ADJOYNYNGE

The first Chaptre.

THAT the honorable and noble aventures of featis of armes, done & achyued by the warres of Fraunce and Inglande, shulde notably be inregistered, and put in perpetuall memory, whereby the prewe & hardy may haue ensample to incourage them in theyr well doyng, I syr Johan Froissart, wyll treat and recorde an hystory of great louage and preyse: but, or I begyn, I require the sauyour of all the worlde, who of nothyng created al thynges, that he wyll gyue me suche grace and vnderstandyng, that I may continue and perseuer in such wyse that who so this proces redeth or hereth, may take pastaunce, pleasure, and ensaumple. It is said of trouth, that al buyldynges are masoned & wroughte of dyuerse stones, and all great ryuers are gurged and assemblede of divers surges and spryngës of water: in lykewyse all sciences are extraught & compiled of diuerse clerkes, of that one wryteth, another parauenture is ignorant; but by the famous wrytyng of auncient auctours, all thyng is ben knowen in one place or other.

WHAN to attaygne to the mater that I haue entreprised, I wyll begyn, fyrst, by the grace of God and the blessed Virgyn our Lady Saynt Mary, from whom all comfort and consolation procedeth, and wyll take my foundation out of the true cronicles somtyme compyled by the right reuerend, discrete and sage maister Johan la Bele, somtyme chanon in Saint Lambartis of Liege, who with good herte & due diligence dyd his true deuoure in wrytyng this noble cronicle, and dyd contynue it all his lyfes days, in folowyng the trouth as nere as he myght, to his great charge and coste in sekyng to procure and to haue the perfight knowledge thereof. He was also in his lyfes days welbeloued, and of the secret counsayle with the lorde sir Johan of Haynaulte, who is often remembred, as reason requyreth, here after in this boke; for of many fayre & noble auentures he was chiefe causer, & to the kyng right nigh, & by whose meanes the said syr Johan la Bele myght well knowe and here of many dyuers noble dedes. The whiche here after shal be declared.

TROUTH it is, that I who have entreprised this boke to ordeyne for pleasure and pastaunce, to the whiche alwayes I have been inclyned, & for that intent I haue folowed and frequented the company of dyuerse noble & great lordes, as well in Fraunce, Inglande, and Scotlande, as in diuerse other countries, and have had knowledge by them, and alwayes to my power iustly haue inquired for the trouth of the dedis of warre and auentures that haue fallen, and specially syth the great batell of Poytyers, where as the noble kynge Johan of France was takyn prisoner, as before that tyme I was but of a yonge age or vnderstandyng. Howe be it I toke it on me assoone as I come from scole, to wryte and recite the sayd boke, & bare the same compyled into Ingland, and presented the volume thereof to my Lady Phelyppe of Heynaulte, noble quene of Inglande, who right amyably receyved it to my great profite & avauncement.

AND it may be so, that the same boke is nat as yet examyned nor corrected so iustely as suche a case requyreth: for featis of armes derely bought & achyued, the honor therof ought to be gyuen & truly deuided to them that by prowes & hard trauayle haue deserued it. Therfore to acquyte me in that bihalfe, & in folowyng the trouth as near as I can, I Johan Froissart have entrepryesed this hystory on the forsaid ordynaunce & true fundacion, at the instaunce and request of a dere lorde of myn, Robert of Namure, knight, lorde of Bewfort, to whom entierly I owe loue and obeysaunce, & God graunt me to do that thyng that may be to his pleasure. Amen.

Here spekethe the auctour of suche as were most valiant knyghtis to be made mencion of in this boke. Capitulo II.

ALL noble hertis, to encorage & to shewe them ensample and mater of honour, I Syr Johann Froissart begynne to speke after the true report and relation of my master Johan la Bele, somtyme Chanon of Saynte Lambertis of

moved to quarters larger than the first occupied by it, and three presses were kept busy. By the end of 1892 Morris had become his own publisher, and after that time all the Kelmscott books were published by him except in cases of special arrangement. A few copies, usually less than a dozen, of nearly all the books were printed on vellum and sold at a proportionately higher price than the paper copies. The volumes were bound either in vellum or half holland, these temporary and unsatisfactory covers probably having been chosen on account of the strength and slow-drying qualities of the ink used, a note to the prospectus of the *Chaucer* stating that the book would not be fit for ordinary full binding with the usual pressure for at least a year after its issue. The issue prices charged for the books were not low, but certainly not exorbitant when time, labour, and expense of producing them are taken into consideration. They were prizes for the collector from the beginning, the impossibility of duplicating them and the small editions sent out giving them a charm and a value not easily to be resisted, and Morris himself and his trustees adopted measures tending to protect the collector's interests. After the death of Morris all the woodblocks for initials, ornaments, and illustrations were sent to the British Museum and were accepted, with the condition that they should not be reproduced or printed from for the space of one hundred years. The electrotypes were destroyed. The matter was talked over with Morris during his lifetime and he sanctioned this course on the part of the trustees, its aim being to keep the series of the Kelmscott Press "a thing apart and to prevent the designs becoming stale by repetition." While there is a fair ground for the criticism frequently made that a man urging the necessity of art for the people showed inconsistency by withdrawing from their reach art which he could control and deemed valuable, it must be remembered that in his mind the great result to be obtained was the stirring up the people to making art for themselves. Morris rightly counted the joy to be gained from making a beautiful thing as far higher than the joy to be gained from seeing one. He was never in favour of making a work of art "common" by reproducing or servilely imitating it. He had shown the printers of books his idea of the way they should manage their craft, now let them develop it themselves along the lines pointed out for them. And whether he was or was not consistent in allowing the works of the Kelmscott Press to be cut off from any possibility of a large circulation, his was the temperament to feel all the delight to be won from exclusive ownership. He had the true collector's passion for possession. If he was bargaining for a book, says his biographer, he would carry on the negotiation with the book tucked tightly under his arm, as if it might run away. His collection of old painted books gave him the keenest emotions before and after his acquisition of them. Of one, which finally proved unattainable, he wrote,

"*Such* a book! *my* eyes! and I am beating my brains to see if I can find any thread of an intrigue to begin upon, so as to creep and crawl toward the possession of it." It is no matter for wonder if in imagination he beheld the love of bibliophiles for his own works upon which he had so ardently spent his energies, and was gratified by the prevision.

Whether the Kelmscott books will increase or decrease in money value as time goes on is a question that stirs interest in book-buying circles. They have already had their rise and ebb to a certain extent, and the prices brought by the copies owned by Mr. Ellis at the sale of his library after his death indicate that a steady level of interest has been reached among collectors for the time being at least; only five of the copies printed on paper exceeding prices previously paid for them. The presentation copy on vellum of the great *Chaucer* brought five hundred and ten pounds, certainly a remarkable sum for a modern book, under any conditions, and nearly a hundred pounds more than the highest price which Morris himself up to the summer of 1894 had ever paid for even a fourteenth-century book. The paper copy of the *Chaucer* sold at the Ellis sale for one hundred and twelve pounds and a paper copy in ordinary binding sold in America in 1902 for $650, while a paper copy in the special pigskin binding brought $950 the same year. The issue price for the four hundred and twenty-five paper copies was twenty pounds apiece, and for the eight copies on vellum offered for sale out of the thirteen printed, a hundred and twenty guineas apiece. The posthumous edition of *Sigurd the Volsung,* the paper copies of which were issued at six guineas apiece, brought at the Ellis sale twenty-six pounds. *News from Nowhere,* issued at two guineas, has never yet brought a higher price than the five pounds, fifteen shillings paid for it in 1899, while Keats's *Poems* issued at one pound, ten shillings, rose as high as twenty-seven pounds, ten shillings, also in 1899. As a general measure of the advance in the Kelmscott books since the death of Morris, it may be noted that the series owned by Mr. Ellis, excluding duplicates, and including a presentation copy of *Jason* and two fine bindings for the paper and the vellum *Chaucer*, represented a gross issue price of six hundred and twelve pounds, ten shillings, and realised two thousand, three hundred and sixty-seven pounds, two shillings. For one decade of the life of a modern series that is a great record, and it would be a rash prophet who should venture to predict future values.

CHAPTER XI.

LATER WRITINGS.

THE writings of Morris's later years consist, as we have seen, chiefly of prose romances. The little group beginning with *The House of the Wolfings* and ending with *The Sundering Flood* were written with no polemical or proselytising intention, with merely his old delight in story-telling and in depicting the beauty of the external world and the kindness of men and maids. Curiosity had never played any great part in his mental equipment; he cared little to know or speculate further than the visible and tangible surface of life. "The skin of the world" was sufficient for him, and in these later romances all that is beautiful and winning has chiefly to do with the skin of the world presented in its spring-time freshness. The background of nature is always exquisite. With the landscape of the North, which had made its indelible impression upon him, he mingled the scenes—"the dear scenes" he would have called them—of his childhood and the fairer portions of the

Thames shore as he had long and intimately known them; and in his books, as in his familiar letters, he constantly speaks of the weather and the seasons as matters of keen importance in the sum of daily happiness. Thus, whatever we miss from his romances, we gain, what is missing from the majority of modern books, familiarity with the true aspect of the outdoor world. We have the constant sense of ample sky and pleasant air, and green woods and cool waters. The mountains are near us, and often the ocean, and the freedom of a genuine wildwood that is no enchanted forest or ideal vision. Inexpressibly charming are such pictures as those of Elfhild (in *The Sundering Flood)* piping to her sheep and dancing on the bank of the river, on the bright mid-April day, whose sun dazzles her eyes with its brilliant shining; and of Birdalone (in *The Water of the Wondrous Isles)* embroidering her gown and smock in the wood of Evilshaw. What could be more expressive of lovely open-air peace than this description? "Who was glad now but Birdalone; she grew red with new pleasure, and knelt down and kissed the witch's hand, and then went her way to the wood with her precious lading, and wrought there under her oak-tree day after day, and all days, either there, or in the house when the weather was foul. That was in the middle of March, when all birds were singing, and the young leaves showing on the hawthorns, so that there were pale green clouds, as it were, betwixt the great grey boles of oak and sweet-chestnut; and by the lake the meadow-saffron new-thrust-up was opening its blossom; and March wore and April, and still she was at work happily when now it was later May, and the harebells were in full bloom down the bent before her . . . . . and still she wrought on at her gown and her smock, and it was well-nigh done. She had broidered the said gown with roses and lilies, and a tall tree springing up from amidmost the hem of the skirt, and a hart on either side thereof, face to face of each other. And the smock she had sewn daintily at the hems and the bosom with fair knots and buds. It was now past the middle of June hot and bright weather."

And only less delightful than these glimpses of the natural world are the recurring portraits of half-grown boys and girls, all different and all lovable. The sweetness of adolescent beauty had for Morris an irresistible appeal, and while his characters have little of the psychological charm inseparable in real life from dawning qualities and undeveloped potentialities, they are as lovely as the morning in the brightness of hair, the slimness of form, the freedom of gesture with which he endows them. The shapely brown hands and feet of Ursula, her ruddy colour, her slender sturdiness, and brave young laugh are attractions as potent as the more delicate charm of Birdalone's serious eyes and thin face, or Elfhild's flower-like head and tender playfulness; and all these heroines are alike in a fine capability for useful toil and pride in it. When the old carle says to Birdalone, "It will be no such hard life for thee, for I have still some work in me, and thou mayst do something in spite of thy slender and delicate fashion," she replies with merry laughter, "Forsooth, good sire, I might do somewhat more than something; for I am deft in all such work as here ye need; so fear not but I should earn my livelihood, and that with joy." Ursula also knows all the craft of needlework, and all the manners of the fields, and finds nothing in work to weary her; and even in the Maid of *The Wood beyond the World,* with her magic power to revive flowers by the touch of her fingers, is felt the preferable human power to make comfort and pleasantness by the right performance of plain tasks.

Nearly if not quite equal to Morris's expression of love for the beauty of nature and of fair humanity is his expression of the love for beautiful handicraft, to which his whole life and all his writings alike testify. Whatever is omitted from his stories of love and adventure, he never omits to familiarise his readers with the ornament lavished upon buildings and garments and countless accessories; hardly a dozen pages of any one of the romances may be turned before the description of some piece of artistic workmanship is met. Osberne's knife in *The Sundering Flood* is early introduced to the reader as "a goodly weapon, carven with quaintnesses about the heft, the blade inlaid with runes done in gold and the sheath of silver," and the gifts he sends to Elfhild across the flood are "an ouch or chain or arm-ring" fashioned "quaintly and finely," or "fair windowed shoon, and broidered hosen and dainty smocks, and silken kerchiefs"; much is made of his holiday raiment of scarlet and gold, of his flowered green coat, and of the fine gear of gold and green for which Elfhild changes her grey cloak. In *The Story of the Glittering Plain,* filled as it is with the sterner spirit of the sagas, there is still room for much detail concerning the carven panelling of the shut-bed, in which was pictured "fair groves and gardens, with flowery grass and fruited trees all about," and "fair women abiding therein, and lovely young men and warriors, and strange beasts and many marvels, and the ending of wrath and beginning of pleasure, and the crowning of love," and for the account of the painted book, "covered outside with gold and gems" and painted within with woods and castles, "and burning mountains, and the wall of the world, and kings upon their thrones, and fair women and warriors, all most lovely to behold." As for the fair Birdalone, her pleasure in fine stuffs and rich embroideries is unsurpassed in the annals of womankind. The wood-wife with canny knowledge of her tastes brings her the fairy web, declaring that if she dare wear it she shall presently be clad as goodly as she can wish. Birdalone can be trusted to don any attire that meets her fancy (and to doff it as willingly, for she has a startling habit not uncommon with Morris's heroines of stripping off her garments to let the winds of heaven play upon her unimpeded). The wood-wife places the raiment she has brought on Birdalone's outstretched arms, "and it was as if the sunbeam had thrust through the close leafage of the oak, and made its shadow nought a space about Birdalone, so gleamed and glowed in shifty brightness the broidery of the gown; and Birdalone let it fall to earth, and passed over her hands and arms the fine smock sewed in yellow and white silk, so that the web thereof seemed of mingled cream and curd; and she looked on the shoon that lay beside the gown, that were done so nicely and finely that the work was as the feather-robe of a beauteous bird, whereof one scarce can say whether it be bright or grey, thousand-hued or all simple of colour. Birdalone quivered for joy of all the fair things, and crowed in her speech as she knelt before Habundia to thank her." Thus Morris carried into his "pleasure-work of books" the "bread-and-butter work" of which he was hardly less fond.

But in the deeper realities of life with which even romantic fiction may deal, and must deal if it is to lay hold of the modern imagination, these romances are poor. Not one of his characters is developed by circumstance into a fully equipped human being thoroughly alive to the intellectual and moral as to the physical and emotional world. His men and women are eternally young and, with the physical freshness of youth, have also the crude, unrounded, unfinished, unmoulded character of youth. They have all drunk of the Well at the World's End, and the scars of experience have disappeared, leaving a blank surface. The range of their emotions and passions is as simple and narrow as with children, and life as the great story-tellers understand it is not shown by the chronicle of their days. In many of the romances, it is true, the introduction of legendary and unreal persons and incidents relieves the writer from all obligation to make his account more lifelike than a fairy-tale; but Morris is never content to make a fairy-tale pure and simple. Marvellous adventures told directly as to a child are not within his method. One of his critics has described *The Water of the Wondrous Isles* as a three-volume novel in the environment of a fairy-tale, and the phrase perfectly characterises it. A sentimental atmosphere surrounds his figures, and suggests languor and soft moods not to be tolerated by the writer of true fairy-tales, for while love is certainly not alien to even the purest type of the latter, with its witch and its princess and its cruel step-mother and rescuing prince, it is not love as Morris depicts it any more than it is love as Dante or Shakespeare depicts it. In Morris's stories the lovers are neither frankly symbolic creatures of the imagination whose loves are secondary to their heroic or miraculous achievements, and who apparently exist only to give a reason for the machinery of witchcraft, nor are they, like the lovers of the great novels, endowed with thoughtful minds and spiritual qualities. They are too sophisticated not to be more complex. The modern taste is unsympathetic to their endless kissing and "fawning" and "clipping," nor would ancient taste have welcomed their refinements of kindness toward each other or the lack of zest in their adventures. Morris seems to have tried somewhat, as in the case of his handicrafts, to start with the traditions of the Middle Ages and to infuse into them a modern spirit that should make them legitimate successors and not mere imitations of the well-beloved mediæval types. That he did not entirely succeed was the fault not so much of his method as of his deficient insight into human nature. He could not create what he had never closely investigated.

When we read his prose romances, their framework gives many a clue to their ancestry, but it is an ancestry so remote from the interest of the general reader as to puzzle more than charm in its influence upon the modern product. In *The House of the Wolfings, The Roots of the Mountains,* and especially *The Glittering Plain,* we have more or less modernised sagas, obviously derived from the Icelandic literature of which he had been drinking deep. The hero of *The Glittering Plain* is as valorous a youth and as given to brave adventures as the great Sigurd, the environment is Norse, and so are the names of the characters — Sea-eagle, Long-hoary, Grey Goose of the Ravagers, and Puny Fox. Other words and phrases also drawn from the "word-hoard" of the Icelandic tongue are sprinkled over the pages. We find "nithing-stake" and byrny, and bight, spoke-shave and ness and watchet, sley and ashlar and ghyll, used as expressions of familiar parlance. The characters give each other "the sele of the day," retire to shut-beds at night, and look "sorry and sad and fell" when fortune goes against them. They wander in garths and call each other faring-fellow and they yea-say and nay-say and wot and wend. It is not altogether surprising to find some of Morris's most loyal followers admitting that they can make nothing of books written in this archaic prose.

In the subsequent romances the comparative sturdiness imparted by the writings of the North gives place to a mildness and grace suggestive of those early French romances the charm of which Morris had always keenly felt. We still have much the same vocabulary and more or less use of the same magic arts, "skin-changing" holding its own as a favourite method of overcoming otherwise insuperable difficulties; but we have more of the love motive and a clearer endeavour to portray the relations of the characters to each other. In all, however, the French and Scandinavian influences are so mingled with each other and with the element provided by Morris alone, and so fused by his fluent prolix style, as to produce a result somewhat different from anything else in literature, with a character and interest personal to itself, and difficult to imitate in essence, although wofully lending itself to parody. The subject never seems important. There is no sense that the writer was spurred to expression by the pressure of an irresistible message or sentiment. We feel that anything may have started this copious flow of words, and that there is no logical end to them. The title of *The Well at the World's End* was taken from an old Scottish ballad called by that name which Morris had never read, but the title of which struck his fancy, and the book reads as though it had grown without plan from the fanciful, meaningless title.

Of these later romances, *The Glittering Plain* is the most saga-like, and *The Water of the Wondrous Isles* is most permeated by the romantic spirit of the Arthurian legends and their kin. Despite all defects, the latter has a bright bejewelled aspect that pleases the fancy although it does not deeply enlist the imagination. The story is leisurely and wandering. The heroine, Birdalone, some of whose characteristics have already been mentioned, is stolen in her infancy from her home near a town called Utterhay, by a witch-wife who brings her up on the edge of a wood called Evilshaw and teaches her to milk and plough and sow and reap and bake and shoot deer in the forest. When she is seventeen years of age she meets in the forest Habundia, a fairy woman, who gives her a magic ring by which she may make herself invisible and a lock of hair by burning a bit of which she may summon her in time of need. Birdalone soon after escapes from the witch-wife in a magic boat, and passes through fabulous scenes to enchanted islands, where she finds friends and enemies. Three maidens, Atra, Viridis, and Aurea, save her from the latter, and send her forth to find for them their lovers. While on her quest she travels to various isles,—the Isle of the Young and the Old, the Isle of the Queens, the Isle of the Kings, and the Isle of Nothing,—which afford opportunity for strange pictures and quaint conceits but have nothing to do with the narrative. When Birdalone finds the lovers of her friends, the Golden Knight, the Green Knight, and Arthur the Black Squire, called the Three Champions, they are charmed by her beauty and friendliness, and she immediately falls in love with the Black Squire, betrothed of Atra.[1] The Black Squire returns her prompt affection, but has grace to show himself moody and downcast at the thought of breaking faith with his lady. Presently the Three Champions go their ways to find the three maidens who were kind to Birdalone and who are kept on the Isle of Increase Unsought by a witch, sister to Birdalone's early guardian, and Birdalone, weary of waiting for their return, fares forth to meet adventures and lovers

[1] The reader here is expected to note the correspondence between the names of the ladies and the titles of their lovers, and the same correspondence is carried out in the colour of the ladies' garments and the armour of the knights.

in plenty. To all the brave knights and youths who take their turn at wooing her she is pitiful and gentle after her fashion, and thanks them kindly, and praises them and suffers them to kiss her for their comfort, and deems them "fair and lovely and sweet," but keeps her preference for the Black Squire. Now, when the Three Champions come back with their ladies and find Birdalone fled there is much distress among them, and the knights set forth to find her. Meeting with her, they are set upon by the bad Red Knight, into whose custody she has recently been thrown, and Baudoin, the Golden Knight, is killed. Returning with this bad news to the three ladies, the two remaining knights, who have rescued Birdalone and killed the Red Knight, decide to ride back into the latter's domain and make war upon his followers. In the meantime Atra has learned that the Black Squire has transferred his affections from her to Birdalone, and does not attempt to dissemble her grief thereat, none of Morris's characters being gifted in the art of dissimulation, particularly where love is concerned. Birdalone, departing from the course which Morris elsewhere is most inclined to sanction, decides to renounce in Atra's favour, and betakes herself to the town of Greenford, where she is received into the broiderers' guild and works with a woman who turns out to be her own mother, from whom she was stolen by the witch. With her she lives for five years, when sickness slays Audrey, the mother, and Birdalone can no longer resist the temptation to seek her love, the Black Squire, again. So she makes her way once more through marvellous adventures into the old forest of Evilshaw, where she comes again upon her fairy friend Habundia, by whose aid she finds the Black Squire. The latter has met with misfortunes and is lost in the forest, where he falls ill. Birdalone nurses him back to health, and they decide that whether Atra be dead or alive they will have no more parting from one another. They are soon to be put to the test, as in the wood they come upon Atra and their other friends, who have set out to seek them, being anxious for their welfare, and who have been overcome by caitiffs and bound and held prisoners. Arthur and Birdalone rescue them, and all these friends make up their minds to go together and dwell in Utterhay for the rest of their lives. Aurea finds another lover in place of the Golden Knight she has lost, but Atra is faithful in heart to the Black Squire, though able to bear with philosophy his union with Birdalone. Thus they live happily ever after. Upon this skeleton of mingled reality and dream Morris built his general idea of happy love. The tale might easily be twisted into an allegory, since all the creatures of his imagination stand for either the satisfactions or dissatisfactions of the visible world, but nothing is more certain than that he meant no such interpretations to be put upon it. When one of his critics assumed an allegorical intention in the story called *The Wood Beyond the World,* he was moved to public refutation, writing to the *Spectator:* "It is meant to be a tale pure and simple, with nothing didactic about it. If I have to write or speak on social problems, I always try to be as direct as I possibly can." The truth of this is best known by those who most faithfully have followed his writings, and it is entirely vain to try to squeeze from his "tales" any ethical virtue beyond their frank expression of his singularly simple temperament. Nevertheless, like the rest of his work, they reveal in some degree his way of regarding the moral world. As we have seen, Birdalone has her impulse toward renunciation, and for a brief interval one feels that the story possibly may be allowed to run along the conventional lines laid down by the civilised human race for the greatest good of the greatest number. This, however, would have been wholly alien to the writer's temper, and there is no shock to those familiar with this temper in finding that in the end the hero and heroine eat their cake and have it. Renunciation on the side of the unbeloved is effected with grace and nobility, but it is made clear that it is a question of accepting the inevitable in as lofty a spirit as possible. It is perhaps the most obvious moral characteristic of Morris's types in general, that they are no more prone than children to do what they dislike unless circumstance forces them to it. If we were to argue from his romances alone we could almost imagine him contending that what one dislikes in conduct is wrong, just as he did contend that what one dislikes in art is bad. But if his men and women do not willingly renounce, at least they do not exult. The sight of unhappiness pains them. For stern self-denial he substitutes the softer virtues of amiability and sweetness of temper. A high level of kindliness and tenderness takes the place of more compelling and formidable emotions. "Kind," indeed, is one of the adjectives of which one soonest wearies when confined to his vocabulary, and "dear," is another. We read of "dear feet and legs," of dear and kind kisses, of kind wheedling looks, of kind and dear maidens, and dear and kind lads, and everyone is kind and dear who is not evil and cruel. What Morris's romances preach, if they preach anything, is: that we should get from life all the enjoyment possible, hurting others as little as may be consistent with our own happiness, but claiming the satisfaction of all honest desires; that, in thus satisfying ourselves, we should keep toward those about us a kind and pleasant countenance and a consideration for their pain even when our duty toward ourselves forces us to inflict it. It is a narrow and exclusive teaching, and ill adapted to foster freedom of mind and spirit. It is a teaching that provides no breastplate for the buffets of fortune, and sets before one no ideal of intellectual or spiritual life the attainment of which would bring pleasure austere and exquisite. There is no stimulus and no sting in the love depicted. Even its ardour is checked and wasted by its dallying with the external charms that seem to veil rather than to reveal the spirit within the flesh. It is the essence of immaturity. But while we gain from the observation of Morris's childlike characters, playing in a world that knows no conventions and consequently no shame, a foreboding of the weariness that would attend such a life as he plans for them, we are conscious also that he is trying characteristically, to go back to the beginning, and to start humanity aright and afresh ; to show us fine and healthy sons of Adam and daughters of Eve, "living," to use his own words, "in the enjoyment of animal life at least, happy therefore, and beautiful according to the beauty of their race." He sets them among the surroundings he loves, gives them the education he values, and leaves them with us — the blithe children of a new world, whose maturity he is content not to forecast. With such health of body, he seems to say, and such innocence of heart, what noble commonwealth may not arise, what glory may not enter into civilisation ?

CHAPTER XII.

THE END.

THE end with Morris seemed to come suddenly, although for months and even for years there had been warnings of its approach. He had enjoyed — and greatly enjoyed — unusual strength and vitality up to almost his sixtieth year. The seeds of gout were in his constitution, and from attacks of this disease he occasionally suffered, but not until the one occurring in the spring of 1891, just as the Kelmscott Press was getting under way, did they give reason for alarm. At that time other complications were discovered and he was told that he must consider himself an invalid. After this, as we have seen, he plunged with rapture into new undertakings involving the use of all his faculties, and carried them on with no apparent lessening of intellectual vigour. But he had too long overtaxed his physical frame by his extraordinary labours, and especially by his activity in the cause of Socialism, which had led him out in all weathers and under the most adverse conditions.

By the beginning of 1895 he began to show plainly the weakness that had been gaining on him, and to admit it, though still keeping busy at his various occupations. His increasing illness brought home to him the thought of that final check upon his activities which he had always found so difficult to conceive. "If," he said, "it merely means that I am to be laid up for a little while, it does n't so much matter, you know; but if I am to be caged up here for months, and then it is to be the end of all things, I should n't like it at all. This has been a jolly world to me and I find plenty to do in it."

As the folio *Chaucer* advanced through the Press, he grew impatient, no doubt fearing that he would not see its completion, and it is pleasant to read of his gratification when a completed copy reached him, bound in the cover designed by himself. Late in July, 1896, by the recommendation of his physician he took a sea voyage, going to Norway for the bracing influences of its air and associations. No benefit was gained, however, and on his return a congestion of one lung set in that proved unyielding, while his general weakness was such that he was unable to cross the threshold of his room. We find him responding to an old friend who had urged him to try the effect of the pure air of Swainslow, that this was the case and he could not come, but was "absolutely delighted to find another beautiful place which is still in its untouched loveliness." Up to the last he did a little work, dictating the final passage of *The Sundering Flood* less than a month before his death, which occurred in his home at Hammersmith on the morning of the 3rd of October, 1896. He died without apparent suffering, and surrounded by his friends. He had lived almost sixty-three years in the "jolly world" wherein he had found so much to do, but he left the impression of having been cut down in the flower of his life.

His burial was in keeping with those tastes and preferences that had meant so much to him. The strong oak coffin in which he was laid was of an ancient, simple shape, with handles of wrought iron, and the pall that covered it was a strip of rich Anatolian velvet from his own collection of textiles. He was carried from Lechlade station to the little Kelmscott church in an open hay-cart, cheerful in colour, with bright red wheels, and festooned with vines, alder, and bulrushes. The bearers and the drivers of the country waggons in which his friends followed him to his grave were farmers of the neighbourhood clad in their moleskins, people who had lost, said one of them, "a dear good friend in Master Morris." The hearse, with its bright decorations and the little group of mourners wound their way along pleasant country roads, beaten upon by a storm of unusual fury. "The north-west wind bent trees and bushes," writes one of those who were present, "turning the leaves of the bird maples back upon their footstalks, making them look like poplars, and the rain beat on the straggling hedges, the lurid fruit, such as only grows in rural England, —the fruit of privet with ripe hips and haws; the foliage of the Guelder roses hung on the bushes; along the road a line of slabs of stone extended, reminding one of Portugal; ragweed and loosestrife, with rank hemp agrimony, were standing dry and dead, like reeds beside a lake, and in the rain and wind the yokels stood at the cross-roads, or at the openings of the bridle-paths."

In *News from Nowhere* Morris describes Kelmscott Church, with its little aisle divided from the nave by three round arches, its windows, "mostly of the graceful Oxfordshire fourteenth-century type," and the interior trimmed with flowers for a village merry-making. On the day of his burial, by a curious coincidence it was trimmed with fruits of the harvest in preparation for the autumn festival. The service was read by an old schoolfellow and friend, and Morris was left to his rest "from patience and from pain" in the place he had best loved and to which in his final weakness he had longed to return.

In regarding Morris through the medium of his work it is difficult to gain a coherent impression. He turned one side and another to the world with such rapidity of succession as to give a sense of kaleidoscopic change. What new combination of colour and form his activities would take was always impossible to forecast. And the thing that he was doing seemed to him at the time the one thing in the world that was worth doing, the one thing that "a reasonable and healthy man" would make it his pleasure to do. Yet, as we have seen, all these pursuits taken up by him with so much zest and laid down by him with such suddenness, fitted harmoniously and accurately into the plan of his life, which, with the decade of militant Socialism deducted, presented a smooth and even surface, unbroken by any violent change of circumstance or method or motive. He has been described by nearly all who have written of him as "a rebel," and a rebel he was in the true Quixotic sense, his lance in rest to charge at any moment against any windmill of convention that might offend him. A friend who was once talking with him about a forthcoming election to the London School Board, expressing a hope that the progressive party would win,—"Well," said Morris, striding up and down, "I am not sure that a clerical victory would not be a good thing. I was educated at Marlborough under clerical masters, and I naturally rebelled against them. Had they been advanced men, my spirit of rebellion would probably have led me to conservatism merely as a protest. One naturally defies authority, and it may be well that the London School Board should be controlled by Anglican parsons, in order that the young rebels in the schools may grow up to defy and hate church authority." His own "natural" defiance of authority entailed what seems to the ordinary toiler in harness a waste of his extraordinary gifts.

His work was most of it in the experimental stage when he left it. He was too content to point the road without following to the end his own direction. "He did not learn a trade in the natural way, from those who knew, and seek then to better the teaching of his masters," says one of his fellow-workers in arts and crafts, "but, acknowledging no master, except perhaps the ancients, he would worry it out always for himself. He had a wonderful knack of learning that way."[1] He had a wonderful knack also of persuading himself that there was no other to learn, and Goldsmith's criticism of Burke—that he spent much of his time "cutting blocks with a razor"—has been happily applied to him. But it is doubtful whether he would have made as strong an impression on his generation as he did if he had devoted his time to one branch of art and worked along conventional lines. His greatest gift was not so much the ability to produce art, artistic though he was in faculty and feeling, as it was the ability to make people see the difference between the kind of beauty to which his eyes were open and the ugliness commonly preferred to it. Nothing is so convincing as to see a man accomplish with his own hands what he has declared possible for anyone to accomplish. Morris's continual illustration of his theories was perhaps more useful in awakening interest in just the matters which he had at heart than any more patient pursuit of an ideal less readily achieved. He had the habit when listening to questions and criticisms after

[1] Lewis F. Day.

his lectures of tracing charming rapid designs on paper. On a large scale that is what he did throughout his life: lecture people about the way to make things, and by way of proving his point, turn off delightful examples of the things he describes. "It is very easy" he seems to say; "watch me for a moment, and we will then pass on."

Considered superficially, he appeared the very prince of paradox. Art was a word continually on his lips, the future and fortunes of art were constantly in his mind, yet for the greatest art of the world he had few words, and the most passing interest. The names of Raphael and Leonardo, Giotto, Dürer, Rembrandt, Velasquez, were seldom if ever on his lips. Art had for him an almost single meaning, namely, the beauty produced by humble workers as an every-day occurrence and for every day's enjoyment, art by the people and for the people. So individual that he will never be forgotten by those who have once seen him and heard his voice raised in its inevitable protest, he nevertheless preached a kind of communism in which any high degree of individuality must have been submerged.

His preferences among books, as might be assumed, were clearly marked, and a list of his favourite authors contains many contrasts. Once asked to contribute to the *Pall Mall Gazette* his opinions on "the best hundred books," he complied by naming those which, he said, had most profoundly impressed him, excluding all which he considered merely as tools and not as works of art. True to himself, he starts the list with books "of the kind Mazzini calls Bibles," books which are "in no sense the work of individuals, but have grown up from the very hearts of the people." Among these are "the Hebrew Bible (excluding some twice-done parts and some pieces of mere Jewish ecclesiasticism), *Homer, Hesiod, The Edda* (including some of the other early old Norse romantic genealogical poems), *Beowulf, Kalevale, Shahnameh, Mahabharata,* collections of folk tales headed by Grimm and the Norse ones, Irish and Welsh traditional poems."

After these "Bibles" follow the "*real* ancient imaginative works: *Herodotus, Plato, Æschylus, Sophocles, Aristophanes, Theocritus, Lucretius, Catullus.*" The greater part of the Latins were esteemed "*sham* classics." "I suppose," says Morris in his character of reasonable man, "that they have some good literary qualities; but I cannot help thinking that it is difficult to find out how much. I suspect superstition and authority have influenced our estimate of them till it has become a mere matter of convention. Of course I admit the archæological value of some of them, especially *Virgil* and *Ovid.*"

Next in importance to the Latin masterpieces he puts mediæval poetry, Anglo-Saxon lyrical pieces (like the *Ruin* and the *Exile*), Dante, Chaucer, *Piers Plowman, Nibelungenlied,* the Danish and Scotch-English Border Ballads, *Omar Khayyam,* "though I don't know how much of the charm of this lovely poem," he says, "is due to Fitzgerald, the translator"; other Arab and Persian poetry, *Reynard the Fox,* and a few of the best rhymed romances. Mediæval story books follow, the *Morte d'Arthur, The Thousand and One Nights,* Boccaccio's *Decameron,* and the *Mabinogion.* After these, "modern poets" up to his own generation, "Shakespeare, Blake (the part of him which a mortal can understand), Coleridge, Shelley, Keats, Byron." German he could not read, so he left out German masterpieces. Milton he left out on account of his union of "cold classicalism with Puritanism" ("the two things which I hate most in the world," he said).

Pilgrim's Progress heads the department of modern fiction, in which is also included *Robinson Crusoe, Möll Flanders, Colonel Jack, Captain Singleton, Voyage Round the World,* Scott's novels, "except the one or two which he wrote when he was hardly alive," the novels of the elder Dumas (the "good" ones), Victor Hugo, Dickens, and George Borrow. The list concludes with certain unclassified works, Ruskin, Carlyle, the *Utopia,* and Grimm's *Teutonic Mythology.* It may safely be assumed that no other list sent in by the "best judges" who responded to Mr. Stead's request in the least resembled this one, which was compiled with high sincerity and represented Morris quite fairly on the bookish side of his mind. Mr. Mackail mentions also among the volumes oftenest in his hands and "imposed upon his friends unflinchingly" Surtees's famous *Mr. Jorrocks,* and records that he considered *Huckleberry Finn* America's masterpiece. For the Uncle Remus stories he had also a peculiar fondness, and for one of his cotton prints he designed what he called a "Brer Rabbit pattern."

The perversity that one marks in Morris beneath—or, perhaps, on the surface of—his essential seriousness, the tendency to whim and paradox so freely noted by his critics, may be attributed to his extraordinarily childlike spirit. His lack of restraint, his dislike of subtlety, his love of spontaneity, his inability to conform to conventions, his hatred of gloom, austerity, and introspection, his readiness to throw himself into enjoyment of the smallest subject that happened to come within the range of his interest, his unflagging vigour, his unjaded humour, all qualities copiously commented upon by his friends, testify to the youthfulness of his temperament, which was like that of a child, also in a certain apparently unpremeditated reticence, an inability to reveal itself fully or satisfactorily to even his closest intimates. What is most attractive and appealing in him is doubtless due to his freedom from artificialities and from the sophistries that ordinarily come with age, but what is noblest in him, and most impressive in the effect produced by his accomplishment, is due to a quality of which a child is and should be ignorant, a sense of personal responsibility. Without this he would have been a pitiful figure, disoriented, and inharmonious with the world into which he was born.

It was his persistent unwearying effort to set the crooked straight by example as well as by precept, and in defiance of a certain paradoxical mental languor that flowed by the side of his energy and impulse, which made him an influence to be counted with among the many conflicting influences of his generation. While he counselled he produced, while he preached he laboured. Declaring that work could and should be lovely, he demonstrated in his own life how intensely one man loved it. He fought for the principle of art with the ardour other men have shown in fighting for the principle of political liberty. He held himself bound to justify his theories in his own action, and while it would be absurd to claim for him complete consistency and freedom from error in even this, it certainly guided him safely past the quicksands of empty and inflated rhetoric by which the expressed philosophy of his own great masters is marred. It will be remembered by those who share his admiration for Dickens that when the proprietor of Dotheboys Hall wished to teach his pupils to spell "window" he had them clean one. The effectiveness of such a method is deeper than the satire, and Morris was its most convincing exponent. What he learned out of books he tried at once to put into practice. He had the highest ideal of service:

> How crown ye excellence of worth?
> With leave to serve all men on earth,

and nothing deflected him from his efforts thus to

serve in his own person the most crying needs of humanity as he conceived them.

Pretentiousness was his least defect. No priggish sense of virtue interfered with his consecration to what he believed were the highest interests of his fellow-men. The cant of the moralist was absolutely unused by him, and he was innocent of any intention to improve the morals of his companions. Get them happy, he thought, with a faith little less than magnificent, get them happy and they will be good. Nor was he guilty of æsthetic priggishness. Art was the concern of his mind and the desire of his heart, but it was by no means his meat and drink. He liked good food, and was proud of his connoisseurship in matters of cookery, and wines. Few things pleased him better than himself to take the cook's place and prove his practical skill. When asked for his opinions on the subject of temperance, he replied that so far as his own experience went he found his victuals dull without something to drink, and that tea and coffee were not fit liquors to be taken with food. He smoked his briarwood pipe with much satisfaction. In his daily habits he was thoroughly, aggressively human, and in nothing more so than in his candid admiration of the work of his own hands, a feeling in which there was no fatuity.

His biographer comments on the singular element of impersonality in his nature, speaking of him as moving among men and women "isolated, self-centred, almost empty of love or hatred," and quotes his most intimate friend's extreme statement that he lived "absolutely without the need of man or woman." In this idea of him those who knew him best seemed to agree, but from his own letters as represented in the biography, a stranger to him gains a different impression. His letters to his invalid daughter are in themselves sufficient to evoke in the mind of the reader an image of unlimited and poignant tenderness impossible to associate with the aloofness and lack of keen personal sympathy said to be characteristic of him. He did not give himself readily or rashly to intense feelings; but he seemed to feel within himself capacity for emotions of force so violent as to be destructive. When his friend Faulkner was stricken with paralysis and other trouble came upon the family, we find him writing: "It is such a grievous business altogether that, rightly or wrongly, I try not to think of it too much lest I should give way altogether, and make an end of what small use there may be in my life." Leaving out the case of Rossetti, there is no record of his having relinquished any friendship of importance, nor did he weary of constant intercourse with his friends. His habit of breakfasting with Burne-Jones on Sunday mornings and dining with him on Wednesdays was unbroken for many years. "The last three Sundays of his life," says this oldest and closest friend, "I went to him."

Loyalty, sincerity, simplicity, and earnestness, these are the qualities conspicuous in the fabric of his life. His influence upon his generation, so far as it may now be observed, has been definite but diffused. It may be doubted whether he would not have been best pleased to have it so, to know that his name will live chiefly as that of one who stimulated others toward art production of and interest in beautiful handiwork. But the last word to be said about him is that he was greater than his work.

BIBLIOGRAPHY[1]

1. *The Story of the Glittering Plain. Which has been also called The Land of Living Men or The Acre of the Undying.* Written by WILLIAM MORRIS. Small 4to. Golden type. Border 1. 200 paper copies at two guineas, and 6 on vellum. Dated April 4, issued May 8, 1891. Sold by Reeves & Turner. Bound in stiff vellum with wash leather ties.[2]

This book was set up from Nos. 81–84 of *The English Illustrated Magazine,* in which it first appeared; some of the chapter headings were rearranged, and a few small corrections were made in the text. A trial page, the first printed at the Kelmscott Press, was struck off on January 31, 1891, but the first sheet was not printed until about a month later.[3] The border was designed in January of the same year, and engraved by W. H. Hooper. Mr. Morris had four of the vellum copies bound in green vellum, three of which he gave to friends. Only two copies on vellum were sold, at twelve and fifteen guineas. This was the only book with wash leather ties. All the other vellum bound books have silk ties, except *Shelley's Poems* and *Hand and Soul,* which have no ties.

2. *Poems by the Way.* Written by WILLIAM MORRIS. Small 4to. Golden type. In black and red. Border 1. 300 paper copies at two guineas, thirteen on vellum at about twelve guineas. Dated September 24, issued October 20, 1891. Sold by Reeves & Turner. Bound in stiff vellum.

This was the first book printed at the Kelmscott Press in two colours, and the first book in which the smaller printer's mark appeared. After *The Glittering Plain* was finished, at the beginning of April, no printing was done until May 11th. In the meanwhile the compositors were busy setting up the early sheets of *The Golden*

[1] This bibliography is reprinted, with certain slight additions, from the bibliography prepared by S. C. Cockerell for the monograph entitled, "A Note by William Morris on his Aims in Founding the Kelmscott Press."

[2] At the Ellis Sale (1901) a presentation vellum copy brought £114.

[3] The first sheet was printed on the 2d of March, the last on the 4th of April.

Legend. The printing of *Poems by the Way,* which its author first thought of calling *Flores Atramenti,* was not begun until July. The poems in it were written at various times. In the manuscript, *Hafburg and Signy* is dated February 4, 1870; *Hildebrand and Hillilel,* March 1, 1871; and *Love's Reward,* Kelmscott, April 21, 1871. *Meeting in Winter* is a song from *The Story of Orpheus* an unpublished poem intended for the *Earthly Paradise.* The last poem in the book, *Goldilocks and Goldilooks,* was written on May 20, 1891, for the purpose of adding to the bulk of the volume, which was then being prepared. A few of the vellum covers were stained at Merton red, yellow, indigo, and dark green, but the experiment was not successful.[1]

3. *The Love-Lyrics and Songs of Proteus, by Wilfrid Scawen Blunt, with the Love Sonnets of Proteus, by the same author, now reprinted in their full text with many sonnets omitted from the earlier editions.* London, MDCCCXCII. Small 4to. Golden type. In black and red. Border 1. 300 paper copies at two guineas, none on vellum. Dated January 26, issued February 27, 1892. Sold by Reeves & Turner. Bound in stiff vellum.

This is the only book in which the initials are printed in red. This was done by the author's wish.

4. *The Nature of Gothic, a Chapter of the Stones of Venice.* By JOHN RUSKIN. With a preface by William Morris. Small 4to. Golden type. Border 1. Diagrams in text. 500 paper copies at thirty shillings, none on vellum. Dated in preface, February 15, issued March 22, 1892. Published by George Allen. Bound in stiff vellum.

This chapter of the Stones of Venice, which Ruskin always considered the most important in the book, was first printed separately, in 1854, as a sixpenny pamphlet. Mr. Morris paid more than one tribute to it in *Hopes and Fears for Art.* Of him Ruskin said, in 1887, "Morris is beaten gold."

5. *The Defence of Guenevere, and Other Poems.* By WILLIAM MORRIS. Small 4to. Golden type. In black and red. Borders 2 and 1. 300 paper copies at two guineas, 10 on vellum at about twelve guineas. Dated April 2, issued May 19, 1892. Sold by Reeves & Turner. Bound in limp vellum.

This book was set up from a copy of the edition published by Reeves & Turner in 1880, the only alteration, except a few corrections, being in the eleventh line of *Summer Dawn.*[2] It is divided into three parts, the poems suggested by Malory's

[1] At the Ellis Sale a presentation vellum copy brought £60.

[2] In this line as it originally stood, "dawn" was the rhyme provided for "corn." In the new line the rhyme for corn is "daylight new-born;" but Mr. Buxton Forman writes that Morris was wont to declare that "No South Englishman makes any difference in ordinary talk between dawn and morn for instance."

Morte d'Arthur, the poems inspired by Froissart's *Chronicles*, and poems on various subjects. The two first sections have borders, and the last has a half border. The first sheet was printed on February 17, 1892. It was the first book bound in limp vellum, and the only one of which the title was inscribed by hand on the back.

6. *A Dream of John Ball and a King's Lesson*. By WILLIAM MORRIS. Small 4to. Golden type. In black and red. Borders 3a, 4, and 2. With a woodcut designed by Sir E. Burne-Jones. 300 paper copies at thirty shillings, 11 on vellum at ten guineas. Dated May 13, issued September 24, 1892. Sold by Reeves & Turner. Bound in limp vellum.

This was set up with a few alterations from a copy of Reeves & Turner's third edition, and the printing was begun on April 4, 1892. The frontispiece was redrawn from that to the first edition, and engraved on wood by W. H. Hooper, who engraved all Sir E. Burne-Jones's designs for the Kelmscott Press, except those for *The Wood Beyond the World* and *The Life and Death of Jason*. The inscription below the figures,[1] and the narrow border, were designed by Mr. Morris and engraved with the picture on one block, which was afterwards used on a leaflet printed for the Ancoats Brotherhood in February, 1894.

7. *The Golden Legend*. By JACOBUS DE VORAGINE. Translated by William Caxton. Edited by F. S. Ellis. 3 vols. Large 4to. Golden type. Borders 5a, 5, 6a and 7. Woodcut title and two woodcuts designed by Sir E. Burne-Jones. 500 copies at five guineas, none on vellum. Dated September 12, issued November 3, 1892. Published by Bernard Quaritch. Bound in half Holland, with paper labels printed in the Troy type.

In July, 1890, when only a few letters of the Golden type had been cut, Mr. Morris bought a copy of this book, printed by Wynkyn de Worde in 1527. He soon afterwards determined to print it, and on September 11th entered into a formal agreement with Mr. Quaritch for its publication. It was only an unforeseen difficulty about the size of the first stock of paper that led to *The Golden Legend* not being the first book put in hand. It was set up from a transcript of Caxton's first edition, lent by the Syndics of the Cambridge University Library for the purpose. A trial page was got out in March, 1891, and fifty pages were in type by May 11th, the day on which the first sheet was printed. The first volume was finished, with the exception of the illustrations and the preliminary matter, in October, 1891. The two illustrations and the title (which was the first woodcut title designed by Mr. Morris) were not engraved until June and August, 1892, when the third volume was approaching completion. About half a dozen impressions of the illustrations were pulled on vellum. A slip asking owners of the book not to have it bound with pressure, nor to have the edges cut instead of merely trimmed, was inserted in each copy.

---

[1] "When Adam dalf and Eve span, who was thanne the gentleman."

8. *The Recuyell of the Historyes of Troye.* By RAOUL LEFEVRE. Translated by William Caxton. Edited by H. Halliday Sparling. 2 vols. Large 4to. Troy type, with table of chapters and glossary in Chaucer type. In black and red. Borders 5a, 5, and 8. Woodcut title. 300 paper copies at nine guineas, 5 on vellum at eighty pounds. Dated October 14, issued November 24, 1892. Published by Bernard Quaritch. Bound in limp vellum.

This book, begun in February, 1892, is the first book printed in Troy type, and the first in which Chaucer type appears. It is a reprint of the first book printed in English. It had long been a favourite with William Morris, who designed a great quantity of initials and ornaments for it, and wrote the following note for Mr. Quaritch's catalogue: "As to the matter of the book, it makes a thoroughly amusing story, instinct with mediæval thought and manners. For though written at the end of the Middle Ages and dealing with classical mythology, it has in it no token of the coming Renaissance, but is purely mediæval. It is the last issue of that story of Troy which through the whole of the Middle Ages had such a hold on men's imaginations; the story built up from a rumour of the Cyclic Poets, of the heroic City of Troy, defended by Priam and his gallant sons, led by Hector the Preux Chevalier, and beset by the violent and brutal Greeks, who were looked on as the necessary machinery for bringing about the undeniable tragedy of the fall of the City. Surely this is well worth reading, if only as a piece of undiluted mediævalism." 2000 copies of a 4to announcement, with specimen pages, were printed at the Kelmscott Press in December, 1892, for distribution by the publisher.[1]

9. *Biblia Innocentium: Being the Story of God's Chosen People before the Coming of Our Lord Jesus Christ upon Earth.* Written anew for children, by J. W. MACKAIL, Sometime Fellow of Balliol College, Oxford. 8vo. Border 2. 200 on paper at a guinea, none on vellum. Dated October 22, issued December 9, 1892. Sold by Reeves & Turner. Bound in stiff vellum.

This was the last book issued in stiff vellum except *Hand and Soul,* and the last with untrimmed edges. It was the first book printed in 8vo.

10. *The History of Reynard the Foxe.* By WILLIAM CAXTON. Reprinted from his edition of 1481. Edited by H. Halliday Sparling. Large 4to. Troy type, with Glossary in Chaucer type. In black and red. Borders 5a and 7. Woodcut title. 300 on paper at three guineas, 10 on vellum at fifteen guineas. Dated December 15, 1892, issued January 25, 1893. Published by Bernard Quaritch. Bound in limp vellum.

---

[1] This book realised at the Ellis Sale £8.5s. for the paper copy, and £61 in vellum. Since its publication it has sold as low as £2.15s. for paper copies, and £29 for vellum.

About this book, which was first announced as in the press in the list dated July, 1892, William Morris wrote the following note for Mr. Quaritch's catalogue: "This translation of Caxton's is one of the very best of his works as to style; and being translated from a kindred tongue is delightful as mere language. In its rude joviality, and simple and direct delineation of character, it is a thoroughly good representative of the famous ancient Beast Epic." The edges of this book, and of all subsequent books, were trimmed in accordance with the invariable practice of the early printers. Mr. Morris much preferred the trimmed edges.

11. *The Poems of William Shakespeare,* printed after the original copies of *Venus and Adonis,* 1593. *The Rape of Lucrece,* 1594. *Sonnets,* 1609. *The Lover's Complaint.* Edited by F. S. Ellis. 8vo. Golden type. In black and red. Borders 1 and 2. 500 paper copies at twenty-five shillings, 10 on vellum at ten guineas. Dated January 17, issued February 13, 1893. Sold by Reeves & Turner. Bound in limp vellum.

A trial page of this book was set up on November 1, 1892. Though the number was large, this has become one of the rarest books issued from the Press.[1]

12. *News from Nowhere: or, An Epoch of Rest, Being Some Chapters from a Utopian Romance.* By WILLIAM MORRIS. 8vo. Golden type. In black and red. Borders 9a and 4, and a woodcut engraved by W. H. Hooper from a design by C. M. Gere. 300 on paper at two guineas, 10 on vellum at ten guineas. Dated November 22, 1892, issued March 24, 1893. Sold by Reeves & Turner. Bound in limp vellum.

The text of this book was printed before Shakespeare's *Poems and Sonnets,* but it was kept back for the frontispiece, which is a picture of the old manor-house in the village of Kelmscott by the upper Thames, from which the Press took its name. It was set up from a copy of one of Reeves & Turner's editions, and in reading it for the press the author made a few slight corrections. It was the last book except the *Savonarola* (No. 31) in which he used the old paragraph mark ¶, which was discarded in favour of the leaves, which had already been used in the two large 4to books printed in the Troy type.

13. *The Order of Chivalry.* Translated from the French by William Caxton and reprinted from his edition of 1484. Edited by F. S. Ellis. And *L'Ordene de Chevalerie,* with translation by William Morris. Small 4to. Chaucer type, in black and red. Borders 9a and 4, and a woodcut designed by Sir Edward Burne-Jones. 225 on paper at thirty shillings, 10 on vellum at ten guineas. *The Order of Chivalry* dated November

[1] Mr. Ellis's presentation copy sold for £91.

10, 1892, *L'Ordene de Chevalerie* dated February 24, 1893, issued April 12, 1893. Sold by Reeves & Turner. Bound in limp vellum.

This was the last book printed in small 4to. The last section is in 8vo. It was the first book printed in the Chaucer type. The reprint from Caxton was finished while *News from Nowhere* was in the press, and before Shakespeare's *Poems and Sonnets* was begun. The French poem and its translation were added as an afterthought, and have a separate colophon. Some of the three-line initials which were designed for *The Well at the World's End* are used in the French poem, and this is their first appearance. The translation was begun on December 3, 1892, and the border round the frontispiece was designed on February 13, 1893.

14. *The Life of Thomas Woolsey, Cardinal Archbishop of York.* Written by GEORGE CAVENDISH. Edited by F. S. Ellis from the author's autograph MS. 8vo. Golden type. Border 1. 250 on paper at two guineas, 6 on vellum at ten guineas. Dated March 30, issued May 3, 1893. Sold by Reeves & Turner. Bound in limp vellum.

15. *The History of Godefrey of Boloyne and of the Conquest of Iherusalem.* Reprinted from Caxton's edition of 1841. Edited by H. Halliday Sparling. Large 4to. Troy type, with list of chapter headings and glossary in Chaucer type. In black and red. Borders 5a and 5, and woodcut title. 300 on paper at six guineas, 6 on vellum at twenty guineas. Dated April 27, issued May 24, 1893. Published by William Morris at the Kelmscott Press. Bound in limp vellum.

This was the fifth and last of the Caxton reprints, with many new ornaments and initials, and a new printer's mark. It was first announced as in the press in the list dated December, 1892. It was the first book published and sold at the Kelmscott Press. An announcement and order form, with two different specimen pages, was printed at the Press, besides a special invoice. A few copies were bound in half holland, not for sale.

16. *Utopia.* Written by SIR THOMAS MORE. A reprint of the second edition of Ralph Robinson's translation, with a foreword by William Morris.[1] Edited by F. S. Ellis. 8vo. Chaucer type, with the reprinted title in Troy type. In black and red. Borders 4 and 2. 300 on paper at thirty shillings, 8 on vellum at ten guineas. Dated August 4, issued September 8, 1893. Sold by Reeves & Turner. Bound in limp vellum.

This book was first announced as in the press in the list dated May 20, 1893.

[1] This "foreword" is a socialist document occupying pp. III to VIII.

17. *Maud, A Monodrama.* By ALFRED, LORD TENNYSON. 8vo. Golden type. In black and red. Borders 10a and 10, and woodcut title. 500 on paper at two guineas, 5 on vellum, not for sale. Dated August 11, issued September 30, 1893. Published by Macmillan & Co. Bound in limp vellum.

The borders were specially designed for this book. They were both used again in the Keats, and one of them appears in *The Saundering Flood.* It is the first of the 8vo books with a woodcut title.

18. *Gothic Architecture: A Lecture for the Arts and Crafts Exhibition Society.* By WILLIAM MORRIS. 16mo. Golden type. In black and red. 1500 on paper at two shillings and sixpence, 45 on vellum at ten and fifteen shillings. Bound in half holland.

This lecture was set up at Hammersmith and printed at the New Gallery during the Arts and Crafts Exhibition in October and November, 1893. The first copies were ready on October 21st and the book was twice reprinted before the Exhibition closed. It was the first book printed in 16mo. The four-line initials used in it appear here for the first time. The vellum copies were sold during the Exhibition at ten shillings, and the price was subsequently raised to fifteen shillings.[1]

19. *Sidonia the Sorceress.* By WILLIAM MEINHOLD. Translated by Francesca Speranza, Lady Wilde. Large 4to. Golden type. In black and red. Border 8. 300 paper copies at four guineas, 10 on vellum at twenty guineas. Dated September 15, issued November 1, 1893. Published by William Morris. Bound in limp vellum.

Before the publication of this book a large 4to announcement and order form was issued, with a specimen page and an interesting description of the book and its author, written and signed by William Morris. Some copies were bound in half holland not for sale.

20. *Ballads and Narrative Poems by Dante Gabriel Rossetti.* 8vo. Golden type. In black and red. Borders 4a and 4, and woodcut title. 310 on paper at two guineas, 6 on vellum at ten guineas. Dated October 14, issued in November, 1893. Published by Ellis & Elvey. Bound in limp vellum.

This book was announced as in preparation in the list of August 1, 1893.

21. *The Tale of King Florus and the Fair Jehane.* Translated by William Morris from the French of the 13th century. 16mo. Chaucer type. In black and red. Borders 11a and 11,

[1] At the Ellis Sale a copy on vellum (not presentation) brought £9.10s.

and woodcut title. 350 on paper at seven shillings and sixpence, 15 on vellum at thirty shillings. Dated December 16, issued December 28, 1893. Published by William Morris. Bound in half holland.

This story, like the three other translations with which it is uniform, was taken from a little volume called *Nouvelles Françoises en prose du XIIIe siècle*, Paris, Jannet, 1856. They were first announced as in preparation under the heading *French Tales* in the list dated May 20, 1893. Eighty-five copies of *King Florus* were bought by J. & M. L. Tregaskis, who had them bound in all parts of the world. These are now in the Rylands Library at Manchester.

22. *The Story of the Glittering Plain. Which has been also called The Land of Living Men or The Acre of the Undying.* Written by WILLIAM MORRIS. Large 4to. Troy type, with list of chapters in Chaucer type. In black and red. Borders 12a and 12, 23 designs by Walter Crane, engraved by A. Leverett, and a woodcut title. 250 on paper at five guineas, 7 on vellum at twenty pounds. Dated January 13, issued February 17, 1894. Published by William Morris. Bound in limp vellum. Neither the borders in this book nor six out of the seven frames round the illustrations appear in any other book. The seventh is used round the second picture in *Love is Enough*. A few copies were bound in half holland.

23. *Of the Friendship of Amis and Amile. Done out of the ancient French by* WILLIAM MORRIS. 16mo. Chaucer type. In black and red. Borders 11a and 11, and woodcut title. 500 on paper at seven shillings and sixpence, 15 on vellum at thirty shillings. Dated March 13th, issued April 4, 1894. Published by William Morris. Bound in half holland.[1]

A poem entitled *Amys and Amillion,* founded on this story, was originally to have appeared in the second volume of the *Earthly Paradise,* but, like some other poems announced at the same time, it was not included in the book.

20a. *Sonnets and Lyrical Poems by Dante Gabriel Rossetti.* 8vo. Golden type. In black and red. Borders 1a and 1, and woodcut title. 310 on paper at two guineas, 6 on vellum at ten guineas. Dated February 20, issued April 21, 1894. Published by Ellis & Elvey. Bound in limp vellum.

This book is uniform with No. 20, to which it forms a sequel. Both volumes were read for the press by Mr. W. M. Rossetti.

---

[1] This story Morris said he translated in a day and a quarter.

24. *The Poems of John Keats.* Edited by F. S. Ellis. 8vo. Golden type. In black and red. Borders 10a and 10, and woodcut title. 300 on paper at thirty shillings, 7 on vellum at nine guineas. Dated March 7, issued May 8, 1894. Published by William Morris. Bound in limp vellum.

This is now (January, 1898) the most sought after of all the smaller Kelmscott Press books. It was announced as in preparation in the lists of May 27 and August 1, 1893, and as in the press in that of March 31, 1894, when the woodcut title still remained to be printed.[1]

25. *Atalanta in Calydon: A Tragedy.* By ALGERNON CHARLES SWINBURNE. Large 4to. Troy type, with argument and *dramatis personæ* in Chaucer type; the dedication and quotation from Euripides in Greek type designed by Selwyn Image. In black and red. Borders 5a and 5, and woodcut title. 250 on paper at two guineas, 8 on vellum at twelve guineas. Dated May 4, issued July 24, 1894. Published by William Morris. Bound in limp vellum.

In the vellum copies of this book the colophon is not on the eighty-second page as in the paper copies, but on the following page.

26. *The Tale of the Emperor Coustans and of Over Sea.* Done out of ancient French by WILLIAM MORRIS. 16mo. Chaucer type. In black and red. Borders 11a and 11, both twice, and two woodcut titles. 525 on paper at seven shillings and sixpence, 20 on vellum at two guineas. Dated August 30, issued September 26, 1894. Published by William Morris. Bound in half holland.

The first of these stories, which was the source of *The Man Born to be King* in *The Earthly Paradise,* was announced as in preparation in the list of March 31, 1894.

27. *The Wood Beyond the World.* By WILLIAM MORRIS. 8vo. Chaucer type. In black and red. Borders 13a and 13, and a frontispiece designed by Sir E. Burne-Jones, and engraved on wood by W. Spielmeyer. 350 on paper at two guineas, 8 on vellum at ten guineas. Dated May 30, issued October 16, 1894. Published by William Morris. Bound in limp vellum.

The borders in this book, as well as the ten half borders, are here used for the first time. It was first announced as in the press in the list of March 31, 1894. Another edition was published by Lawrence & Bullen in 1895.

---

[1] At the Ellis Sale a paper copy brought £25.10s., while in 1900 one brought £27.5s.

28. *The Book of Wisdom and Lies. A Book of Traditional Stories from Georgia and Asia.* Translated by Oliver Wardrop from the original of Sulkhan-Saba Orbeliani. 8vo. Golden type. In black and red. Borders 4a and 4, and woodcut title. 250 on paper at two guineas, none on vellum. Finished September 20, issued October 29, 1894. Published by Bernard Quaritch. Bound in limp vellum.

The arms of Georgia, consisting of the Holy Coat, appear in the woodcut title of this book.[1]

29. *The Poetical Works of Percy Bysshe Shelley.* Volume I. Edited by F. S. Ellis. 8vo. Golden type. Borders 1a and 1, and woodcut title. 250 on paper at twenty-five shillings, 6 on vellum at eight guineas. Not dated, issued November 29, 1894. Published by William Morris. Bound in limp vellum without ties.

Red ink is not used in this volume, though it is used in the second volume, and more sparingly in the third. Some of the half borders designed for *The Wood Beyond the World* reappear before the longer poems. The Shelley was first announced as in the press in the list of March 31, 1894.[2]

30. *Psalmi Penitentiales. An English rhymed version of the Seven Penitential Psalms.* Edited by F. S. Ellis. 8vo. Chaucer type. In black and red. 300 on paper at seven shillings and sixpence, 12 on vellum at three guineas. Dated November 15, issued December 10, 1894. Published by William Morris. Bound in half holland.

These verses were taken from a manuscript Book of Hours, written at Gloucester in the first half of the fifteenth century, but the Rev. Professor Skeat has pointed out that the scribe must have copied them from an older manuscript, as they are in the Kentish dialect of about a century earlier. The half border on p. 34 appears for the first time in this book.

31. *Epistolade Contemptumundi di Frate Hieronymo da Ferrara Dellordinede Frati Predicatori la Quale Manda ad Elena Buonaccorsi Sua Madre.* Per CONSOLARLA DELLA MORTE DEL FRATELLO, *Suo Zio.* Edited by Charles Fairfax Murray from the original autograph letter. 8vo. Chaucer type. In black and

---

[1] Mr. Vallance says, "This is noteworthy as being the sole instance of a heraldic device among the *published* designs of William Morris."

[2] In the list of Dec. 1st, 1894, the 2d and 3d volumes are announced to follow "early in the New Year." The third volume did not, however, appear until the autumn of 1895.

red. Border 1. Woodcut on title designed by C. F. Murray and engraved by W. H. Hooper. 150 on paper and 6 on vellum. Dated November 30, ready December 12, 1894. Bound in half holland.

This little book was printed for Mr. C. Fairfax Murray, the owner of the manuscript, and was not for sale in the ordinary way. The colophon is in Italian, and the printer's mark is in red.

32. *The Tale of Beowulf.* Done out of the old English tongue by WILLIAM MORRIS and A. J. WYATT. Large 4to. Troy type, with argument, side-notes, list of persons and places, and glossary in Chaucer type. In black and red. Borders 14a and 14, and woodcut title. 300 on paper at two guineas, 8 on vellum at ten pounds. Dated January 10, issued February 2, 1895. Published by William Morris. Bound in limp vellum.

The borders in this book were only used once again, in the Jason. A note to the reader printed on a slip in the Golden type was inserted in each copy. *Beowulf* was first announced as in preparation in the list of May 20, 1893. The verse translation was begun by Mr. Morris, with the aid of Mr. Wyatt's careful paraphrase of the text, on February 21, 1893, and finished on April 10, 1894, but the argument was not written by Mr. Morris until December 10, 1894.

33. *Syr Perecyvelle of Gales.* Overseen by F. S. Ellis, after the edition edited by J. O. Halliwell from the Thornton MS. in the Library of Lincoln Cathedral. 8vo. Chaucer type. In black and red. Borders 13a and 13, and a woodcut designed by Sir E. Burne-Jones. 350 on paper at fifteen shillings, 8 on vellum four guineas. Dated February 16, issued May 2, 1895. Published by William Morris. Bound in limp vellum.

This is the first of the series to which *Sire Degrevaunt and Syr Isumbrace* belong. They were all reprinted from the Camden Society's volume of 1844, which was a favourite with Mr. Morris from his Oxford days. *Syr Perecyvelle* was first announced in the list of December 1, 1894. The shoulder-notes were added by Mr. Morris.

34. *The Life and Death of Jason,* A Poem by WILLIAM MORRIS. Large 4to. Troy type, with a few words in Chaucer type. In black and red. Borders 14a and 14, and two woodcuts designed by Sir E. Burne-Jones and engraved on wood by W. Spielmeyer. 200 on paper at five guineas, 6 on vellum at twenty guineas. Dated May 25, issued July 5, 1895. Published by William Morris. Bound in limp vellum.

This book, announced as in the press in the list of April 21, 1894, proceeded slowly, as several other books, notably the Chaucer, were being printed at the same time. The text, which had been corrected for the second edition of 1868, and for the edition of 1882, was again revised by the author. The line fillings on the last page were cut on metal for the book, and cast like type.

29a. *The Poetical Works of Percy Bysshe Shelley.* Volume II. Edited by F. S. Ellis. 8vo. Golden type. In black and red. 250 on paper at twenty-five shillings, 6 on vellum at eight guineas. Not dated, issued March 25, 1895. Published by William Morris, Bound in limp vellum without ties.

35. *Child Christopher and Goldilind the Fair.* By WILLIAM MORRIS. 2 vols. 16mo. Chaucer type. In black and red. Borders 15a and 15, and woodcut title. 600 on paper at fifteen shillings, 12 on vellum at four guineas. Dated July 25, issued September 25, 1895. Published by William Morris. Bound in half holland, with labels printed in the Golden type.

The borders designed for this book were only used once again, in *Hand and Soul.* The plot of the story was suggested by that of Havelok the Dane, printed by the Early English Text Society.

29b. *The Poetical Works of Percy Bysshe Shelley.* Volume III. Edited by F. S. Ellis. 8vo. Golden type. In black and red. 250 on paper at twenty-five shillings, 6 on vellum at eight guineas. Dated August 21, issued October 28, 1895. Published by William Morris. Bound in limp vellum without ties.

36. *Hand and Soul.* By DANTE GABRIEL ROSSETTI. Reprinted from *The Germ,* for Messrs. Way & Williams, of Chicago. 16mo. Golden type. In black and red. Borders 15a and 15, and woodcut title. 300 paper copies and 11 vellum copies for America. 225 paper copies for sale in England at ten shillings, and 10 on vellum at thirty shillings. Dated October 24, issued December 12, 1895. Bound in stiff vellum, without ties.

This was the only 16mo book bound in vellum. The English and American copies have a slightly different colophon. The shoulder-notes were added by Mr. Morris.

37. *Poems Chosen out of the Works of Robert Herrick.* Edited by F. S. Ellis. 8vo. Golden type. In black and red. Borders 4a and 4, and woodcut title. 250 on paper at thirty shillings, 8 on vellum at eight guineas. Dated November 21, 1895, issued February 6, 1896. Published by William Morris. Bound in limp vellum.

This book was first announced as in preparation in the list of December 1, 1894, and as in the press in that of July 1, 1895.

38. *Poems Chosen out of the Works of Samuel Taylor Coleridge.* Edited by F. S. Ellis. 8vo. Golden type. In black and red. Borders 13a and 13. 300 on paper at a guinea, 8 on vellum at five guineas. Dated February 5, issued April 12, 1896. Published by William Morris. Bound in limp vellum.[1]

This book contains thirteen poems. It was first announced as in preparation in the list of December 1, 1894, and as in the press in that of November 26, 1895. It is the last of the series to which Tennyson's *Maud,* and the poems of Rossetti, Keats, Shelley, and Herrick belong.

39. *The Well at the World's End.* By WILLIAM MORRIS. Large 4to. Double columns. Chaucer type. In black and red. Borders 16a, 16, 17a, 17, 18a, 18, 19a, 19, and four woodcuts designed by Sir E. Burne-Jones. 350 on paper at five guineas, 8 on vellum at twenty guineas. Dated March 2, issued June 4, 1896. Sold by William Morris. Bound in limp vellum.

This book, delayed for various reasons, was longer on hand than any other. It appears in no less than twelve lists, from that of December, 1892, to that of November 26, 1895, as "in the press." Trial pages, including one in a single column, were ready as early as September, 1892, and the printing began on December 16th, of that year. The edition of *The Well at the World's End,* published by Longmans, was then being printed from the author's manuscript at the Chiswick Press, and the Kelmscott Press edition was set up from the sheets of that edition, which, though not issued until October, 1896, was finished in 1894. The eight borders and the six different ornaments between the columns appear here for the first time, but are used again in *The Water of the Wondrous Isles,* with the exception of two borders.

40. *The Works of Geoffrey Chaucer.* Edited by F. S. Ellis. Folio. Chaucer type, with headings to the longer poems in Troy type. In black and red. Borders 20a to 26, woodcut title, and eighty-seven woodcut illustrations designed by Sir E. Burne-Jones. 425 on paper at twenty pounds, 13 on vellum at 120 guineas. Dated May 8, issued June 26, 1896. Published by William Morris. Bound in half holland.

The history of this book, which is by far the most important achievement of the Kelmscott Press, is as follows:

As far back as June 11, 1891, Mr. Morris spoke of printing a Chaucer with a black-letter fount, which he hoped to design. Four months later, when most of the Troy type was designed and cut, he expressed his intention to use it first on

---

[1] Dull red silk ties. Gold lettering on back.

John Ball, and then on a Chaucer, and perhaps a *Gesta Romanorum.* By January 1, 1892, the Troy type was delivered, and early in that month two trial pages, one from *The Cook's Tale* and one from *Sir Thopas,* the latter in double columns, were got out. It then became evident that the type was too large for a Chaucer, and Mr. Morris decided to have it re-cut in the size known as pica. By the end of June he was thus in possession of the type which, in the list issued in December, 1892, he named the Chaucer type. In July, 1892, another trial page, a passage from *The Knight's Tale*, in double columns of fifty-eight lines, was got out, and found to be satisfactory. The idea of the Chaucer as it now exists, with illustrations by Sir Edward Burne-Jones, then took definite shape.

In a proof of the first list, dated April, 1892, there is an announcement of the book as in preparation, in black-letter, large quarto, but this was struck out, and does not appear in the list as printed in May, nor yet in the July list. In that for December, 1892, it is announced for the first time as to be in Chaucer type "with about sixty designs by E. Burne-Jones." The next list, dated March 9, 1893, states that it will be a folio, and that it is in the press, by which was meant that a few pages were in type. In the list dated August 1, 1893, the probable price is given as twenty pounds. The next four lists contain no fresh information, but on August 17, 1894, nine days after the first sheet was printed, a notice was sent to the trade that there would be 325 copies at twenty pounds, and about sixty woodcut designs by Sir Edward Burne-Jones. Three months later it was decided to increase the number of illustrations to upwards of seventy, and to print another 100 copies of the book. A circular letter was sent to the subscribers on November 14th, stating this, and giving them an opportunity of cancelling their orders. Orders were not withdrawn, the extra copies were immediately taken up, and the list for December 1, 1894, which is the first containing full particulars, announces that all paper copies are sold.[1]

Mr. Morris began designing his first folio border on February 1, 1893, but was dissatisfied with the design and did not finish it Three days later he began the vine border for the first page, and finished it in about a week, together with the initial word "Whan," the two lines of heading, and the frame for the first picture, and Mr. Hooper engraved the whole of these on one block. The first picture was engraved at about the same time. A specimen of the first page (differing slightly from the same page as it appears in the book) was shown at the Arts and Crafts Exhibition in October and November, 1893, and was issued to a few leading booksellers, but it was not until August 8, 1894, that the first sheet was printed at 14, Upper Mall. On January 8, 1895, another press was started at 21, Upper Mall, and from that time two presses were almost exclusively at work on the Chaucer. By September 10th, the last page of *The Romaunt of the Rose* was printed. In the middle of February, 1896, Mr. Morris began designing the title. It was finished on the 27th of the same month and engraved by Mr. Hooper in March. On May 8th, a year and nine months after the printing of the first sheet, the book was completed. On June 2nd, the first two copies were delivered to Sir Edward Burne-Jones and Mr. Morris. Mr. Morris's copy is now at Exeter College, Oxford, with other books printed at the Kelmscott Press.

Besides the eighty-seven illustrations designed by Sir Edward Burne-Jones, and

[1] Also that 7 of the 8 vellum copies have been subscribed for.

engraved by W. H. Hooper, the Chaucer contains a woodcut title, fourteen large borders, eighteen different frames around the illustrations, and twenty-six large initial words designed for the book by William Morris. Many of these were engraved by C. E. Keats, and others by W. H. Hooper and W. Spielmeyer.

In February, 1896, a notice was issued respecting special bindings, of which Mr. Morris intended to design four.

Two of these were to have been executed under Mr. Cobden-Sanderson's direction at the Doves Bindery, and two by Messrs. J. & J. Leighton. But the only design that he was able to complete was for a full white pigskin binding, which has now been carried out at the Doves Bindery on forty-eight copies, including two on vellum.[1]

41. *The Earthly Paradise.* By WILLIAM MORRIS. Volume I. *Prologue: The Wanderers.* March: *Atalanta's Race. The Man Born to be King.* Medium 4to. Golden type. In black and red. Borders 27a, 27, 28a, and 28, and woodcut title. 225 on paper at thirty shillings, 6 on vellum at seven guineas. Dated May 7, issued July 24, 1896. Published by William Morris. Bound in limp vellum.

This was the first book printed on the paper with the apple water-mark. The seven other volumes followed it at intervals of a few months. None of the ten borders used in the *Earthly Paradise* appear in any other book. The four different half-borders round the poems to the months are also not used elsewhere. The first border was designed in June, 1895.

42. *Laudes Beatæ Mariæ Virginis.* Latin poems taken from a Psalter written in England about A.D. 1220. Edited by S. C. Cockerell. Large 4to. Troy type. In black, red, and blue. 250 on paper at ten shillings, 10 on vellum at two guineas. Dated July 7, issued August 7, 1896. Published by William Morris. Bound in half holland.

This was the first book printed at the Kelmscott Press in three colours.[2] The manuscript from which the poems were taken was one of the most beautiful of the English books in Mr. Morris's possession, both as regards writing and ornament. No author's name is given to the poems, but after this book was issued the Rev. E. S. Dewick pointed out that they had already been printed at Tegernsee in 1579, in a 16mo volume in which they are ascribed to Stephen Langton. A note to this effect was printed in the Chaucer type in December 28, 1896, and distributed to the subscribers.

41a. *The Earthly Paradise.* By WILLIAM MORRIS. Volume II. April: *The Doom of King Acrisius. The Proud King.*

[1] In the prospectus the price for full white tooled pigskin binding executed under Mr. Cobden-Sanderson's direction is given at £13.

[2] The quotations heading each stanza are in red, the initial letters pale blue, the remaining text in black.

Medium 4to. Golden type. In black and red. Borders 29a, 29, 28a, and 28. 225 on paper at thirty shillings, 6 on vellum at seven guineas. Dated June 24, issued September 17, 1896. Published by William Morris. Bound in limp vellum.

43. *The Floure and the Leafe, and The Boke of Cupide, God of Love, or The Cuckow and the Nightingale.* Edited by F. S. Ellis. Medium 4to. Troy type, with note and colophon in Chaucer type. In black and red. 300 on paper at ten shillings, 10 on vellum at two guineas. Dated August 21, issued November 2, 1896. Published at the Kelmscott Press. Bound in half holland.

Two of the initial words from the Chaucer are used in this book, one at the beginning of each poem. These poems were formerly attributed to Chaucer, but recent scholarship has proved that *The Floure and the Leafe* is much later than Chaucer, and that *The Cuckow and the Nightingale* was written by Sir Thomas Clanvowe about A.D. 1405–10.

44. *The Shepheardes Calender: Conteyning Twelve Aeglogues, Proportionable to the Twelve Monethes.* By EDMUND SPENCER. Edited by F. S. Ellis. Medium 4to. Golden type. In black and red. With twelve full page illustrations by A. J. Gaskin. 225 on paper at a guinea, 6 on vellum at three guineas. Dated October 14, issued November 26, 1896. Published at the Kelmscott Press. Bound in half holland.

The illustrations in this book were printed from process blocks by Walker & Boutall. By an oversight, the names of author, editor, and artist were omitted from the colophon.

41b. *The Earthly Paradise.* By WILLIAM MORRIS. Volume III. May: *The Story of Cupid and Psyche. The Writing on the Image.* June: *The Love of Alcestis. The Lady of the Land.* Medium 4to. Golden type. In black and red. Borders 30a, 30, 27a, 27, 28a, 28, 29a, and 29. 225 on paper at thirty shillings, 6 on vellum at seven guineas. Dated August 24, issued December 5, 1896. Published at the Kelmscott Press. Bound in limp vellum.

41c. *The Earthly Paradise.* By WILLIAM MORRIS. Volume IV. July: *The Son of Crœsus. The Watching of the Falcon.* August: *Pygmalion and the Image. Ogier the Dane.* Medium 4to. Golden type. In black and red. Borders 31a, 31, 29a, 29, 28a, 28, 30a, and 30. Dated November 25, 1896, issued January

22, 1897. Published at the Kelmscott Press. Bound in limp vellum.

41d. *The Earthly Paradise.* By WILLIAM MORRIS. Volume V. September. *The Death of Paris. The Land East of the Sun and West of the Moon.* October: *The Story of Acontius and Cydippe. The Man Who Never Laughed Again.* Medium 4to. Golden type. In black and red. Borders 29a, 29, 27a, 27, 28a, 28, 31a, and 31. Finished December 24, 1896, issued March 9, 1897. Published at the Kelmscott Press. Bound in limp vellum.

41e. *The Earthly Paradise.* By WILLIAM MORRIS. Volume VI. November: *The Story of Rhodope. The Lovers of Gudrun.* Medium 4to. Golden type. In black and red. Borders 27a, 27, 30a, and 30. Finished February 18, issued May 11, 1897. Published at the Kelmscott Press. Bound in limp vellum.

41f. *The Earthly Paradise.* By WILLIAM MORRIS. Volume VII. December: *The Golden Apples. The Fostering of Aslaug.* January: *Bellerophon at Argos. The Ring Given to Venus.* Medium 4to. Golden type. In black and red. Borders 29a, 29, 31a, 31, 30a, 30, 27a, and 27. Finished March 17, issued July 29, 1897. Published at the Kelmscott Press. Bound in limp vellum.

45. *The Water of the Wondrous Isles.* By WILLIAM MORRIS. Large 4to. Chaucer type, in double columns, with a few lines in Troy type at the end of each of the seven parts. In black and red. Borders 16a, 17a, 18a, 19, and 19a. 250 on paper at three guineas, 6 on vellum at twelve guineas. Dated April 1, issued July 29, 1897. Published at the Kelmscott Press. Bound in limp vellum.

Unlike *The Well at the World's End*, with which it is mainly uniform, this book has red shoulder-notes and no illustrations. Mr. Morris began the story in verse on February 4, 1895. A few days later he began it afresh in alternate prose and verse; but he was again dissatisfied, and finally began it a third time in prose alone, as it now stands. It was first announced as in the press in the list of June 1, 1896, at which date the early chapters were in type, although they were not printed until about a month later. The designs for the initial words "Whilom" and "Empty" were begun by William Morris shortly before his death, and were finished by R. Catterson-Smith. Another edition was published by Longmans on October 1, 1897.

41g. *The Earthly Paradise.* By WILLIAM MORRIS. Volume VIII. February: *Bellerophon in Lycia. The Hill of Venus. Epilogue. L'Envoi.* Medium 4to. Golden type. In black and red. Borders 28a, 28, 29a, and 29. Finished June 10, issued September 27, 1897. Published at the Kelmscott Press. Bound in limp vellum.

The colophon of this final volume of *The Earthly Paradise* contains the following note: "The borders in this edition of *The Earthly Paradise* were designed by William Morris, except those on page 4 of Volumes ii., iii., and iv., afterwards repeated, which were designed to match the opposite borders, under William Morris's direction, by R. Catterson-Smith, who also finished the initial words 'Whilom' and 'Empty' for *The Water of the Wondrous Isles.* All the other letters, borders, title-pages, and ornaments used at the Kelmscott Press, except the Greek type in *Atalanta in Calydon*, were designed by William Morris."

46. Two trial pages of the projected edition of Lord Berners's Translation of Froissart's Chronicles. Folio. Chaucer type, with heading in Troy type. In black and red. Border 32, containing the shields of France, the Empire, and England, and a half-border containing those of Reginald, Lord Cobham, Sir John Chandos, and Sir Walter Manny. 160 on vellum at a guinea, none on paper. Dated September, issued October 7, 1897. Published at the Kelmscott Press. Not bound.

It was the intention of Mr. Morris to make this edition of what was since his college days almost his favourite book a worthy companion to the Chaucer. It was to have been in two volumes folio, with new cusped initials and heraldic ornament throughout. Each volume was to have had a large frontispiece designed by Sir Edward Burne-Jones; the subject of the first was to have been St. George, that of the second Fame. A trial page was set up in the Troy type soon after it came from the foundry, in January, 1892. Early in 1893 trial pages were set up in the Chaucer type, and in the list for March 9th of that year the book is erroneously stated to be in the press. In the three following lists it is announced as in preparation. In the list dated December 1, 1893, and in the three next lists, it is again announced as in the press, and the number to be printed is given as 150. Meanwhile the printing of the Chaucer had been begun, and as it was not feasible to carry on two folios at the same time, the Froissart again comes under the heading "in preparation" in the lists from December 1, 1894, to June 1, 1896. In the prospectus of *The Shepheardes Calender,* dated November 12, 1896, it is announced as abandoned. At that time about thirty-four pages were in type, but no sheet had been printed. Before the type was broken up, on December 24, 1896, thirty-two copies of sixteen of these pages were printed and given as a memento to personal friends of the poet and printer whose death now made the completion of the book impossible. This suggested the idea of printing two pages for wider distribution. The half-border had been engraved in April, 1894, by W. Spielmeyer, but the large border only existed as a drawing. It was engraved with great skill and spirit by C. E. Keates, and the two pages were printed by Stephen Mowlem, with the help of an apprentice, in a manner worthy of the designs.

47. *Sire Degrevaunt.* Edited by F. S. Ellis after the edition printed by J. O. Halliwell. 8vo. Chaucer type. In black and red. Borders 1a and 1, and a woodcut designed by Sir Edward Burne-Jones. 350 on paper at fifteen shillings, 8 on vellum at four guineas. Dated March 14, 1896, issued November 12, 1897. Published at the Kelmscott Press. Bound in half holland.

This book, subjects from which were painted by Sir Edward Burne-Jones on the walls of the Red House, Upton, Bexley Heath, many years ago, was always a favourite with Mr. Morris. The frontispiece was not printed until October, 1897, eighteen months after the text was finished.

48. *Syr Ysambrace.* Edited by F. S. Ellis after the edition printed by J. O. Halliwell from the MS. in the Library of Lincoln Cathedral, with some corrections. 8vo. Chaucer type. In black and red. Borders 4a and 4, and a woodcut designed by Sir Edward Burne-Jones. 350 on paper at twelve shillings, 8 on vellum at four guineas. Dated July 14, issued November 11, 1897. Published at the Kelmscott Press. Bound in half holland.

This is the third and last of the reprints from the Camden Society's volume of Thornton Romances. The text was all set up and partly printed by June, 1896, at which time it was intended to include *Sir Eglamour* in the same volume.

49. *Some German Woodcuts of the Fifteenth Century. Being thirty-five reproductions from books that were in the library of the late William Morris.* Edited, with a list of the principal woodcut books in that library, by S. C. Cockerell. Large 4to. Golden type. In red and black. 225 on paper at thirty shillings, 8 on vellum at five guineas. Dated December 15, 1897, issued January 6, 1898. Published at the Kelmscott Press. Bound in half holland.

Of these thirty-five reproductions twenty-nine were all that were done of a series chosen by Mr. Morris to illustrate a catalogue of his library, and the other six were prepared by him for an article in the fourth number of *Bibliographical* part of which is reprinted as an introduction to the book. The process blocks (with one exception) were made by Walker & Boutall, and are of the same size as the original cuts.

50. *The Story of Sigurd the Volsung and the Fall of the Niblungs.* By William Morris. Small folio. Chaucer type, with title and headings to the four books in Troy type. In black and red. Borders 33a and 33, and two illustrations designed by Sir Edward Burne-Jones and engraved by W. H. Hooper. 160

on paper at six guineas, 6 on vellum at twenty guineas. Dated January 19, issued February 25, 1898. Published at the Kelmscott Press. Bound in limp vellum, with blue silk ties.

The two borders used in this book were almost the last that Mr. Morris designed. They were intended for an edition of *The Hill of Venus,* which was to have been written in prose by him and illustrated by Sir Edward Burne-Jones. The foliage was suggested by the ornament in two Psalters of the last half of the thirteenth century in the library at Kelmscott House. The initial A at the beginning of the third book was designed in March, 1893, for the Froissart, and does not appear elsewhere.

An edition of *Sigurd the Volsung,* which Mr. Morris justly considered his masterpiece, was contemplated early in the history of the Kelmscott Press. An announcement appears in a proof of the first list, dated April, 1892, but it was excluded from the list as issued in May. It did not reappear until the list of November 26, 1895, in which, the Chaucer being near its completion, *Sigurd* comes under the heading "in preparation," as a folio in Troy type, "with about twenty-five illustrations by Sir Edward Burne-Jones." In the list of June 1, 1896, it is finally announced as "In the press," the number of illustrations is increased to forty, and other particulars are given. Four borders had then been designed for it, two of which were used on pages 470 and 471 of the Chaucer. The other two have not been used, though one of them has been engraved. Two pages only were in type, thirty-two copies of which were struck off on January 11, 1897, and given to friends, with the sixteen pages of Froissart mentioned above.

51. *The Sundering Flood.* Written by WILLIAM MORRIS. Overseen for the press by May Morris. 8vo. Chaucer type. In black and red. Border 10, and a map. 300 on paper at two guineas. Dated November 15, 1897, issued February 25, 1898. Published at the Kelmscott Press. Bound in half holland.

This was the last romance by William Morris. He began to write it on December 21, 1895, and dictated the final words on September 8, 1896. The map pasted into the cover was drawn by H. Cribb for Walker & Boutall, who prepared the block. In the edition that Longmans are about to issue the bands of robbers called in the Kelmscott edition Red and Black Skinners appear correctly as Red and Black Skimmers. The name was probably suggested by that of the pirates called "escumours of the sea" on page 154 of *Godfrey of Boloyne.*

52. *Love is Enough, or the Freeing of Pharamond; A Morality.* Written by William Morris. Large 4to. Troy type, with stage directions in Chaucer type. In black, red, and blue. Borders 6a and 7, and two illustrations designed by Sir Edward Burne-Jones. 300 on paper at two guineas, 8 on vellum at ten guineas. Dated December 11, 1897, issued March 24, 1898. Published at the Kelmscott Press. Bound in limp vellum.

This was the second book printed in three colours at the Kelmscott Press. As explained in the colophon, the final picture was not designed for this particular edition.

53. *A Note by William Morris on his Aims in Founding the Kelmscott Press. Together with a Short Description of the Press,* by S. C. COCKERELL. And an Annotated List of the Books Printed Thereat. Octavo. Golden type, with five pages in the Troy and Chaucer types. In black and red. Borders 4a and 4, and a woodcut designed by Sir E. Burne-Jones. 525 on paper at ten shillings, 12 on vellum at two guineas. Dated March 4, issued March 24, 1898. Published at the Kelmscott Press. Bound in half holland.

Various Lists, Leaflets, and Announcements Printed at the Kelmscott Press :

Eighteen lists of the books printed or in preparation at the Kelmscott Press were issued to booksellers and subscribers. The dates of these are May, July, and December, 1892 ; March 9, May 20, May 27, August 1, and December 1, 1893; March 31, April 21, July 2, October 1 (a leaflet), and December 1, 1894; July 1 and November 26, 1895; June 1, 1896; February 16 and July 28, 1897. The three lists for 1892, and some copies of that for March 9, 1893, were printed on Whatman paper, the last of the stock bought for the first edition of *The Roots of the Mountains.* Besides these, twenty-nine announcements, relating mainly to individual books, were issued ; and eight leaflets, containing extracts from the lists, were printed for distribution by Messrs. Morris & Co. The following items, as having a more permanent interest than most of these announcements, merit a full description :

1. Two forms of invitation to the annual gatherings of the Hammersmith Socialist Society on January 30, 1892, and February 11, 1893. Golden type.

2. A four-page leaflet for the Ancoats Brotherhood, with the frontispiece from the Kelmscott Press edition of *A Dream of John Ball* on the first page. March, 189 Golden type. 2500 copies.

3. An address to Sir Lowthian Bell, Bart., from his employees, dated 30th June, 1894. Eight pages. Golden type. 250 on paper and 2 on vellum.

4. A leaflet, with fly-leaf, headed *An American Memorial to Keats,* together with a form of invitation to the unveiling of his bust in Hampstead Parish Church on July 16, 1894. Golden type. 750 copies.

5. A slip giving the text of a memorial tablet to Dr. Thomas Sadler, for distribution at the unveiling of it in Rosslyn Hill Chapel, Hampstead. November, 1894. Golden type. 450 copies.

6. Scholarship certificates for the technical Education Board of the London County Council, printed in the oblong borders designed for the pictures in Chaucer's Works. One of these borders was not used in the book, and this is its only appearance. The first certificate was printed in November, 1894, and was followed in January, 1896, by eleven certificates; in January, 1897, by six certificates; and in February, 1898, by eleven certificates, all differently worded. Golden type. The numbers varied from 12 to 2500 copies.

7. Programmes of the Kelmscott Press annual *Wayzgoose* for the years 1892–95. These were printed without supervision from Mr. Morris.

8. Specimen showing the three types used at the Press for insertion in the first edition of Strange's *Alphabets* March, 1895. 2000 ordinary copies and 60 on large paper.

9. Cards for Associates of the Deaconess Institution for the Diocese of Rochester. One side of this card is printed in Chaucer type ; on the other there is a prayer in the Troy type enclosed in a small border which was not used elsewhere. It was designed for the illustrations of a projected edition of *The House of the Wolfings,* April, 1897. 250 copies.

INDEX.

Messrs. MORRIS & COMPANY have appointed as their general agent Mr. A. E. Bulkley of 42 East 14th St., New York City, and he will be pleased to give all information respecting the various fabrics, etc., designed by the late Mr. Morris and sold by MORRIS & COMPANY. These may also be obtained of Mr. A. H. Davenport, 96–98 Washington St., Boston.

MEMOIRS OF FRANÇOIS RENÉ, VICOMTE DE CHÂTEAUBRIAND

Sometime Ambassador to England. Being a Translation of "Les Mémoires d'Outre-Tombe," by ALEXANDER TEIXEIRA DE MATTOS. With illustrations from contemporary sources. Six volumes (sold in sets only). 8°. Each . . net, $3 75

"Though some critics have denied that Châteaubriand was truly great, it has never occurred to any critic to deny that he was truly interesting—the most impressive, if not the most important, literary figure of his period. Wherever he went, and whatever he did, he was always the centre of the picture—the very type of the dramatist's 'sympathetic hero.' That is the chief secret of the fascination of his pages. A picturesque personality is presented in them, in the romantic manner, by the hand of a consummate artist."—*London Times.*

THE YOUTH OF LA GRANDE MADEMOISELLE (1627–1652)

By ARVÈDE BARINE. Authorized English Version by L. G. MEYER. 8°. With frontispiece and about 25 illustrations from contemporaneous sources . . . . . net, $

All French history is interesting, but there are few of its pages more fascinating than the kaleidoscopic career of La Grande Mademoiselle. She was related to Louis XIII. by both father and mother; she was the richest heiress in France; she aspired to be an empress, a nun, a political power. Her memoirs give unique and valuable pictures of life at the Court of Anne of Austria, and of the wars of the Fronde, in which she played a manly part.

STUDIES OF A BIOGRAPHER

By LESLIE STEPHEN, author of "Hours in a Library," etc. New Series. Two volumes in a box, each . . net, $2 00

The works of this writer need no comment. By way of suggesting the nature of the contents of these volumes, a few of the titles are given: The Browning Letters; John Donne; John Ruskin; William Godwin's Novels; Walter Bagehot; Thomas Henry Huxley.

"Stephen is one of the soundest of our critics. . . . His cool, shrewd judgment is refreshing in its contrast to the tall talk which has been only too common with modern biographers. . . . The author belongs to the psychological school of critics."—*The Athenæum.*

G. P. PUTNAM'S SONS, NEW YORK AND LONDON

www.ingramcontent.com/pod-product-compliance
Lightning Source LLC
LaVergne TN
LVHW010741120826
845150LV00009B/1264

* 9 7 8 1 4 2 5 5 7 3 3 8 6 *